BULLITT FOUNDATION,

THANK YOU FOR THE

OVER THE YEARS.

OUR BEST,

ISS _____

Sustainable Solutions:

Let Knowledge Serve the City

LET KNOWLEDGE
SERVE
THE CITY

EDITED BY **B.D. WORTHAM-GALVIN, JENNIFER H. ALLEN**
AND **JACOB D.B. SHERMAN**

Greenleaf
PUBLISHING

© 2016 Greenleaf Publishing Limited

Published by Greenleaf Publishing Limited
Aizlewood's Mill
Nursery Street
Sheffield S3 8GG
UK
www.greenleaf-publishing.com

The right of B.D. Wortham-Galvin, Jennifer Allen and Jacob D.B. Sherman to be identified as Editors of this Work has been asserted by them in accordance with sections 77 and 78 of the Copyright, Designs and Patents Act 1988.

Cover by Sadie Gornall-Jones
Printed and bound by Printondemand-worldwide.com, UK.

MIX
Paper from
responsible sources
FSC® C004959

British Library Cataloguing in Publication Data:
  A catalogue record for this book is available from the British Library.

  ISBN-978-1-78353-3691 [hardback]
  ISBN-978-1-78353-4012 [PDF ebook]
  ISBN-978-1-78353-5736 [ePub ebook]

Contents

Acknowledgements

As the chapters in this volume demonstrate, credit for Portland State University's successes in sustainability research and engagement is due to the many faculty, students, staff, administrators and community partners who, over the past two decades, have demonstrated a deep commitment to creating collaborative solutions to the ecological, economic, and social challenges of our time. To each of you, thank you for your efforts. This meaningful work has built a strong foundation for PSU's ongoing work toward building a more equitable and vibrant community.

There are several individuals whose significant leadership and dedication to advancing the University's work in these areas during their time at PSU deserves specific recognition. Without their willingness to provide thought leadership and to invest often-scarce resources to advance sustainability scholarship and practice, PSU would not be where it is today. Judith Ramaley laid the foundation for PSU's commitment to community-engaged learning; Bill Feyerherm made key investments in faculty, graduate students and in incentives for interdisciplinary sustainability research; Roy Koch played a essential role in ensuring that sustainability was recognized as a priority for PSU and that it became the focus of the $25 million challenge gift from the James F. and Marion L. Miller Foundation. George Pernsteiner, Marvin Kaiser, Nohad Toulan, and Scott Dawson demonstrated foresight in backing the creation of sustainability programs. Finally, Michele Crim and Robyn Pierce led early efforts to ensure sustainability principles guided PSU facilities and operations. We want to thank each of these individuals for making sustainability and community engagement flourish as an area of excellence at PSU. PSU's current administration has demonstrated continued commitment to advancing sustainability efforts; in particular we want to recognize President Wim Wiewel and Vice President Jon Fink for their leadership and support.

The editors also want to acknowledge the support provided by their family members in the course of this book project; to Ed Galvin, Wayne Luscombe and Martha Sherman, our heartfelt thanks. The editors also want to acknowledge graduate student Genevieve Harding's sterling logistical support and her hard work keeping us organized and attentive to important details; thanks, Genevieve!

Finally, we would like to thank the trustees and staff of the James F. and Marion L. Miller Foundation for their willingness to invest in building PSU's capacity to serve the community through our sustainability programs. We hope that the stories included in this book attest to PSU's commitment to live up to this potential.

Foreword

Wim Wiewel
President, Portland State University

Sustainability—environmental, economic and civic—has been a core focus of Portland State University for decades. It was formally endorsed by the university's leadership in 2007 and given a tremendous boost by a $25 million gift from a local foundation the following year. PSU's dedication to sustainability concepts and practices developed over a long institutional history in tandem with the university's close relationship with Portland and the surrounding area.

PSU's motto, "Let Knowledge Serve the City," speaks to our deep and unique engagement with our region. This ongoing, mutually beneficial linkage emerged in part from the institution's contentious history of origin. Started as an extension center in 1946 to serve returning World War II veterans, and initially intended to go out of business after a few years, Portland State kept growing. It grew despite opposition from other state universities and the former State Board of Higher Education – all of whom wanted to see PSU go away.

To ensure survival, PSU from the beginning created strong partnerships with civic, business, labor, and political sectors in the Portland region. Connecting education with "real life" was in our DNA from the beginning. It was formalized in a major curriculum change in the mid-1990s that elevated community engagement as a central ethos for the university and its faculty and students. Promotion and tenure criteria were changed to reward civic engagement. New core curricula were developed to ensure students spent considerable time outside the classroom on community projects and service.

Oregon and Portland's long-standing "green" focus initially centered on preservation of nature and open space, reflected in the Urban Growth Boundary, permanent public ownership of all ocean beaches, and the nation's first required bottle deposit bill. It has evolved in recent years into concerns about climate change; Portland was the first city in the U.S. to adopt a Climate Action Plan and has a very aggressive pro-bicycle and public transportation policy. With that level of community concern, it's no surprise that PSU had many faculty teaching about and researching principles of environmentalism and sustainability. The politically progressive nature of the city further contributed to having faculty broaden the concept to issues of environmental justice and social equity.

Thus, sustainability has deep roots and a large number of faculty engaged with long-lasting connections to many local, regional, and national organizations. But PSU and Portland, while still frontrunners, are far from rare. Most colleges and universities use various forms of green branding to appeal to today's students. Competition for environmental and sustainability research dollars can be fierce, prompting universities to stake their claim as leaders in the field. And it's not just students and faculty. The Climate Leadership Network of Second Nature, for example, has more than 650 signatories for its Carbon Commitment—an attempt to reduce greenhouse gas emissions by having universities pledge to develop Climate Action Plans related to energy purchases, travel and buildings, as well as curriculum.

Universities remain society's primary centers of research, thought and creativity. As such they play a critical leadership role in the complex arena of sustainability. As you will read in this book, Portland State University embraces this role and the positive changes it can bring about for the city, the region and the world.

Introduction to the "Sustainable Solutions" Series

Jennifer Allen, David Ervin, B.D. Wortham-Galvin, and Jacob Sherman

This book tells the story of building the platform for sustainability programs at Portland State University. There has been a rapid increase in academic sustainability programs in the U.S. and overseas as well as increasing evidence that community-engaged learning is a particularly powerful experience for students and faculty. As both enrollment and budget pressures grow in higher education, we believe universities, their communities, and governing and funding organizations can learn valuable lessons from Portland State University's approach, our successes, and perhaps even more from our continuing struggles in sustainability programming and community-engaged scholarship and teaching. In the end, any university that seeks to advance scholarship and education in these areas must find its own best path. However, some overarching principles can assist that journey and avoid wasting valuable resources while improving progress in addressing escalating sustainability problems and forging successful university–community partnerships. In particular, our experience suggests that building a solid foundation for organizational growth requires close adherence from the outset to the central precepts of sustainability science—involving a range of natural and social science disciplines, promoting problem-based scholarship, involving relevant stakeholders, and adaptive management.

Context and motivation

Powerful trends in society often catalyze new academic initiatives. Witness the information technology (IT) revolution and the subsequent growth in computing and information science programs. The explosion in academic sustainability programs and in efforts to work in a more co-productive manner with community partners may be the latest set of university and college initiatives responding to societal pressures. Here we examine the development of the sustainability efforts in higher education and the emergence of community engagement as a central tenet of effective learning.

Spurred initially by the realization that resource depletion and environmental degradation threaten the long-term survival of natural and human systems around the globe (WCED, 1987; NRC, 1999), the sustainability movement now incorporates social, cultural, and economic issues as well. Some scholars dub it the latest "megatrend imperative" for business, following a pattern similar to the quality and IT revolutions that reshaped industry over the last 30 years (Lubin and Esty 2010). Governments—from local agencies to the United Nations—businesses, and non-governmental organizations are all exploring and expanding sustainability-related programs. This diverse array of organizations looks to higher education for research capacity and training of professionals to advance their myriad efforts in sustainability.

The rapid expansion of the American Association for Sustainability in Higher Education (AASHE) suggests that academia is accepting the challenge to integrate sustainability considerations into its research, teaching, and operations. Beginning as the Education for Sustainability (EFS West) organization in 2001 serving western states and Canada, AASHE transitioned into a national organization in 2006. It serves as the first professional higher education association for the college and university sustainability community and has grown to 840 member schools as of 2014 (AASHE, 2014). In 2006, AASHE held its first national conference and 650 students, faculty and university operations staff attended from colleges and universities across North America and beyond. Two years later, attendance for the conference tripled to over 1,700, rising to over 2,000 for the 2014 conference (AASHE, 2014).

While this burst in interest is impressive, the development of successful academic sustainability programs poses three nontrivial challenges. First, the scientific theory and methodology to conduct sustainability scholarship in teaching and research remains nascent. A large eclectic literature has emerged on sustainability over the last few decades, including National Research Council reports that have helped lay a foundation for understanding the scope of this field (e.g., NRC 1999, 2014). However, a tight paradigm that would provide a common foundation and methods for analysis has not yet evolved. While that diversity may reflect the all-encompassing nature of the topic, it leaves the field in a considerable state of flux (Clark and Dixon, 2003). Without clear guidance, academic institutions generally "learn by doing," an exercise in adaptive management that can be successful but also involves mis-steps and corrective actions. Second, implementing successful academic sustainability programs requires new institutions and organizational developments to foster interdisciplinary and transdisciplinary scholarship. Although the National Science Foundation has sponsored such efforts, e.g., the Integrative Graduate Education, Research and Training (IGERT) and Research

Traineeship (NRT) programs, academia—and especially its governance structures—is still dominated by individual disciplines. Third, sustainability scholarship generally involves interdisciplinary systems' approaches to "wicked" problems (Rittell and Weber, 1973; Batie, 2008) that impose high up-front costs. This in turn requires seed funding for investments in cross-disciplinary integrative teams. Although such approaches arguably yield more systemic and durable solutions to today's vexing issues, sources of funding for such efforts are few.

It is important to stress that Portland State University is a comparatively young university, especially in research capacity. Founded as an extension college in 1946 to serve veterans of World War II, PSU only achieved university status in 1969. This relative immaturity as a research institution carries both advantages and limitations in building academic sustainability programs, as we will demonstrate in this volume. What some may not appreciate is that PSU has been a leader for decades in creating educational programs consistent with sustainability principles. For example, PSU launched the nation's first multidisciplinary environmental science PhD degree in 1971. Since 1994, PSU's general education "University Studies" program has been organized around interdisciplinary approaches that advance students' abilities and understanding related to inquiry and critical thinking, communication, diversity, and ethics and social responsibility. The legacy of these early commitments to interdisciplinarity may well have set the stage for the acceptance by faculty, administrators, staff and students of more recent sustainability programming.

PSU also had a distinguished history of community engagement and problem solving, core elements of implementing successful sustainability programs. Consistently ranked in the top ten US universities for its service learning efforts, PSU takes seriously the education of its students through experiential learning (Shandas, 2008). The senior Capstone requirement in the University Studies program is designed to build cooperative learning communities by taking students out of the classroom and into the field. The Community Watershed Stewardship program, recipient of the Jimmy and Rosalynn Carter Partnership Award for Campus–Community Partnerships in 2008, is a long-standing partnership between PSU and the City of Portland's Bureau of Environmental Services to engage Portlanders in enhancing the health of watersheds while promoting public awareness of the value of these natural systems. As will be discussed later, this orientation to engagement also paid dividends in securing the Miller Foundation Challenge Grant.

In Chapter 1, "Building sustainability scholarship: Lessons from Portland State University," Allen and Ervin map the history of PSU's engagement in sustainability, reviewing the reasoning behind the decision to create a cross-cutting initiative integrating sustainability across the campus in academic programs, centers of community service, and PSU's own footprint. The chapter shares lessons learned from PSU's experience that may be of value to other institutions interested in building their academic sustainability programs. In Chapter 2, "Engaging undergraduates across a four-year general education curriculum," Estes *et al.* describe how PSU scaffolds student community engagement in sustainability-related courses across a four-year general education curriculum, arguing that the role of community engagement in a course should parallel the students' developing understanding of complex issues of sustainability and their capacity to apply that knowledge to real-world issues and concerns. The authors emphasize the importance of balancing prescriptive course sequencing with opportunities for students and faculty to explore emerging issues and interests as they arise. In Chapter 3, Jones and Brown argue that because business schools influence future business behavior through pedagogy and curricula they therefore have a responsibility to educate business leaders who recognize that true success depends on a sustainability model with multiple stakeholders, not just a profitable bottom line. This chapter tells the story of integrating sustainability principles into a core business course, and how various attributes of the academic environment interacted to create a successful model that can be studied by others, in the hope of achieving similar results.

In Chapter 4, Burns *et al.* describe an innovative program based on a partnership between PSU's Leadership for Sustainability Education program and the City of Portland and Portland Public Schools. The Learning Gardens Lab (LGL) serves as a site for teaching, community-based learning, and research related to food- and garden-based education for undergraduate and graduate students at PSU. LGL has also been the context for longitudinal research investigating how garden-based education impacts middle school students' motivation, learning, and achievement. This chapter highlights the transformational work at LGL, and discusses challenges inherent to building capacity to support community partnerships for sustainability.

In Chapter 5, Spring and Samuelson focus on understanding the complexity of university–community partnership arrangements, specifically the paucity of knowledge regarding the essential leadership roles that college students can play within partnerships. Portland State's Student Leaders for Service program has effectively utilized student leaders to support and deepen its partnership infrastructure for more than ten years; this chapter explores the impact of students on community–university partnerships and sustainability.

In Chapter 6, Spalding and Wise examine the potential to enhance sustainability initiatives through partnerships with Enrollment Management and Student Affairs (EMSA) divisions while simultaneously strengthening student recruitment, retention, learning, and success. Using PSU's EMSA assessment initiative as a case study for measuring sustainability practices and impacts on student learning, the chapter offers recommendations for designing large-scale sustainability assessments across campus. In Chapter 7, DeLaTorre and Neal describe how faculty members at PSU have emphasized sustainable community development principles in their approaches to teaching and research in the field of gerontology; their strategies have included carrying out translational research with the long-term aim of improving the health of the public, integrating aging in local policy and practice, and offering service-learning opportunities for students and citizens that incorporate sustainable development principles into projects aimed at preparing communities for population aging. In Chapter 8, McClintock *et al.* share the experiences of a group of PSU student and faculty scholar-activists in developing "food justice dialogues," an action research effort to probe the disconnects between the sustainable food movement and food justice; this effort focused on building meaningful relationships and establishing individual and communal understandings of how to develop and apply an anti-oppression lens to food systems work.

In Chapter 9, Ferry and Palleroni discuss the objectives and complexities of the emerging field of public interest design through an examination of the range of initiatives undertaken by the Center for Public Interest Design (CPID) in its inaugural year. This chapter explores how establishing CPID—the first of its kind in the country—has cleared a path for others to follow, making it an ideal model from which to learn and anticipate the trajectory of non-traditional architecture practices.

In the US in general, the gap between official plans and policies and their implementation is so well known that virtually every effort to draft or update a city plan begins with a promise that it will not sit on a shelf and collect dust. In Chapter 10, Liberty and Walton discuss the processes and achievements of the Urban Sustainability Accelerator program, which was formed precisely to help urban areas in the United States translate their sustainability plans, policies, and goals into the reality of a more sustainable city.

In Chapter 11, Sherman and Beaudoin argue that higher education has a role to play in addressing complex sustainability problems, and describe two programs run by the Institute for Sustainable Solutions that broker and support community–university partnerships aimed at translating research to action. This chapter explores key issues that universities must face if they want to play an active role in resolving society's urban sustainability challenges, providing insight on how some barriers are addressed at PSU and uncovering systemic challenges that remain.

The themes that emerge from these chapters are summarized and reflected upon in the afterword, which also sets the stage for Volume II of the "Sustainable Solutions" series: *Community–University Partnerships*. The authors and editors of this volume hope that others can learn from our experiences and that these stories can contribute to an ongoing dialogue about how universities and communities can work together to advance sustainable solutions.

References

AASHE (Associate for the Advancement of Sustainability in Higher Education). (2014). Annual Report. Retrieved from: http://www.aashe.org/files/aashe_annual_report_2014.pdf

Batie, S. (2008). Wicked Problems and Applied Economics. *American Journal of Applied Economics*, 90(5), 1,176-1,191.

Clark, W.C., & Dickson, N.M. (2003). Sustainability science: The Emerging Research Program. Proceedings of the National Academy of Sciences 100(14): 8,059-8,061.

Lubin, D.A., & Esty, D.C. (2010). The Sustainability Imperative. *Harvard Business Review*. May

NRC (National Research Council). (1999). *Our Common Journey: A Transition Toward Sustainability*. Washington, DC: National Academies Press.

NRC (National Research Council). (2014). Pathways to Urban Sustainability: Perspective from Portland and the Pacific Northwest: Summary of a Workshop. Washington, DC: National Academies Press. Retrieved from: http://www.nap.edu/openbook.php?record_id=18704

Rittel, H., & Webber, M. (1973). "Dilemmas in a General Theory of Planning." *Policy Sciences.* (5): 155-169.

Shandas, V. (2008). Fostering green communities through civic engagement: Community-based environmental stewardship in the Portland area. *Journal of the American Planning Association,* 74(4), 408-418.

WCED (World Commission on Environment and Development) (1987). *Our Common Future.* New York: United Nations.

1

Building sustainability scholarship

Lessons from Portland State University

Jennifer H. Allen and David Ervin[1]

The chapter describes the development of PSU's sustainability programs between 2000 and 2015, distilling the key methodological and organizational principles that underpin the development of these programs. The chapter describes the trajectory of development over a 15-year period; the initial efforts focused on engaging faculty, administrators, and students with community partners in an early planning process, developing principles, credibility, and commitment by all parties, building internal capacity with multidisciplinary institutions and activities, and launching some early projects that demonstrated our capacity to deliver quality research and instruction. Later developments involved the significant transformation of the sustainability program after PSU's receipt of the $25 million challenge gift from the

1 We owe a deep debt of gratitude to the faculty, administrators, students, operations staff, and community partners too numerous to mention who have aided our journey in building academic sustainability programs at Portland State University over the last decade. This exploration has been one of the most rewarding intellectual and personal experiences of our careers. The genesis of this paper came from a keynote presentation by Ervin to the Sustainable Michigan Endowed Project 2009 Academy sponsored by Michigan State University. We thank Sandra Batie for motivating this analysis and reporting of building Portland State University's academic sustainability programs.

James F. and Marion L. Miller Foundation in 2008. We also relate the steps taken at Portland State University to address each of the challenges noted in the introduction: how to "learn by doing" and take an adaptive management approach, given the nascent state of the scientific theory and methodology for conducting sustainability scholarship in teaching and research; the importance of developing new institutions and organizational approaches to foster interdisciplinary and transdisciplinary scholarship; and the need to address the barriers to interdisciplinary, problem-based scholarship and teaching. The story is essentially one of adaptive management because uncertainty pervades the field of sustainability, meaning that both targets and methods require periodic revision based on emerging information and learning.

We appreciate that our case is in some ways unique and cannot be generalized per se. However, we feel that our experiences at Portland State University, both the successes and continuing struggles, offer lessons and principles that can assist other higher education institutions in their sustainability journeys. We also hope the insights will be of use to potential private and public funders of academic sustainability projects and diverse community organizations who want higher education to help them solve complex real-world problems.

The building blocks of early program development

The introductory chapter to this book maps out key institutional developments starting in the 1970s that laid the foundation for PSU's sustainability programs. Building on this work, several key actions and investments gave the sustainability programs early momentum. As often happens at universities, student activism was an instrumental driver in the early stages of sustainability programming at Portland State University. In 2000, a group of students assembled to voice their dissatisfaction with the state of recycling on campus, forming an ad hoc group to investigate potential improvements and recommended using some of their student fees to finance a new position in campus operations in charge of sustainability activities. The Student Senate approved their recommendation and the Vice President for Administration and Finance matched their commitment with additional funding, maintaining this pledge despite tough budget cuts in 2000–01. PSU's first operations sustainability coordinator started in the fall of 2001, after a national search that attracted over 100 applicants.

Lesson 1: Early leadership by students and administrators were key elements in successfully launching PSU's sustainability programs.

Simultaneously, many faculty members and multidisciplinary teams were developing research and education projects with sustainability issues and concepts at their core. For example, a team of faculty and graduate students were invited to work with the Mt. Hood National Forest to develop a set of sustainability indicators for managing the forest (Ervin *et al.*, 2012), while the development of a sustainable business initiative in the School of Business Administration eventually led to recurring top 25 "Beyond Grey Pinstripes" rankings for PSU's leadership in integrating sustainability into the business curriculum.[2] PSU's urban ecology research consortium, launched around this time, has also since received national recognition (Yeakley, 2012).

Despite the growing portfolio of sustainability research projects, and rising demands by students and community partners to do more such projects, there was little institutional capacity to coordinate and leverage such efforts across campus. Recognizing this void and the unrealized opportunities it represented, in 2001 two faculty members (including one of the authors of this chapter) met with several deans to propose hiring an academic sustainability coordinator so that there would be someone who would, as the faculty members saw it, "wake up everyday thinking about how to advance PSU's academic sustainability programs." The deans endorsed this proposal, recognizing that the Portland region was gaining a national and international reputation for developing innovative sustainability institutions and practices, and that PSU had an obligation to assist public and private entities in achieving their sustainability aspirations—consistent with the university's motto, "Let Knowledge Serve the City."

PSU's Provost at the time similarly recognized the importance of enhancing institutional support for sustainability programs and conducted an internal competitive process to select the first Coordinator of Academic Sustainability Programs (CASP). One of the co-authors of this chapter (Ervin) was selected, starting in this role in September 2002.[3] In addition to the CASP's half-time salary, the Provost and the Office of Research and Sponsored Projects provided a small operations budget and support for two graduate assistants; while this limited resource base forced a lean approach focused on building social networks on and off campus, these relationship-focused strategies yielded significant dividends in the long run.

The CASP needed to invest in several years of trust building to reassure faculty across campus that he would not favor departments in his home college. Placing the CASP position in the Office of the Vice Provost for Research and Graduate Studies conveyed its campus-wide responsibilities and signaled that helping PSU develop a scholarly research agenda would be an integral part of the effort. The position's main responsibilities were to identify the various strands of sustainability scholarship on campus (including pockets of excellence that could grow with additional support), facilitate dialogue among faculty, students, and community partners on potential academic scholarship initiatives, and work with the

---

2 The Aspen Institute, "Beyond Grey Pinstripes: MBA Survey Archives." http://bit.ly/1NsRZe3, accessed May 13, 2016.

3 The other co-author, Allen, joined PSU part-time in 2003 to work with the CASP on program development activities.

operations sustainability coordinator to make the campus a laboratory for education, research, and community outreach.

An example of an early effort to build faculty community was a book group that provided a forum for discussion and exploration across a broad set of disciplines. The overarching goal of such efforts to build relationships and trust among faculty, administrators, students, and staff was to build a diverse coalition that could develop a common set of principles for advancing sustainability scholarship at PSU. The sense of connection and community that grew from these efforts laid the foundation for rich interdisciplinary efforts in later years.

> *Lesson 2: Early investment in developing social capital across the campus community to engender trust—an essential but often neglected component of effective sustainability programs—can pay long-run dividends.*

Defining the relevant boundaries and content that sustainability programs should encompass is a common and ongoing challenge for these programs, as sustainability concepts can encompass the natural and social sciences, engineering, professional schools, the humanities, and the arts. An important early step in helping to define PSU's sustainability focus was to conduct an online survey of faculty in 2003 to inventory existing research projects, courses, and outreach programs that had "significant" sustainability content. Lacking a precise set of criteria and metrics to judge relevance to sustainability, the survey offered a general description of core sustainability concepts, defining sustainability as a "quest that requires the integration of environmental protection, social equity, and economic viability to meet the needs of present generations without compromising the ability of future generations to meet their needs," and allowed responding faculty to judge whether their work fit in that domain. While it was clear that this process would likely capture more activities than PSU could reasonably support if we were to succeed in bringing rigor and focus to the sustainability programs, the process was important to identify faculty members who felt they were involved in sustainability-related scholarship and to begin the process of building a social network of campus scholars who could contribute to program development. The survey findings were categorized under common themes such as urban planning, water resources, business sustainability, and several others. Respondents were invited to provide feedback on these themes through a sustainability website. Using a fairly open-ended approach to collect a broad base of information and then iteratively refining PSU's areas of focus represented the important sustainability principle of using adaptive management when faced with uncertainties (Castle *et al.*, 1996).

While defining which topics should be included and which left out made this exercise a challenging one, the effort helped paint a rough picture of which areas had a critical mass of talent and resources and which areas offered a comparative advantage for PSU if given additional internal and external support. The inventory also helped identify areas that would most likely not be competitive due to few participating faculty or a lack of internal or external funding opportunities. This allowed university administrators to evaluate where to allocate effort and resources to best achieve the institution's goals of building academic sustainability programming that reflected areas where PSU had strong scholarship and competitive expertise. In addition, the inventory helped generate information PSU could use to describe academic sustainability expertise to community partners and potential funders.

An important constituency in support of developing PSU's sustainability programs were community partners who expressed a need for high-quality education programs on sustainability practice for working professionals. In response to this demand, in 2003 PSU launched a Professional Certificate in Sustainability in collaboration with a local consulting group. The program, which attracted a broad range of students from business, government, utilities, and non-profits as well as a number of PSU graduate students, paired university faculty and practitioners as instructors to provide the students with a perspective that bridged academic and experiential perspectives. Although receiving high student evaluations, the program was suspended after two years because of insufficient enrollment to cover administrative costs; lack of adequate marketing and communications support and insufficient resources to manage the program wholly in-house likely contributed to the suspension, as other competitor programs that emerged shortly thereafter were able to attract viable enrollments for a number of years.

An internationally oriented sustainability initiative launched in 2004 to develop partnerships with international universities around web-based sustainability curricula faced similar challenges; while some enduring partnerships emerged from this effort, including a student and faculty exchange with Tongji University in Shanghai, China, this broader effort faltered in part because the core sustainability research and educational capacity at PSU was still emergent when it was launched. As that capacity has grown, PSU has developed a number of successful international sustainability activities, including an eco-city and climate action governance program in Vietnam (Halimi et al., 2016), and urban planning programs in China; the success of these efforts has been largely due to the leadership of specific faculty who have prioritized the development of the institutional relationships needed to support such programs.

> *Lesson 3: Focus early investments on a few key strategic priorities and avoid activities—even if worthy—that require more program resources than are available in the initial stages of program development.*

While the certificate and international programs noted above were not successful, several important capacity-building activities were conducted during those same years that helped form a broader foundation of sustainability scholarship. These activities—four of which are described below—were guided by some of the core sustainability concepts referenced previously, such as involving a range of hard and soft science disciplines, promoting problem-based scholarship, adaptive management, and involving relevant stakeholders.

The first effort, focused on social sustainability, was initiated by a small group of faculty and students who felt that PSU's sustainability agenda was overly dominated by the environmental and economic dimensions without sufficient attention to social sustainability aspects such as equity and diversity. With the CASP's encouragement, this group requested support from the Vice Provost for Research and Graduate Studies to start a "Social Sustainability Research/Teaching Group" to advance scholarship in this area. The group received support for two course releases and a graduate research assistant (GRA) to develop one or more new interdisciplinary courses on social sustainability and to develop and submit interdisciplinary grant proposals. The group—which came to be known as the Social Sustainability Colloquium—has maintained solid participation from 20–25 faculty, students, and community partners in their regular seminars, has created an interdisciplinary team-taught social sustainability course, and helped foster the publication of several scholarly publications on social sustainability (e.g., Dillard *et al.*, 2009; Dujon *et al.*, 2015). This effort has helped elevate this often-neglected aspect of sustainability at PSU and has helped the university develop a truly integrated "triple bottom line" approach to the subject.

The second effort, focused on curricular development, was initiated by a cross-campus faculty group who felt PSU should offer an integrated core of graduate courses in sustainability theory and methods to students in all fields; this effort reflected a concern that the scattered curricular offerings available at the time did not cover all salient sustainability topics in a rigorous fashion. During 2003–04, a subgroup of faculty deliberated on the structure and content of a curriculum to remedy this deficiency and proposed the creation of a "Graduate Certificate in Sustainability" that would include three core courses on the environmental, social, and economic dimensions of sustainability (four credit hours each), and a fourth core course that integrated all aspects into a systems-approach problem-solving exercise. Students could choose two electives from qualifying courses to complete the certificate's required 21–23 credit hours. The faculty group's rationale for pursuing this cross-cutting approach was that sustainability is an overarching construct that applies to all fields rather than being just the responsibility of a single department or college. The Vice Provost for Research and Graduate Studies provided course releases for four faculty members to develop the core courses; the investment of resources in these course releases signaled the importance of the effort in the eyes of key leaders at PSU. Several of the core courses include a project that involves problem-based research, often in conjunction with community partners, which PSU considers to be an integral feature of sustainability science and curricula.

The certificate was quite successful in its early years, with strong enrollment and student evaluations. However, when demand began to regularly exceed the spaces available in the classes, offering additional sections without additional faculty resources became an obstacle. In addition, two of the core courses were initially taught by multidisciplinary teams, an approach well received by students and faculty. However, team teaching raised resource allocation issues in terms of how to share student credit hours and fund multiple instructors for one course. Neither of these issues has been satisfactorily resolved at the time of writing.

The third activity, the book group described briefly in a previous section, involved a group of faculty, graduate students, and staff that met regularly in the student-operated, sustainability-oriented cafe to discuss popular and scientific writings on sustainability topics, such as Jared Diamond's Collapse (2005) and Gunderson and Holling's edited volume Panarchy (2002). In terms of format, a volunteer would offer a 10–15 minute summary and interpretation of the reading, followed by an intense but unstructured discussion for the remainder of the hour. Attendance was robust, ranging from eight to approximately 20 faculty members, graduate students and staff despite the 8 am start time (which hindered some with early morning child care duties from attending). Informal feedback from participants suggested this was one of the most intellectually invigorating forums on campus, helping to build the credibility and reputation of sustainability scholarship on campus.

The fourth initiative, a strategic planning effort, grew out of a sense that, despite the inventory and other activities described above, PSU's academic and operational sustainability efforts were not guided by a clear vision. PSU hired a professional facilitator in early 2005 to help better articulate PSU's sustainability mission by bringing together approximately 40 faculty, administrators, staff, students, and community partners to deliberate PSU's desired role in advancing sustainability scholarship and practice. Participants were chosen for their knowledge and experience in the field and with an eye to including all relevant stakeholder perspectives. A professional communications consultant was also hired to help record and interpret the views expressed in the workshop. The exercise focused on identifying assets/attributes, principles and lessons that should inform the development of PSU's sustainability programs. An intense conversation yielded wide-ranging and divergent ideas that often animated discussions about sustainability; the facilitator helped the participants winnow the broad range of concepts down to several principles that all could support.

> *Lesson 4: Having a neutral facilitator to guide strategic conversations, identify promising ideas, and cull the non-productive notions is a valuable investment; the neutrality of the position allows faculty to focus on areas of common interest rather than on defending disciplinary or other turf.*

Based on the workshop discussion, a "Declaration of Support for Sustainability at Portland State University" was crafted to provide a concise statement of consensus values that should underpin sustainability scholarship and practice at PSU. Four critical actions were defined to guide program development:

• Infuse sustainability into all colleges, schools and programs

• Develop a sustainable physical campus that is an example to other institutions

- Make PSU a living laboratory and demonstration model for sustainable processes and practices, e.g., sustainable food procurement contracts

- Develop core multidisciplinary research competencies in key sustainability areas, e.g., green building.

Over the next month, approximately 800 signatures of support were collected in person or via a public website; signatories included the Provost, Vice Provost for Research, a majority of the deans, and a diverse group of faculty, students, and operations staff. The document was endorsed unanimously by the student senate, while, as one might expect, the faculty senate engaged in a vigorous discussion of the need for such an action. When several faculty senators claimed the Declaration represented an "ideological agenda", the CASP responded by framing it as a scholarly agenda. Eventually, the faculty senate endorsed the Declaration by a 70–30% margin, helping to further legitimize sustainability research and education as part of PSU's core academic programs.

> *Lesson 5: Using core concepts from sustainability science—involving a range of natural and social science disciplines, promoting problem-based scholarship, adaptive management, and involving relevant stakeholders—helped assure that each new research, education, and outreach activity advanced the institution's base of sustainability scholarship.*

The conversations that took place as part of the strategic planning process made it clear that the scholarly agenda surrounding sustainability must explicate and analyze the roles of values and ethics in creating more sustainable development—a central proposition in moving toward transdisciplinary science (Max-Neef, 2005). It is important to note that engaging in dialogue about ethics and values does not mean that academic scholars should advocate certain sets of values and ethics over others, in effect giving preference to certain groups in society over others; rather, it means that the resolution of complex problems inevitably involves a host of often conflicting values by affected stakeholders and these need to be made explicit. If the origins and effects of these values and ethics are not openly and rigorously analyzed, the potential to make progress on resolving such complex problems will be significantly restricted, if not completely precluded. Furthermore, the exercise of science always involves some underlying values, though rarely stated by the researchers. By explicitly embracing social sustainability topics as described above, and taking on research projects such as the Mount Hood assessment of stakeholder values, PSU engaged directly with such issues.

> *Lesson 6: Advancing academic sustainability scholarship requires that the fundamental role of values and ethics be dealt with openly and rigorously.*

Using the momentum and ideas from the strategic planning and engagement processes, PSU's vision and mission in sustainability were defined in 2006 as follows:

- PSU Sustainability Vision—To be an internationally recognized university known for excellence in student learning, innovative research, and community engagement that simultaneously advances economic vitality, environmental health, and quality of life.

- PSU Sustainability Mission—To serve as a leading academic laboratory for developing sustainable processes and practices using multi-disciplinary approaches in partnership with business, government, and other organizations. (Ervin and Allen, 2006).

In addition to confirming PSU's commitment to making sustainability a campus-wide, interdisciplinary effort, the strategic planning process also identified the need to further institutionalize the coordination of sustainability programs across campus to help reduce the unavoidable transaction costs of doing interdisciplinary work. In 2006, the Center for Sustainable Processes and Practices (CSP2) was established to address these needs; staffed by several part-time positions, including the CASP (co-author Ervin), Associate Director (co-author Allen), and an assistant. CSP2 was intended to serve as the institutional home of academic sustainability programs, to facilitate rigorous, cross-disciplinary research with environmental, social and economic components, to serve as the locus for collaborative research and dialogue with academic and community participants, to provide a focal point for institutional support for building sustainability scholarship resource base, and to serve as a portal for community engagement. An example of this last role was the Associate Director's involvement in the establishment and subsequent management of the Built Environment and Sustainable Technologies (BEST) Signature Research Center, a collaborative research center involving PSU, Oregon State, University of Oregon and Oregon Institute of Technology.

All of the academic sustainability activities conducted to this point had been supported by relatively small budgets from the Provost and the Vice Provost for Research and Graduate Studies. However, to achieve the vision and mission defined above, more substantial investments in human and physical capital were required; this investment process began with the Provost and Vice Provost for Research providing $100,000 of funding in 2005–06 to seed promising areas of sustainability scholarship. An initial RFP received an overwhelming response from the faculty, indicating a pent-up demand for such investments in sustainability scholarship. This early offering solicited research proposals that were interdisciplinary and were focused on outcomes that would advance our understanding of critical sustainability issues.

A second RFP process, sponsored by CSP2 for awards of up to $10,000, shifted the focus from supporting research to building PSU's capacity in areas that promised to be competitive for extramural support. Although the decision-making process was challenging, selecting the recipients of these early RFPs helped develop criteria for evaluating future investments in sustainability scholarship by PSU faculty that aligned with community interests and PSU's areas of competitive core capacity.

The RFP process and earlier inventory exercises helped define six initial "thrust" areas of interdisciplinary research at PSU: green science and technology development, integrated water resource management, sustainable urban design, sustainable business models, social sustainability, and intelligent urban transportation systems. In addition to the projects supported under the RFPs, CSP2 facilitated the development of several projects that exemplified the university's commitment to interdisciplinary and problem-based approaches and to using the campus and the city as a living laboratory, consistent with the tenets of the Sustainability Declaration. These included a project on ecoroof design and evaluation using one of the campus dormitories as the project site, and a project assessing occupant productivity in green buildings; both projects involved University, industry, government, and foundation partnerships.

In addition to the establishment of CSP2, several important steps toward building PSU's capacity in the sustainability realm took place in 2007 and 2008. In the fall of 2007, sustainability was endorsed as an institutional priority at a senior administration retreat, an action that catalyzed a number of initiatives to further integrate sustainability across campus. In addition, the Provost asked CSP2's Associate Director to convene an interdisciplinary group of faculty with demonstrated interest in sustainability to further refine PSU's focal areas of strength in sustainability research and identify where up to ten additional sustainability faculty positions would best leverage these strengths by filling capacity gaps and building critical mass.

The faculty brought together for this effort became known as the "Ad Hoc Group", and represented yet another valuable investment in building social capital across campus. The group identified four focal areas encompassing the thematic areas previously identified—coupling of human and natural systems, sustainability in urban and urbanizing communities, metrics and evaluation, and mechanisms that effect change and foster engagement at the individual, organizational, societal, and ecosystem levels—and identified areas of expertise that would help deepen and strengthen PSU's expertise in these areas if additional faculty positions were added.

The Ad Hoc group's report was presented to the Provost in January 2008, at about the same time that the trustees of the Portland-based James F. and Marion L. Miller Foundation approached the Provost and senior development staff with a startling opportunity. The trustees had decided that they wanted to make a ten-year, $25 million contribution to an institution that could have a transformational impact on Portland and the region. The trustees had each independently identified PSU as an institution that they felt had significant potential to lead this type of transformational change. In the course of discussions between the trustees, the Provost, and senior development staff, PSU's sustainability programs emerged as the priority area of opportunity for this investment. Factors that contributed to the decision to fund this area were the significant level of campus engagement and institutional groundwork that had been laid for the sustainability programs over the previous years, as well as the strong alignment between PSU's sustainability activities and the priorities and leadership in the broader Portland community.

>*Lesson 7: The investments of time and resources PSU administration, faculty, and students made to develop sustainability priorities in times of scarcity laid a critical foundation that positioned PSU for the investment of significant resources when the opportunity arose.*

The Miller Foundation gift was announced in September 2008, significantly elevating the level of institutional energy and activity in this area. To date, this is the largest philanthropic gift PSU has received. By structuring the $25 million gift as a ten-year challenge grant, the Miller Foundation intended PSU to use the gift to build institutional capacity and to leverage the gift through additional external funds. The gift stipulated that PSU raise an additional $2.5 million for sustainability programs every year in order to receive the following year's $2.5 million allocation.

PSU's proposal to the Miller Foundation that sustainability be the focus of their gift indicated that the funds would be invested in enhancing the student experience, expanding faculty excellence in research and teaching, and strengthening community engagement (Portland State University Miller Proposal, 2008). While it was recognized that a broader planning effort would be needed to help guide this level of investment, provisional outcomes were indicated in the proposal for each of these areas. Specific investments would be made in key staff including a student leadership position and communications and development staff. A search was already under way for a full time Director of CSP2 at the time the proposal was submitted and this position would also be supported under the grant.

A strategic planning process to guide the implementation of the gift was launched in the fall of 2008, in parallel with the identification and prioritization of investments for the first year of the gift. While there had been extensive outreach across campus preceding the Miller gift, several sessions were held to which all faculty were invited to provide input on PSU's priority opportunities and areas for investment in the sustainability arena. While primarily intended to provide input to the planning process, these sessions were in and of themselves extremely valuable exercises, as they offered the opportunity for faculty to meet each other and get to know the full range of interest and activity on campus—an ongoing challenge at a large and complex university. A number of research partnerships were forged from the relationships that were initiated at these gatherings. As with the aforementioned book discussion group, events that build social capital are essential to the success of interdisciplinary work.

>*Lesson 8: Offering formal and informal opportunities for faculty from different schools and disciplines to meet and share their work is a critical ingredient for interdisciplinary success.*

Building on these meetings, a broad RFP was issued in the fall of 2008 for a total of $1.5 million in Miller Foundation funding to ensure that the full range of sustainability activities, expertise, and opportunities on campus were identified. The criteria used to guide the RFP built on the principles that had been established in previous years, including an emphasis on interdisciplinary work, community engagement, capacity building efforts, and "catalytic" opportunities that would set the stage for external funding. Although there was a very short timeline for proposal development, almost 100 proposals were submitted in response to the RFP, totaling over $7 million in funding requests. This was an early signal that while $2.5 million a year represents a significant investment, it was not sufficient to respond to the full range of opportunities to assist sustainability scholarship at PSU. The review process for the proposals engaged internal and external experts in the fields represented by the proposals in a "single blind" review process; not surprisingly, many more proposals were favorably reviewed than could be supported through the grant. As a result, the process of prioritizing and awarding the first round of funding was both exhilarating and immensely frustrating, as many worthy projects went unfunded at that juncture.

Projects receiving support addressed a number of themes, with a key criteria for funding being capacity building, inter-disciplinary engagement, and leveraging of additional external funds. Funded projects focused on research related to sustainable water management under climate change, ecosystem service changes from dam removal, the establishment of a green building research laboratory, development of a sustainable transportation roadmap, planning and offering a "smart grid" research seminar, sustainable high-performance computing, renewable clean petroleum fuels, and support for faculty in the humanities to explore their role in the sustainability arena. While some of the themes that had emerged in earlier stages of sustainability programming are evident, the first RFP also supported a few initiatives that were emergent but that seemed promising, such as the humanities effort and the ecosystem services focus.

The strategic planning process during the first year of the Miller gift brought home the importance and the challenge of identifying priority areas for concentrated investment in order to ensure that resources are leveraged and that they result in long-term institutional capacity. As has been noted previously, the nature of sustainability as an integrative and all-encompassing concept makes it difficult to place boundaries on what is "in" and what is "out"—and, particularly when there are significant resources on the table, everyone would like to be "in" on the opportunity. Given PSU's long-standing support for an integrative approach that acknowledges the social, economic, and environmental aspects of sustainability, there was a strong push to provide resources to the social sciences and engage the humanities. On the other hand, there were more external funding resources available for engineering and some of the "hard" sciences, including in PSU's case significant matching bonds in the engineering arena. Navigating a course that leveraged institutional capacity building in terms of social capital development as well as providing for more "speculative" investments has been an ongoing challenge.

It is important to emphasize that many sustainability initiatives continued without direct support from the Miller gift. The development of a campus-wide learning outcome around sustainability that was adopted in March 2009 by the faculty senate was under way before the Miller gift and represents an important effort to fully institutionalize sustainability into the undergraduate curriculum. The campus operations aspect of sustainability efforts also proceeded apace prior to the Miller gift; while cooperation between the academic and operational efforts had been an early hallmark of PSU's sustainability strategies, this relationship has been enhanced through efforts to expand student learning opportunities related to campus-based projects such as the development of the PSU "Ecodistrict" and related activities such as the development of the Living Lab program that provides resources both from the Miller gift and from campus operational funding to more fully develop the campus as a learning laboratory for students. These significant ongoing efforts reflect the cumulative effects of building capacity among faculty with strongly-held values about the importance of sustainability scholarship and practice.

> *Lesson 9: Bringing focus to sustainability programs so that they reflect the specific assets and character of an institution is essential in order to build competitive capacity; however, the tension between focus and inclusion can be an ongoing challenge.*

Providing mechanisms for students to become engaged and to self-organize has become an important element of PSU's efforts in recent years, including the hiring of a Student Leadership and Outreach Coordinator based in Enrollment Management and Student Affairs (EMSA) to lead a student-focused Sustainability Leadership Center (see Chapter 6). The launch of an "Eco-wiki"—primarily designed and managed by students—provided an important communications portal for sustainability-related activities; channels for student-focused communication have evolved over the years and now include a regular e-newsletter.

An investment in the first year of the gift that attracted significant engagement from students was support for an "Idea Generator" where students presented their proposals for sustainability-related funding. This effort, in addition to generating significant energy among the students, also provided a locus around which student leadership could coalesce. Over time the value of providing a more structured process to better align projects with broader university needs became clear, and in recent years a Living Lab program has been established that provides a process to link PSU's Campus Sustainability Office with students to work on priority projects.

> *Lesson 10: Providing mechanisms for students to engage as fully as possible in sustainability programs leverages one of the core strengths of a university—its students—and allows their ideas to be incorporated into interdisciplinary curricula and research programs.*

The Miller gift also helped launch a faculty Fellows program in 2008, initially providing partial salary support for selected faculty to build their sustainability scholarship and to facilitate their campus leadership roles in fostering interdisciplinary research, education, and outreach. The number of Fellows was significantly expanded in later years, though most of them did not receive any direct salary support. The expansion of faculty engagement beyond those involved in the early phases was important to build the human capital base that can push the programs to the next level across campus, and address issues of succession and ongoing innovation in research and curricula. However, starting with a core group of faculty who were self-motivated and willing to put in the time to build the infrastructure was a critical first step.

The role of the Fellows program in providing ongoing guidance and governance for the sustainability programs is still being refined and clarified; a particular challenge has been finding the balance in the roles of Fellows between supporting PSU's broader sustainability efforts and providing resources that advance their own specific research interests.

> *Lesson 11: Faculty engagement was critical at all stages of PSU's sustainability program development, regardless of whether funds were available to support their efforts; however, investment of financial resources sends an important message about the value of faculty time and effort.*

As described in earlier sections, PSU already had an active sustainability research enterprise under way prior to the Miller gift. Describing a specific example may be helpful in conveying how Miller Foundation funds have been used to further foster and advance interdisciplinary scholarship. In the fall of 2007 (prior to the Miller Challenge Grant), a seven-member faculty team submitted a pre-proposal to the National Science Foundation's Integrative Graduate Education Research Traineeship (IGERT) program to establish an interdisciplinary PhD-level program focusing on ecosystem services management. Their pre-proposal was not selected for full proposal development. After a second unsuccessful submission in 2008, the seven co-principal investigators prepared an education and research capacity building proposal on ecosystem services management for the initial Miller Foundation RFP. The main objectives included the creation of an interdisciplinary course that would involve student teams analyzing the ecosystem service effects of the Marmot Dam removal on the Sandy River in Oregon, the largest dam removal in the nation at that point. Following sustainability science concepts, the course instruction and student projects would involve extensive engagement with public and private organizations involved in the dam removal. The proposal was funded for $115,000 and provided course release monies for the participating faculty to build the interdisciplinary course pedagogy and subject matter. Surprisingly, within only three weeks of advertising the new course, 16 graduate students from a diversity of programs signed up for this experimental offering. The students worked in teams of three or four on specific issues, such as stakeholder involvement in the dam removal decision process. In co-teaching the course, the core team built important social capital and increased their knowledge of interdisciplinary science and ecosystem services subject matter. The course received high evaluations by the students, and one group's project won the Sigma Chi award in the PSU student competition.

In 2009, the core team, joined by another eight associated faculty members, resubmitted an IGERT pre-proposal. With the benefit of the experience and knowledge gained through the Miller-funded project activities, they were subsequently invited to submit a full proposal by NSF. The proposed program would create four new interdisciplinary courses and use team approaches to problem-based scholarship on ecosystem service challenges in urbanizing areas with 12 local, state, and federal community partners. The proposal, entitled "Ecosystem Services for Urbanizing Regions (ESUR)," was selected by NSF for funding in 2010 and awarded $3 million to create a "PhD plus" interdisciplinary training program—the only IGERT awarded to Portland State University.

To date, the IGERT program has 29 PhD students enrolled with a team of 31 diverse faculty from five colleges who advise, teach or assist the students in conducting interdisciplinary research projects. CSP2, which was renamed the Institute for Sustainable Solutions in 2010, has been instrumental in bolstering student research support for the IGERT program as it addresses key priorities of the Miller Challenge grant. The success of the IGERT program and of other research initiatives, such as PSU's transportation programs, illustrate that areas where faculty are already working together or where there is strong faculty leadership provide the strongest base for program enhancement. However, efforts to develop a cohesive research effort in other areas such as water resources have been less successful in articulating a shared research agenda that encompasses the various areas of research. Ultimately, faculty leadership, their willingness to invest time and effort in building research agendas, and their openness to other disciplinary perspectives and paradigms are essential ingredients for success.

> *Lesson 12: While having financial resources to invest in supporting faculty research can provide useful incentives to engage in collaborative work, such resources cannot substitute for the leadership that must be provided by individual and groups of faculty to build effective collaborative, interdisciplinary programs.*

PSU has also learned some lessons about the need to have alignment between program leadership, institutional identity, and programmatic priorities. In 2010 internationally recognized ecological economist Robert Costanza was appointed Director of CSP2, which was soon to be renamed the Institute for Sustainable Solutions (ISS). Costanza's stature brought increased attention to PSU and its sustainability efforts, and his long-standing engagement in ecosystem service research contributed to PSU's profile in this arena.

The importance of having leadership committed to the capacity building intention of the Miller gift became clear during Costanza's tenure as Director. While having a Director who was a well-recognized scholar brought prominence to the position and the institution, more attention was needed on issues of basic institutional capacity, given where PSU was in its development of sustainability programs. Recognizing that these issues were not a priority focus for Costanza and that a more PSU-centric approach was needed in order to achieve these capacity building goals, co-author and former Associate Director of CSP2 Jennifer Allen was appointed Interim Director in late 2011 and appointed Director in 2012.

Lesson 13: Be true to your institution's identity and candid about its most important needs—"growing your own" leadership can help ensure ownership and alignment with your institution's priorities.

The value of taking a proactive and aggressive approach to communicating about sustainability efforts on campus cannot be understated. Communication was always seen as an important investment, from the engagement of a communications consultant during the 2005 strategic planning process to the investment in strong communications staff at ISS in more recent years. However, given the decentralized structure of universities, the difficulty of getting the attention of busy faculty, staff, students, and community partners, and the complex nature of sustainability itself, effective communication is both essential and challenging.

Building capacity across campus, while maintaining a clear and identifiable sustainability enterprise, also presents a complex set of opportunities and challenges. The Declaration of Support for Sustainability noted above laid out important guiding principles for the development of sustainability programs at PSU: the opportunity to view it as a campus-wide program and to find ways to harness the assets of the campus toward excellence in this area. A few examples that demonstrate this approach include ISS's partnership with the School of Business Administration to support the Impact Entrepreneurs social entrepreneurship program; the investment in faculty lines and research efforts such as the Green Portable Classroom that helped lay the foundation for the establishment of the Center for Public Interest Design; and the support for the Student Sustainability Center's coordinator based in EMSA noted above. In each of these cases, timely investments helped build programs in a way that ensured their integration with key communities of interest.

These investments, while aligned with the Miller gift's intention to build the institution's capacity, also highlight an ongoing challenge that ISS has faced: developing and maintaining an identity of its own while serving as a catalyst and steward for programs based in other campus units. Crafting a communications strategy that honors both of these dynamics and that provides sufficient understanding of the value of units like ISS in building overall institutional capacity also continues to be a work in progress.

Engaging faculty, students, and staff in communicating externally about PSU's efforts at conferences and in other venues has also been a critical factor in raising the university's profile in this area. Given limited resources for travel and conference attendance, ISS's ability to provide such support has facilitated these opportunities. The work that has been done to raise PSU's profile in the sustainability arena may also have helped contribute to PSU securing several interdisciplinary research grants.

> *Lesson 14: Clear and ongoing communication about program activities and approaches is particularly important when taking an embedded and distributed approach to sustainability; in addition, maintaining a unit's identity while taking a campus-wide approach can pose ongoing communication challenges. Engaging representatives of PSU in other venues to spread the word of our work has also been an important factor in raising the profile of this program.*

ISS has moved in recent years toward developing more intentional and sustained partnerships with key community organizations to help provide for more cumulative impact and to create systems that allow for iterative problem solving over time. For example, as described in Chapter 11, ISS has partnered with the Bullitt Foundation to invest in support for faculty and staff to work with the City of Portland's Bureau of Planning and Sustainability to identify key research questions related to the city's Climate Action Plan; ISS then has played a role in identifying faculty whose expertise and interests align with these areas and has brokered a process to further refine research questions and provide support to faculty and students to work on these topics. While PSU has a long-standing tradition of community partnerships, this approach differs in the value-added role that ISS plays in supporting the partnership, and in its focus on ongoing dialogue and development of a shared research agenda that can build over time. In 2015, ISS established an advisory council made up primarily of community partners to help provide ongoing guidance on where ISS should focus its work and investments to ensure it is responsive to priority community needs. Almost all of those invited to join the council agreed, including sustainability leaders from government agencies, non-profits, and the private sector. This provides one indication of the value the community sees in the work ISS has done over the years in helping build meaningful community connections.

This brokering role with the community parallels the role that CSP2/ISS has played within the university over the past decade—particularly in institutions like universities, which are organized around multiple disciplines, have a number of schools or colleges, and which increasingly are organized around performance-based budget models which provide few incentives for collaborative work. Having a unit that can help to build connections and defray some of the transaction costs of doing interdisciplinary and collaborative work can be a major asset. However, upper administration must recognize and value that role, with ongoing resource commitments, for it to flourish.

Lesson 15: Having a unit that can play a brokering role between the community and PSU as well as across the campus provides a critical infrastructure that can help facilitate deeper and stronger partnerships and champion interdisciplinary and collaborative work.

While progress has been made on interdisciplinary work, challenges remain. ISS hosts the Graduate Certificate in Sustainability described above, which as noted has faced a number of challenges in terms of support for team teaching, ability to respond when additional course sections were needed, and cohesion across the program. In recent years ISS has worked with faculty to design new certificates in focused areas that transcend traditional disciplines, including an undergraduate sustainability certificate and graduate energy and food systems certificates. After a decision by PSU's deans that such programs needed to be hosted within credit-granting units, ISS worked to identify logical homes for these programs that would allow them to maintain an interdisciplinary approach. For the food systems certificate, ISS worked with the deans of the four schools and colleges involved in the program to craft a memorandum of understanding (MOU) that established coordinating mechanisms to support the program and attempted to mitigate the institutional pressure to capture student credit hours. This approach may provide a model for similar certificates in sustainability fields.

ISS also has taken the lead to collect data related to the challenges of doing interdisciplinary work in order to provide a more objective basis for exploration of strategies to support such work. A focus group of faculty from a broad set of disciplines indicated both strong interest to engage in interdisciplinary research and teaching, and frustration with the institutional structures—such as budgeting that puts primary focus on generation of student credit hours within each college over other forms of academic productivity and performance—that make such work challenging. While the MOU for the food systems certificate noted above may mitigate some of the pressures related to programs that engage multiple units, more needs to be done to reward and incentivize such work if the institution is serious about advancing integrative efforts.

Work also remains to be done in ensuring that basic sustainability literacy is part of every student's experience at PSU. The Student Sustainability Center in EMSA (see Chapter 6) has helped expand the exposure of students to these concepts, and in 2009 PSU adopted a campus-side sustainability learning outcome; however, while the undergraduate University Studies general education program has been very successful in ensuring that community-engaged learning is part of the undergraduate experience (see Chapter 2), sustainability is not a learning outcome of the program. While the process of developing the undergraduate certificate has helped to better define how the campus-wide learning would translate into measurable indicators and competencies, PSU still lacks a mechanism to ensure that all students are exposed to sustainability concepts. Until PSU adopts sustainability as a core goal of the institution that exposure will likely remain inadequate. It would certainly seem appropriate that each PSU graduate have meaningful training in sustainability theory and practice given Portland's international leadership role in sustainable development. In doing so, the faculty and administration will likely discover innovative ways to deliver interdisciplinary education that helps achieve PSU's aspiration of become a leading urban research university.

> *Lesson 16: Having a unit that can champion collaborative and interdisciplinary work is beneficial, but cannot substitute for broader institutional commitments to advancing these efforts by adopting core values, addressing organizational disincentives, and providing of adequate resources.*

Overarching lessons and remaining challenges

The development of PSU's sustainability programs described in this chapter has been a process of ongoing learning and adaptation toward achieving our long-term aspiration to be a national leader in sustainability scholarship. While substantial progress has been made, challenges remain. As for embedding institutional change as programs mature, engaging new leaders, indeed champions, will be key (Ostrom, 2009). That leadership may be fostered most effectively by empowering all parts of the academy to play roles in innovating sustainability programs. One of the overarching lessons in Portland State University's journey to advance sustainability scholarship is the importance of engaging a wide diversity of students, staff, faculty, and administrators.

The lessons that we have highlighted in this chapter reflect our experience and assessment of some of the key considerations other institutions might take into account in building their academic sustainability enterprises. Some of our learning may have applicability and value for other academic institutions, but generalization must proceed cautiously. We recognize that each institution has its own unique culture, context, and characteristics, and that sustainability initiatives should take these factors into account in order to ensure that they are aligned with, and leverage, the institution's key assets and aspirations. Indeed, the process of discovering the best path forward for a college or university should make full use of their experiential knowledge, one of the canons of sustainability theory and practice.

References

Batie, S. (2008). Wicked Problems and Applied Economics. *American Journal of Agricultural Economics*, 90(5), 1,176-1,191.

Castle, E., Berrens, R., & Polasky, S. (1996). Economics of Sustainability. *Natural Resources Journal*, 36(Fall), 715-730.

Clark, W., & Dixon, N. (2003). Sustainability science: The emerging research program. *Proceedings of the National Academy of Science*, 100(14), 8,059-8,061.

Diamond, J. (2005). *Collapse: How Societies Choose to Fail or Succeed*. New York: Viking Press.

Dillard, J., Dujon, V., & King, M. (Eds.). (2009). *Understanding the Social Dimensions of Sustainability*. Oxford: Routledge.

Dujon, V., Dillard, J., & Brennan, E. (2015). *Social Sustainability: A Multilevel Approach to Social Inclusion*. Oxford: Routledge.

Ervin, D. & Allen, J. (2006). PSU Sustainability Program Overview, Portland State University. Retrieved from http://www.pdx.edu/sustainability/sites/www.pdx.edu.sustainability/files/Public%20presentation%20on%20PSU%27s%20sustainability%20programs%2C%20November%202006.pdf

Ervin, D., Larsen, G., & C. Shinn, C. (2012). Simple Ecosystem Service Valuation Can Impact National Forest Management. *Essay for American Association of Environmental and Resource Economists Newsletter*, Spring, 17-22.

Gunderson, L., & Holling, C.S. (Eds.). (2002). *Panarchy: Understanding Transformations in Natural and Human Systems*. Washington, DC: Island Press.

Halimi, S., Babcock, J., & Ingle, M. (2016). Promoting international urban sustainability through innovative community–university partnership: The case of Hoi An, Vietnam. In B.D. Wortham-Galvin, J. Allen & J. Sherman, *University–Community Partnerships*. Sheffield, UK: Greenleaf Publishing.

Lubin, D.A., & Esty, D.C. (2010). The Sustainability Imperative. *Harvard Business Review*, May, 42-50.

Max-Neef, M.A. (2005). Foundations of Transdisciplinarity: Commentary. *Ecological Economics*, 53, 5-16.

National Research Council (1999). *Our Common Journey: A Transition Toward Sustainability*. Washington, DC: National Academies Press.

National Research Council (2014). *Pathways to Urban Sustainability: Perspective from Portland and the Pacific Northwest: Summary of a Workshop*. Washington, DC: National Academies Press.

Ostrom, E. (2009). A General Framework for Analyzing the Sustainability of Socio-Ecological Systems. *Science*, 325(July), 419-422.

Portland State University Miller Proposal (2008). James F. and Marion Miller Foundation proposal for establishing a World Class Center for Sustainability at Portland State University. Retrieved from: http://www.pdx.edu/sustainability/envisioning-background-material

Rittel, H., & Webber, M. (1973). Dilemmas in a General Theory of Planning. *Policy Sciences*, 5, 155-169.

Shandas, V., & Messer, W.B. (2008). Fostering green communities through civic engagement: Community-based environmental stewardship in the Portland area. *Journal of the American Planning Association*, 74(4), 408-418.

Yeakley, J.A. (2012). Research on urban ecosystems. In: D. Roix (Ed.), *Regional Conservation Strategy for the Greater Portland-Vancouver Region* (pp. 106-109). Portland: The Intertwine Alliance.

2

Sustainable community-based learning

Engaging undergraduates across a four-year general education curriculum

J.R. "Jones" Estes, Jeff Gerwing, and Celine Fitzmaurice

Wandering the hallways of Cramer Hall on any weekday morning, one is likely to encounter the hum of a University Studies class in session. Within these classrooms, students from various majors are grouped around tables, engaged in dialogue or working on projects related to pressing social and environmental themes. These courses, with titles like "Healthy People, Healthy Places," "Global Environmental Change," and "Indigenous Gardens and Food Justice," form the backbone of University Studies, a unique general education program at Portland State University. While the course themes vary tremendously, all of the courses are designed to help students develop the knowledge and skills to engage in civic life and bring their disciplinary expertise to bear on real-world problems. The faculty represent individuals from a range of disciplines and academic ranks who contribute their own academic knowledge, community contacts, and passions to the course design.

This chapter describes how we scaffold student community engagement in sustainability-related courses across a four-year general education curriculum. We argue that the role of community engagement in a course should parallel both developing student understanding of complex sustainability issues and student capacity to apply that knowledge to multiple contexts. Learning about sustainability issues inspires an eagerness among students in first and second year courses "to do something" to make the world a better place. In these courses, assigned community-engagement projects nurture that eagerness while providing a supportive and structured platform where students develop their abilities to analyze sustainability-related issues, assess the implications of action for diverse stakeholders, and communicate across differences in values and cultures. Through these transformative projects, students develop a deeper understanding of course content, build a better understanding of the complexities of meaningful and responsible community engagement, and gain transferable knowledge and skills.

Program history and overview

University Studies was established as the general education program for Portland State University in 1994. Informed by the growing literature of the scholarship of teaching and learning, University Studies was created to replace the distribution or cafeteria models of general education with an interdisciplinary, student-centered, and community-based learning experience. At the heart of the program are its four learning goals: Critical Inquiry and Thinking, Communication, Respect for the Diversity of Human Experience, and Ethics and Social Responsibility. The curricula is delivered over four years, or levels, of the student experience from freshmen through senior year. Each level of the program is structured differently with continuity provided by the shared learning goals and a student-centered emphasis on learning communities within a seminar format.

Figure 2.1 illustrates how students progress through the program. In the first year students take Freshmen Inquiry, a year-long, theme-based seminar, as a 36-student cohort taught by the same professor. Sophomore Inquiry courses are also theme-based and limited to 36 students; however, rather than remain a cohort with a single professor, students choose three courses from among the themes. As a result, students have the opportunity to explore three different themes of interest over the course of the year. Unique to Freshmen and Sophomore Inquiry is the role of peer mentors. In Freshmen Inquiry, upper division undergraduates lead subsections of 12 students, twice a week, in activities developed by the professor that support the learning goals of the course. In Sophomore Inquiry, these subsections meet once a week and are led by a graduate student. Once the three Sophomore Inquiry courses are complete, students choose one of these themes to examine more deeply as a junior. Thus, the Junior Cluster requirement is comprised of three courses grouped around a theme that builds upon their chosen Sophomore Inquiry theme. In the senior year, students choose from a variety of Capstone course options to complete their general education. While Capstone courses vary in theme, every course is linked to a community partner with whom students engage in a large-scale community based learning project. While the structure of the University Studies program is prescribed, the topics of study are up to the student's interests. Similarly, the themes developed and taught at each level are the product of faculty interest.

Figure 2.1 The University Studies program at a glance

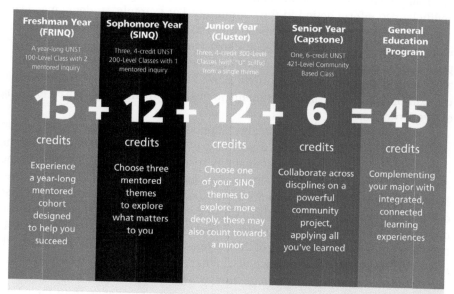

Freshman Year (FRINQ)	Sophomore Year (SINQ)	Junior Year (Cluster)	Senior Year (Capstone)	General Education Program
A year-long UNST 100-Level Class with 2 mentored inquiry	Three, 4-credit UNST 200-Level Classes with 1 mentored inquiry	Three, 4-credit 300-Level Classes (with "U" suffix) from a single theme	One, 6-credit UNST 421-Level Community Based Class	
15 +	**12** +	**12** +	**6** =	**45**
credits	credits	credits	credits	credits
Experience a year-long mentored cohort designed to help you succeed	Choose three mentored themes to explore what matters to you	Choose one of your SINQ themes to explore more deeply, these may also count towards a minor	Collaborate across discplines on a powerful community project, applying all you've learned	Complementing your major with integrated, connected learning experiences

Scaffolding sustainability education

It has helped that the educational objectives of the four University Studies' learning goals are symbiotic with the goals of sustainability education. Both seek to empower and prepare students to address the big questions and wicked problems of the twenty-first century through building student capacity. Thus the program has always had sustainability-related courses at each of its levels. However, with the rise of sustainability as a distinct area of academic inquiry, the program's course offerings addressing issues of sustainability have clarified and grown significantly. For example, in 2009 sustainability was adopted as a university-wide learning outcome, expanding the opportunities to create and collaborate across campus on the development of sustainability-related curriculum within and beyond the University Studies program. This is to say, the curricula described below did not form itself neatly and whole. It evolved over time within the context of the campus and community work described in other chapters.

Levels

Within the framework of the four University Studies' goals, the Sustainability Freshmen Inquiry course provides students with background knowledge on sustainability-related issues. Students then use that knowledge to develop a sustainability lens to inform action in the community. For example, students may learn about water use around the world and then examine how that use intersects with issues of economic, environmental, and social justice to create their own antiwater privatization event. The unique, year-long cohort structure of Freshmen Inquiry, along with its peer mentor component, allows faculty to pace content and scaffold the skill-building necessary for students to engage in community-based learning at a variety of depths.

In the Environmental Sustainability Sophomore Inquiry, students engage in the same process within the ten-week frame of the course. This short time frame fosters an intensive focus on sustainability-related challenges. For students who choose Environmental Sustainability as their Junior Cluster theme, there are over 30 classes offered by 17 departments from which students create their own course of study through their choice of three Cluster courses. Providing students with an opportunity to study sustainability issues in-depth based upon their own interests cultivates student understanding of the range, scale, and complexity of sustainability issues. These courses introduce disciplinary understandings of sustainability, range in size, and do not include a mentor section.

In the Senior Capstone course, students integrate knowledge from their University Studies and major courses and apply it to a sustainability-related concern. Capstone courses are small by design, with a typical course size of 15 students. Examples of sustainability-themed Capstone courses include "Sustainable Living" and "Grant Writing for Language Sustainability." When students arrive at the Capstone, the emphasis shifts from gaining knowledge and skills for community-based learning to applying the knowledge and skills gained through an extended community-based learning project. The Capstone experience highlights the challenges and rewards of addressing local sustainability issues in collaboration with community members. Ultimately, the course provides students a real world context for their work.

Within this four-year model, Freshmen Inquiry and the Capstone are the program's signature experiences that bookend the student's' general education journey. However, the student-centered nature of the program fosters the common practices of community-based learning and critical self-reflection that are key to sustainability education throughout the four years.

Application

In University Studies, with multidisciplinary faculty that rotate in and out, tapping the interests of faculty in identifying themes that translate well into community-based learning projects has been key to building a robust sustainability curriculum. At Portland State, the themes of food systems, water use, and climate change are prevalent across the University Studies sustainability curriculum.

Early and frequent opportunities for community-based learning lay the essential groundwork for deep community work in the Capstone and in life beyond the University. Consequently, the Freshmen through Junior Cluster course offerings provide students with an opportunity to build toward a significant community-based learning project through a variety of "soft" partnership experiences. These include:

- Utilizing internal campus partners for students to engage with existing campus programs

- Employing existing community events

- Exposing students to active community projects through site visits

- Matching small groups of students to community partners with a well-developed volunteer infrastructure

- Asking students to identify their own community partners

Within the context of a course, these five straightforward approaches to community-based learning offer faculty a variety of ways to introduce students to engagement and developing self-understanding and agency within the context of course material with minimal additional effort. Within the context of the program, they provide the foundation for students to engage more deeply with a Capstone community partner. A variety of community-based learning experiences provides students with the opportunity to engage with multiple aspects of sustainability, naturally engage student interest, and lend themselves to projects of varying levels of sophistication and community engagement. The most essential element to the success of a community-based project rests within the instructions of the assignment it fulfills. Specifically, every community-based activity requires that the students articulate the components of critical self-reflection and connection to the course material.

First year

In Freshmen Inquiry, few students have engaged in community-based activities on their own and even fewer have done so explicitly for the purpose of learning. Consequently, in this first year, we scaffold their community-based experiences. The first quarter introduces students to the concept of community-based learning through two community-based assignments, such as a site visit and a small group research project.

For example, students are assigned a text such as *The Omnivore's Dilemma* (Pollan, 2007) that explores interactions among the environmental, social, and economic aspects of our industrial food system. Community-based projects provide opportunities for students to connect their classroom learning to the "real world" by exploring how themes raised in the book play out in local food systems. In one course, students complete a "Food System Inquiry," in small teams and develop a research question related to food and food systems that can be answered using data that they collect themselves. Questions that students have addressed include:

- Are supermarket prices more expensive downtown than in the suburbs of Portland?

- What would be the cost of switching a "typical" student diet to organic?

- What is the difference in costs between shopping at a farmer's market and a supermarket?

- Can one actually save money by eating a vegetarian (or even a reduced-meat) diet?

In another Freshmen Inquiry, also working in small groups, students are asked to visit a local farmer's market and interview proprietors using questions they developed while reading *The Omnivore's Dilemma* (2007), then analyze their findings against Pollan's and formally present their findings to the class. Asking students to reflect and relate these activities to the course materials, along with considering their role in completing the project, in formal and informal written reflections and class discussions, are key to their impact. Combining these two components facilitates student recognition of their role and responsibility in their own learning.

Continuing the pattern of two community-based projects within ten weeks, winter term students are assigned activities such as participating in a campus-wide Day of Service, visiting an art museum exhibition that relates to the course, and visiting a local non-profit doing work on an issue related to that term's course content.

Through the established expectation of community-based assignments, by spring term, students are primed for a more involved and independent community-based learning project. In one class this may be a student-planned and led social change event while in another course students are key partners in a community festival. Regardless of the type of community-based activities across sections of the Sustainability courses, the Freshmen Inquiry year culminates in an ePortfolio where students compile their work and reflections from throughout the year. Because students have been practicing critical self-reflection throughout the year in a variety of contexts, the final step of formally organizing and articulating how their work exemplifies the four University Studies goals provides students with a deeper understanding of themselves as learners.

Second and third year

In the Environmental Sustainability Sophomore Inquiry, students continue developing their understanding of themselves as connected members of the community and environment. At this level, students experience increased independence and responsibility for forming their own path of community-engagement. The term begins with students conducting a resource audit—water, for example—of their personal use that they then analyze using course readings and present back to the class. Next, students create their own small-group, community-based learning projects. This process includes choosing a sustainability-related issue and researching it to develop a local action plan. That action plan may be either an intervention/behavior change campaign or assisting a community organization. Once the action is complete, students evaluate the efficacy of their intervention and develop suggestions for further action at local and global levels.

After completing the Environmental Sustainability Sophomore Inquiry, students move into the Junior Cluster where they participate in community-based learning activities as diverse as the 30 courses offered within the Cluster. For example, from Fundamentals of Environmental Design (Architecture) to Literature and Ecology (English) to Indigenous and Systems Perspectives on Sustainability (Systems Science), the course offerings at the Junior level encourage students to explore the multitude of disciplinary perspectives on sustainability and creating meaningful community engagement experiences.

Senior year

Building on the groundwork of the previous three levels, Senior Capstone courses ask students to apply the knowledge and skills developed in their previous coursework to the completion of an in-depth community-based project. Each course partners with a local organization addressing critical community needs. Working in interdisciplinary teams, students apply sophisticated sustainability concepts to real world problems identified by the community partners. Sample concepts include a "commons approach" to managing and preserving shared resources or "just sustainability" as it relates to production, distribution, and access to food. Ultimately, the Capstone situates sustainability concepts studied over the four-year program in on-the-ground practice while fostering connections with community partners that often last beyond graduation.

"Reclaiming the Commons" is an example of a sustainability-focused Capstone that allows students to bring together their previous community-based learning experiences to create a culminating experience. In this class students learn about the political and economic history of the commons and consider ways to manage and sustain our shared ecological, cultural and societal resources moving forward. The course was inspired by an emerging global movement to embrace a commons framework for raising consciousness and action related to sustainability. This diverse community of scholars and activists refers to the commons as "things that we inherit and create jointly, and that will (hopefully) last for generations to come" (On The Commons, 2015). The commons includes the interconnected ecosystems services that sustain life on the planet as well as shared social creations such as art, scientific research, public spaces and libraries. A commons-based approach questions how the enclosure of various aspects of the commons has benefitted the market at the expense of communities and future generations. It does not limit itself to ecological sustainability. For this reason it provides a connecting point for students of various disciplines to apply their expertise to multiple dimensions of sustainability.

A number of activities guide student exploration of this theme over the course of the term. Early in the term, students participate in a facilitated workshop in which they jointly brainstorm and cluster various aspects of the commons into categories. This helps them to name what they value and wish to preserve for themselves and future generations. Toward the midpoint of the term, students form into teams and teach their peers about the commons through a series of "Common Teach-ins." Through the "teach-ins," student teams share information about a threat to the commons and analyze the efforts of local commons-based movements to address these threats. Finally, these same teams engage in a community-based learning partnership to raise public awareness of the commons and contribute to the collaborative management of our shared resources. Final projects have included a social media campaign to raise awareness of wetlands, a video highlighting the importance of policy efforts to protect our commonwealth, and a literacy campaign to strengthen the educational programming of an underserved elementary school.

In this course, we often reflect on the motto "We're all better off when we are all better off." Effectively managing and preserving our commonwealth for ourselves and future generations requires a significant transition in the way we view our world. Moving from "me to we" means thinking and acting outside of an individual and market-based paradigm. In short, it means prioritizing the common good over individual gain. While this approach can be easiest to grasp and enact at an individual or local-scale, students recognize that advocating for national and international policies will ensure the sustainable management of our commonwealth for all of earth's citizens and for generations to come.

Challenges and opportunities

As individual learners, students come to understand the value of experiential learning at different points. For many freshmen, the background knowledge necessary to engage with and analyze sustainability issues is new and shocking. We have found that by taking freshmen out of the classroom and beyond the course books, community-based learning counteracts the development of passivity, hopelessness, or cynicism. However, as a largely transfer institution, the majority of students graduated by Portland State enter after their first year. Scaffolding the community-based learning for these students is much more difficult because we do not know what community-based learning experience, if any, they bring with them. Currently, transfer students, either as sophomores or juniors, enter the sustainability curriculum without the broad, foundational exploration of sustainability and community-based learning provided in Freshmen Inquiry. While the majority of Portland State students will continue to enter into the sustainability curriculum at a variety of levels, as a program we are exploring the development of a bridge course to serve as a transition and ensure that students are equally prepared to do the engaged work required at the junior and senior levels.

Our transfer students also miss the practice of creating an ePortfolio that occurs in the Freshmen Inquiry course. As a program, we have begun moving the ePortfolio component up through each level to support students in developing an on-going practice of critical self-reflection and to maximize their opportunity to make connections among all of their coursework and experiences. To assist with this, Portland State recently licensed an online learning platform designed for this purpose.

The transformative role of community-based learning for students is well established; however, its impact on faculty can be overlooked. For the faculty practicing community-based learning, there is a level of risk-taking and vulnerability that requires support. Most disciplinary cultures neither prepare nor reward the work inherent in innovative and collaborative models of curriculum development. Furthermore, transformational learning can be messy because it pushes students and because it takes them outside the predictability of the classroom. We have found the practice of deep and ongoing faculty development support, including frequent formative assessment, crucial to the program. Examples include the programmatic practice of formal reflective retreats, informal "brown bag" lunches, as well as one-on-one support as necessary. This high level of ongoing professional development support is possible because the sustainability curriculum is one theme of many that benefits from the University Studies program's commitment to faculty development.

Because faculty are supported, we see high levels of innovation, independence, and ingenuity. The drawback to our "grassroots" approach to course development and community-based projects may, at times, result in lack of coordination among courses working in similar community contexts/neighborhoods. The Learning Gardens Lab described in Chapter 4 is one attempt to turn this challenge into an opportunity.

Conclusion

Our flexible and graduated approach to community-based learning moves students from an introductory understanding of sustainability to deep engagement in sustainability through community-based experiences. When developing a community-based curriculum within the framework of sustainability education, we have found the importance of balancing prescriptive course sequencing with opportunities for students and faculty to be "free-range" and explore emerging issues and interests as they arise. Capstone programs are increasing nationally and, perhaps because they are intensive to develop, it is understandable that an institution may decide that a Capstone course is enough to instill the skills and values of community engagement. We argue the opposite: that the Capstone experience is a product of students' previous community-based learning and that providing students with consistent and frequent opportunities to learn in community is essential to students maximizing the potential that a Capstone course offers.

One may compare the University Studies program to a living organism. While the basic framework of the program has remained stable since its inception, the content of the curriculum is constantly growing and evolving based on emerging issues. Over the past 15 years, courses with a sustainability theme have multiplied and rooted themselves in the curriculum. The curriculum is dynamic and flexible. Therefore, a faculty member can easily adapt or create a course to respond to emerging topics. Similarly, the program's focus on community engagement and civic agency lends itself well to sustainability topics. Our interdisciplinary nature allows for a holistic exploration of sustainability that draws on the disciplinary knowledge and skills of students and faculty alike. Finally, the program's emphasis on community engagement and civic agency provides students with the opportunity to apply their knowledge to any area or problem utilizing a sustainability lens—a perspective that serves us all well.

References

Bollier, D. (2003). *Silent Theft*. New York: Routledge Press.

On The Commons. (2015) *About us*. Retrieved from: http://www.onthecommons.org/about-commons

Pollan, M. (2007). *The Omnivore's Dilemma: A Natural History of Four Meals*. New York: The Penguin Group.

3

SBA Undergraduate Business Strategy/Capstone Program

The value of working with community-based partners

William Jones and Darrell Brown

This chapter describes the conversion of a traditional lecture-based business strategy course into an innovative community-based learning (CBL) course. The business strategy course is designed to be the final course that undergraduate business majors take and is considered to be a "capstone" course; a course in which students integrate the learning they have accumulated throughout their academic careers. The course, as converted into a CBL course, integrates broad general education goals and traditional business strategy content through a community-based project with explicit deliverables, based on opportunities or problems identified by community partners. Significantly, these changes allowed the business strategy course to serve as the university capstone (required of all Portland State University undergraduate students) while simultaneously improving the experience that students received in the business capstone. We provide a historical view of the conversion so that other institutions considering such a change can learn from our experience.

At Portland State University (PSU) all undergraduates must take a university-mandated capstone class prior to graduation.[1] This capstone is the culminating portion of the University Studies (UNST) program, which is the general education program for undergraduate students.[2] The UNST capstone requires engagement with a community partner, has students work in cross-disciplinary teams, and produces a deliverable at the end of the term. The UNST learning goals, which are capstone goals as well, are communication, inquiry and critical thinking, the diversity of human experience, and ethics and social responsibility. UNST capstones are very small six-credit classes, with approximately 20 students per section, with the vast majority taught by part-time adjunct instructors. The subject matter of these capstones requires no disciplinary background. As such, UNST capstones tend toward a broadening experience around service learning with community partners that work to address many of the challenges of contemporary society. The classes are highly varied, which makes assuring students of a community based learning (CBL) experience relating to their academic education problematic.

In the School of Business Administration (SBA), all business undergraduates take a core set of courses that provide a broad business education and then specialize in one of seven "disciplines" such as finance, accounting, or marketing. The business strategy course is the culminating core course, required of all undergraduate business majors.

The primary learning goal supported by the course is "theory to action", which reflects the SBA's objective of having students understand how to take their academic experience and bring it to life in practice. Prior to the changes described in this chapter, students were confined to working on academic cases and text-related activities.

The remainder of this chapter is divided into two primary sections. The first relates the process of establishing the CBL course that currently exists. This section is framed around the "barriers" encountered and negotiated during the process. The second section describes the implementation and continuing evolution of the course since its inception in fall term of 2011. The types of activities required for implementation subdivide this section.

Section 1: Creating the CBL business strategy course

To describe how the course change occurred, we focus on the primary barriers, or difficulties encountered. The barriers ranged from funding to institutional

---

1 There are a relatively small number of undergraduates who attend the Honors College. Those students do not take the UNST program and are not required to take a UNST capstone course

2 For a comprehensive description of the UNST curriculum, see Chapter 2 of this volume.

structures to territorial perspectives. More specifically, the main barriers to be dealt with were:

1. **Funding**. The SBA needed two new full-time tenure-related faculty plus a full-time support person.

2. **Institutional structures**. Two university-wide faculty committees, one PSU administrative committee, the SBA Faculty Council, and PSU Faculty Senate needed to approve the change.

3. **Territoriality**. The UNST faculty and administrators had to relinquish some of the content and structure of the capstones. The business strategy faculty in the SBA had to give up some business strategy content to include the CBL content.

We discuss each barrier individually.

Barriers: funding

At PSU, as in most universities, the pay structure for faculty in different roles and different departments varies widely. To move the capstones from adjuncts teaching UNST classes to tenure line professors teaching in the business school requires significantly increased amounts of funding. In addition to funding two tenure-line faculty, the move from UNST, which has infrastructure to support CBL, to the SBA with no such infrastructure, required hiring a full-time support person.

Moving from the 20-student classes in UNST to 35-student classes in the SBA mitigated part of the funding increase. Ultimately, the funding for the new tenure-line faculty came from:

- Savings from hiring fewer adjunct faculty in the SBA due to the new tenure-line faculty

- Hiring fewer adjunct faculty in UNST due to the reduced number of course sections taught by UNST

- Additional funds from the central administration. The Provost's commitment to two new tenure lines in the SBA was a crucial piece of the funding puzzle.

Barriers: institutional structures

The logistics of getting approval to teach the UNST capstone class in the SBA included committees within the School and across the campus. As faculty have control over the curriculum and the UNST capstone is a part of the undergraduate requirements for graduating from PSU, changes such as this receive considerable oversight. We address each level of oversight below.

The University Studies Council, a standing committee of the Faculty Senate, controls the UNST curriculum. In order to meet the Council's concerns, we consulted extensively with the faculty and staff who coordinate and implement many of the existing UNST capstones. A lead SBA faculty member, who had considerable experience teaching SBA business strategy, worked for almost a year developing and testing a syllabus that would be true to the UNST goals while meeting the expanded goals of the new SBA capstone. UNST staff provided considerable support and one particularly experienced staff member was detailed part-time to provide SBA support for developing this syllabus. After numerous iterations, the team created a syllabus that addressed the UNST concerns while meeting the needs of the faculty teaching business strategy.

Including a significant CBL project was integral to creating a successful syllabus and course. After receiving assurance from the UNST staffers who assisted in converting the class from UNST to SBA, the University Studies Council approved the syllabus.

Concurrently with working for the approval of the University Studies council, we needed to work with the SBA Undergraduate Curriculum Committee (UCC) to get its approval for the course changes. This committee approves all significant course changes in the SBA. A number of issues concerned the UCC including:

- How to assign teaching loads (typical tenure-line faculty loads are 20 credits per year; shifting from four credits per class to six credits per class makes annual loads irregular)

- Whether it was possible to reduce the strategy content and maintain the course's integrity

- How to create an infrastructure to facilitate engaging with community partners, and perhaps most importantly

- Why we would make this change.

We agreed to assign course loads in three-year cycles, with two years of teaching 18 credits (three sections) and one year teaching 24 credits (four sections). The syllabus development by our lead faculty, in consultation with other SBA faculty teaching the course, assured the UCC that the course's integrity could be maintained.

As a result of the UCC's concern about the ability of individual faculty members to keep up with all their other duties and adequately work with community partners, we requested and received a full-time person to oversee the CBL-oriented portion of all of the sections of our course. This person would nurture, coordinate, and oversee the SBA-community partner relationships. A person dedicated to cultivating and maintaining these relationships addressed the UCC's concern.

The final issue concerning the UCC was the most important: why make this change at all? There were two perspectives to consider:

- Why would the University want to move some of its undergraduate general education requirement into the SBA, and

- Why would the School be interested in taking over that requirement?

From the University's perspective, the ability to have tenure line faculty teaching a course designed to be an "integrative cumulating experience" appealed to the administration. Most UNST capstones (over 60%) are taught by adjuncts and the administration wanted to have more students receive this experience with full time faculty. In addition, the ability to bring the capstone into a school such as the SBA allowed the capstone to have content that relied on the students having some baseline academic experience. UNST capstones had no coursework prerequisites and therefore could not assume any content knowledge by the students, meaning the students could often take an "academic capstone" that had no relationship to their academic background.

From the SBA's perspective, combining the business capstone with the university capstone made the university capstone more relevant to many students. One of the goals of the SBA, as a school, is to provide opportunities for the students to translate their theoretical learning into practical applications. Revising the university capstone to include a significant CBL experience incorporating their SBA academic learning ensures that every student has a "theory to practice" experience in their academic career. Other benefits include increasing the number of relationships between community partners and the school and the addition of two tenure-line faculty to bolster the research productivity of the school.

The process of addressing all the concerns of the UCC and, subsequently the SBA Faculty Council, took significant time and energy. At the end of the process, however, the SBA support was strong. The addition of two tenure-line faculty plus a full-time support person, combined with improving the student experience through a well-designed CBL course, made implementing the change appealing to the SBA faculty.

Meeting the concerns of the University Undergraduate Curriculum Committee (UUCC) proved to be less onerous, as the Committee's concerns centered on whether the course, as re-constituted, had an adequate syllabus and whether it duplicated other courses on campus. As the new course covered the content from the old course, and the addition of CBL to the content made the course more rather than less unique, the UUCC gave its approval with little debate.

The final institutional hurdle was the university's Faculty Senate. This group's primary concern revolved around the history of the UNST capstone. As originally conceived, the capstone would bring students from a wide range of backgrounds to work together with a community partner. One of the consequences of this was that the capstone would have no academic prerequisites, other than the students' senior standing. While this resulted in students with diverse backgrounds being drawn together, students could not be relied upon to have any content knowledge, so the CBL projects could not expect students to apply their learning content, only their learning processes.

Moving the capstone into the business school assured that all students would have a common base of business knowledge. The Faculty Senate was concerned that having only business students would result in a lack of diversity in academic backgrounds. While the academic diversity was reduced compared to capstones that drew from across the campus, we argued that bringing students from all the business disciplines resulted in sufficient diversity. We showed that in the applied field of business many other disciplines are embedded, for example marketing includes design, psychology, and communication, finance includes economics and math, etc. The Faculty Senate accepted the course change with the recommendation that non-business students with sufficient business background be accepted on a case-by-case basis into the SBA capstones.

Barriers: territoriality

Both UNST and SBA faculty felt that their academic territories were potentially threatened. The UNST faculty takes great pride in their conception and delivery of the capstones. They use terms like "transformational" and "life-changing" when describing student experiences in the capstone. The capstone goals are process-oriented and only overlap partially with the SBA learning goals. We came to an understanding with UNST by addressing these issues directly, acknowledging the concern that the SBA might be unprepared to meet the UNST goals without help from the UNST faculty, and being cognizant of our need to adapt. Another UNST concern was that we were taking approximately 700 students per year from their capstones. This meant that there would be a number of course sections that would need to be eliminated. This was a real impact that could not be mitigated.

The SBA faculty had to add a time-consuming CBL project to an already content-heavy course. Moving from a four-credit course to a six-credit course provided some, but inadequate, relief. In addition, to meet some of the UNST capstone learning goals, a new set of cases oriented to those goals were added to the course; this meant that the SBA capstone course had to be reworked to eliminate some of the business strategy content material. This led to conflicts among the faculty as they debated what was absolutely necessary for an adequate education for business students.

Each person had content they felt was vital, while confronted with the reality that some items had to be eliminated. Ultimately, the faculty created a syllabus that was acceptable to all faculty members.

Section 2: Implementing the CBL business strategy course

The revised business strategy course, hereinafter called BA495 (the course number per the academic bulletin) was first implemented in the fall term, 2011. We now have 16 academic terms of experience, with over 250 community partners and nearly 3,000 students. The remainder of this section discusses our experience and the evolution of BA495 based on this experience. Specifically we address:

- Course stakeholders

- Course administration

- Course delivery and modification

- Challenges, and

- Best practices

Course stakeholders

The revised BA495 course transformed the traditional BA495 course in two fundamental ways. It introduced community partners (called "clients" in BA495) into the
classroom, adding a third stakeholder to the traditional student/instructor stakeholder relationship. It also added new content requirements, that of meeting learning goals of both SBA and UNST.

Integrating the client into BA495 while preserving the unique quality of the client as an outsider over which the student and instructor ultimately had no control
was accomplished in part by defining each stakeholder's goals, roles, and activities.

We chose a consultant/client model as the dominant classroom organizational
theme. This model outlined specific roles for each stakeholder:

- **Instructor**: delivers academic content; advises student project team; assesses
  and grades capstone products; minimal direct client contact.

- **Student team**: independent of client (not an intern or employee); conducts
  research and analysis, crafts strategic recommendations based on client's
  business goals.

- **Client**: identifies problem or opportunity for student focus; engages with,
  but independent from, student team; reviews/comments on products.

Figure 3.1 outlines the new set of relationships introduced by the capstone client.
Though the relationship between instructor and student represented in intersection #4 remains the same as the traditional BA495 course, it was no longer the main
area of learning. It was replaced by intersection #7 where all stakeholders inter-
sected. That is, intersection #7 is where instruction and advising, student learning
and work, and client engagement come together to accomplish the desired learning goals of the capstone program. This shift of the main focus of learning from
intersection #4 to intersection #7 is crucial in moving from a traditional course to
a truly CBL course.

Figure 3.1 Stakeholder engagement diagram

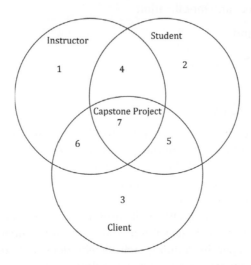

Table 3.1 more precisely outlines the goals, roles, and activities of these new relationships. Student and instructor interaction continued some of the same traditional roles and activities of a normal class, but the client required a different set of relationships that affected the three categories (goals, roles, activities).

Table 3.1 Capstone stakeholder goals and activities

Stakeholder	Goal(s)	Roles	Activities	Evaluation and assessment
Faculty	1. Teach business strategy syllabus 2. Application of SBA and UNST learning goals	1. Conducts classroom instruction 2. Evaluates course work, both individual and team	1. Teach strategy concepts 2. Advise student(s), team(s) 3. Review, comment, score student and team assignments 4. Limited client interaction	1. AoL assessment 2. Assessment of Capstone Project deliverables

Stakeholder	Goal(s)	Roles	Activities	Evaluation and assessment
Student	1. Application core and discipline competencies 2. Collaboration 3. Problem solving 4. Meet client goals	1. Recipient of instruction 2. Responsible for team and individual work 3. Work with client following consultant/ client model	1. Teamwork 2. Independent research, analyses, key findings 3. Presentation 4. Client project preparation	1. Course Evals (SBA, UNST) 2. Grading 3. AoL assessment
Client (community partner) work	1. Client engagement 2. Receive useful consulting services	1. Limited classroom access 2. Work closely with student project team (client/consultant model) 3. Not involved in academic course-work	1. Active engagement (attend presentations and meetings) 2. Review, comment, provide feedback student prepared documents 3. limited instructor interaction	1. Client experience survey

The instructor and student roles in the new BA495 followed traditional pedagogy of teaching content and learning concepts, respectively. Adding the client relationship added new goals, roles, and activities to meet client stakeholder requirements. Essentially they were the following:

- Incorporation of the UNST and SBA learning goals
- Communication between client, faculty, and student
- Collaboration within the student project team, and
- Engagement between client and student capstone project team

Although it is important to assess student accomplishments for existing courses, it is particularly critical to do so for a new course. The SBA did so by adding assessment tools to specifically target accomplishments that could not otherwise be determined through traditional assessment methods. The added assessment tools included:

- UNST course evaluation
- Client experience survey, and
- Evaluation of the quality of the team's final deliverable to client[3]

---

3 This assessment was still under development as of the summer of 2015.

Course administration

Given the complexity and scope of the client relationships, a program coordinator was hired for the following primary duties:

- Manage clients

- Manage adjuncts

- Interface with UNST Campus-wide Capstone Coordinator

- Archive documentation

- Represent BA495 capstone program on campus-wide committees, and

- Teach BA495 courses

Client management

Performing client recruiting well is a key to program success. The BA495 program recruits between 60 and 70 clients a year. The actual number of eligible clients, however, must be larger to account for client attrition and representation from a wide range of businesses and organizational sectors.

Since BA495 is offered every term, client recruitment is a year-round activity. Though we recruit from all sectors including private, non-profit, and public organizations we have guidelines that direct the recruiting.

We initially have focused on serving entities who either are certified Women/Minority Business enterprises (WMBE) or that cannot hire or contract for professional consulting services. While our clients remain overwhelmingly in this underserved camp, we have recruited businesses that can afford professional consulting services because they meet our other selection criteria, which include the following:

- Select clients located within the greater Portland Metropolitan Region. This ensures that students experience face-to-face meetings and have access to the client's organization via mass-transit should team members not have other means of transportation.

- Select clients from all sectors and corporate organizations (e.g., non-profit, for-profit, public agency, etc.), business cycles (e.g., pre-revenue start-up, growing, mature, dissolution or ending organization, etc.) and sizes.

- Consider specific business services client requests to make sure it fits our students' capabilities.

Client recruitment is a multiple-step process involving marketing, meeting, application, and selection. Direct marketing to clients and membership organizations (chambers of commerce, business associations, trade organizations, etc.) remains the main source of client recruitment. We have also developed informal agreements with several organizations that support the type of clients that fit our client profile. Increasingly, though, word-of-mouth, and direct referrals from previous clients have aided client recruitment.

The program coordinator meets with all potential clients to discuss the program in detail, the services that the client is seeking, and what we expect from the client. Candidates then submit an application where they describe the organization, their goals and what they seek by way of business services from the student capstone team.

The final step in the recruitment process is application review and eligibility determination. The main factors determining eligibility are a cogent organization description including any long and short-term goals, and a description of the project and business services the client seeks from the capstone course. If the application is complete, they are considered eligible and are put into the applicant pool for review and selection prior to each term.

Eligibility, however, does not mean an organization will be a client. Actual client selection is based upon a set of selection criteria beginning about six weeks prior to the following term. We use six criteria to select a diverse set of clients from the client pool.

- Client demographics: minority, women-owned, underrepresented groups, etc.[4]

- Organizational structure: for profit, non-profit, public agency, public authority, etc.

- Organization size: employees, locations, revenue, etc.

- Organization maturity: pre-revenue, start-up, expansion, dissolution, etc.

- Organization business needs, and

- Faculty knowledge and expertise

Except for the underserved criterion, which is considered most important, the other criteria are not weighted. The list of clients selected from the eligibility pool is sent to instructors teaching the next term. They select three clients[5] who they want to work with. The project coordinator introduces the clients to the instructor and the faculty member is thereon responsible for direct client contact.

---

4 While we strive to address the needs of underrepresented groups, clients not from underrepresented groups are not automatically eliminated from further consideration due to the desire to address diversity in the other selection criteria.

5 Each client provides a capstone project. Often, the capstone project is subdivided into components, such as a marketing plan for a business and an assessment of community impacts of the business, with a student team assigned to each component. Each class may have as many as seven student teams, working on different components of the three client capstone projects.

At term-end the program coordinator distributes the client experience survey and conducts any client follow-up. The online survey includes both Likert-scale and open-ended questions. To date, the client response rate has been over 95% due in large part to client follow-up through email and telephone calls.

Adjunct management

Adjunct faculty teach approximately 20% of the SBA course sections. These faculty add significant value to the program, as they typically come with significant practical experience. They are often able to engage the clients in ways full-time faculty may not. Some adjuncts are consultants, so they bring direct experience with the consultant role that their students will be performing.

To prepare adjuncts to teach BA495, the program coordinator uses an on-boarding procedure that includes business concept review, client management, case study and textbook review, and basic teaching practices.

The program coordinator monitors all adjuncts' teaching capability. Adjuncts are formally evaluated using SBA and UNST course evaluations, input from UNST's capstone director, and the BA495 program coordinator's observations. Generally, the adjunct's first time teaching the course is one of adjustment to the unique format. With feedback from other instructors, UNST capstone director, and program coordinator we have found that most instructors can successfully teach the course.

Client document archiving

The program coordinator collects and archives electronic files of all team prepared deliverables (e.g., presentations, work scopes, financials, final reports). These documents offer academic research on CBL goals as well as course assessment opportunities.

Additional functions of the program coordinator

UNST plays a critical role in BA495 capstone program through financial support and guidance. The project coordinator meets with the Capstone Director on a scheduled and as-needed basis. Much of the interaction between UNST and BA495 is to investigate and implement ways to improve UNST goal achievement.

As a part of PSU's campus-wide focus on CBL, the program coordinator participates in several CBL-related committees. The most critical committee is PSU's Partnership Council, whose mission is to publicize PSU's CBL success and also to share best practices with other PSU CBL activities.

Finally, the program coordinator teaches two sections each year. Teaching provides direct feedback on how the program is going from multiple angles.

Course delivery

Course delivery follows the structure defined in the syllabus. Like other SBA courses the program has well-defined learning goals, academic texts, assignments, and grading designed to help assess the students' learning goal achievement. Where it differs is in the CBL component, which requires significant time on completing the client project work.

During the first year the new BA495 was offered academic content, not client project work, dominated classroom time. That focus, while important, did not allow students sufficient time on the client project. Essentially, the CBL goal could not be met. Students spent too much time on individual assignments and academic content at the expense of the client project.

To better align classroom activities with course goals, faculty experimented by removing or restructuring content not directly relevant to the client project and learning goals. These activities resulted in more direct links between actual CBL and the course goals.

Project teamwork is now the course's main focus. While academic content is used to reinforce the strategy concepts that students apply to the project, it supports rather than dominates the student's work.

Class structure

A typical class has between 30 and 35 students, with three clients and teams of 10–12 students. Before student teams are formed, clients make an in-class presentation about their organization and the project and business services they are seeking from the students. The instructor forms teams based on student preference, appropriate team size and business disciplines needed for the client project. Teams select a project coordinator (PC) who becomes the main client contact throughout the project.

Class sessions and "homework" are a combination of academic content and direct client work. The academic work includes individual student assignments (e.g., weekly write-ups and essays, quizzes, classroom participation). Students are graded individually based on how well they perform in each of the individual assignments.

Students also collaborate on the client project. Students receive a project grade that may vary within a group based on peer reviews, conducted both mid-term and post-term, and instructor's observations.

The following activities constitute the group project activities.

- Perform secondary and primary research
- Develop a work scope based on client's goals
- Conduct up to four in-class presentations to their clients

- Prepare a final consultant report that encompasses project work and strategic recommendations developed to meet the client's goals

Evaluation

Evaluation is critical to measuring students' learning goal achievement. Currently we use the following evaluation tools:

- UNST Learning Goals: UNST student surveys
- SBA Learning Goals: SBA student surveys
- Client Satisfaction: Client Experience Survey

Assessment results

The learning goal assessments have mixed results, which may point to the continuing challenge of creating a successful CBL course. Below are two examples.

At the end of each term all BA495 students fill out a UNST capstone evaluation. The evaluation focuses on the four UNST capstone learning goals previously described.

The average of our faculty's UNST evaluation scores consistently lag behind campus-wide average scores. While course modifications mentioned previously and support from UNST administrators have narrowed the gap, it continues.

Client satisfaction presents a wholly different picture. Client experience surveys indicate clients rate extremely high (between 85 and 92%) their satisfaction with:

- Overall project
- Effectiveness in meeting client goals
- Desire to participate in another project, and
- Willingness to recommend program to another client

Challenges

Though we have achieved success in a number of areas, challenges administering the course continue. Some challenges have partial solutions, while others continue with no solution yet identified.

Academic vs. project

There continues to be concern that we still have not identified the appropriate ratio of academic and applied content in the course. While BA495 must continue to include business strategy concepts, faculty differ regarding the number of concepts and level of detail necessary. Some possible solutions to this include continuing to modify academic content, or alternatively, providing the academic content in a prior class, leaving BA495 as strictly a capstone course. Regardless of the solution, students need business strategy knowledge to successfully complete this course.

Assessment

Assessments, as noted above, indicate that the course meets client goals, but has not yet fully met UNST goals. We continue to work with UNST to improve the assessment scores. UNST goals are broad and, while not necessarily conflicting with BA495, they may not yet be fully aligned either. Given the broad mission of the course, this vexing issue is likely to continue, taking more time to resolve.

New modes of delivery

As the SBA increases the number of teaching platforms available to students we have followed suit by developing both hybrid and fully online BA495 classes. These modes of delivery present challenges unique to these platforms including:

- Addressing learning goals related to team collaboration
- Identifying the appropriate division of course work between in-class and online platforms for a hybrid course
- Connecting the instructor to the student teams
- Determining client recruitment selection criteria for online and hybrid courses, and
- Learning goal assessment

Lessons learned

We have identified a number of lessons learned when creating and implementing the BA495 CBL course.

The most important are:

- Address each institutional barrier with a spirit of cooperation and collaboration
- Accept and request support from individuals who are part of the infrastructure; use their expertise and knowledge of the system to guide you through the process

- Understand the overall infrastructure through which the changes must be guided well; many complications can be avoided by rigorously following the appropriate channels

- Identify the program goals and assessments to measure the goals

- Develop a syllabus that integrates program goals, content (academic and applied), and assignments for both individual student and team collaboration

- Hire a program coordinator to manage the program's logistical and administrative operations, client recruitment, assessment, outreach, and teaching

- Recruit clients willing to engage with the students and attend in-class sessions. Both elements are critical to project success

- Create recruiting collateral such as application, non-disclosure agreement, and marketing materials

- Develop a client database that at a minimum is searchable, relational, and can generate simple statistics and frequencies

- Develop an on-boarding program for new faculty unfamiliar with teaching a course involving CBL

- Hold regularly scheduled meetings with faculty teaching BA495. This is especially critical at the initial stages of course roll-out, but it should continue as the program matures.

- Archive project documents, which will allow future research and assessment

- Create a follow-on internship program for capstone students to continue working with the client to implement the strategic recommendations

Conclusion

Transformation of the traditional BA495 course to a CBL-based one has been and continues to be a challenge both from an institutional as well as the academic perspective. We have received strong support from PSU academic and administrative communities, and we expect it to continue as long as we make progress toward meeting the UNST learning goal scores that our program currently lacks.

From the academic perspective we feel we are providing an excellent program. It prepares the students for professional business careers by requiring them to apply their academic coursework in an applied or "clinical" setting. It simulates as closely as possible what they will encounter when they graduate and enter the workforce.

4

Cultivating sustainability
A decade of innovation and community partnerships at the Learning Gardens Laboratory

Heather Burns, Sybil Kelley, and Dilafruz Williams

Just beyond brightly colored welcome signs at the entrance of the Learning Gardens Laboratory (LGL), visitors are greeted with a lengthy and vibrant hedgerow. This hedgerow is a strip of trees and other plants that edges a grassy field and provides habitat for a variety of life. This particular hedgerow is full of maturing persimmon and fig trees, elderberry, gooseberry, currents, lavender, yarrow, sage, and a myriad of other flowers, herbs, and groundcovers. Just five years ago, this hedgerow resembled nothing more than a collection of stick-like plants. Today however, as bees buzz, and volunteers scavenge for a berry snack, this hedgerow is an apt and visual metaphor for the growth of the Learning Gardens Laboratory. Our work here is diverse, multi-layered, textured, complex and challenging. It also attracts all kinds of beneficial participants and produces both food and incredible beauty. As an edge, or a place of increased diversity and creativity, this hedgerow also mimics the many edges of the Learning Gardens Lab: on the edge of several large universities, a diverse neighborhood community and a public school system. The Learning Gardens Lab is unique in that it is built on strong partnerships that provide the foundation of success for this four-acre (1.6 hectare) garden-based education site. Our mission is to support academic achievement, leadership development, and a local sustainable food system by providing garden-based education for public school students and their families, university students, and community members. Portland State University has partnered with Portland Public Schools, the City of Portland, Oregon State University, and the local community to develop a variety of garden-based educational programs at LGL, which advance the development of sustainable food systems and sustainability education (See Figure 4.1). In this chapter we share the emerging story of the Learning Gardens Laboratory including how it was initially envisioned and brought to life by PSU faculty. We will also discuss the partners and programs that are part of this garden-based education site, some of the values and systems that underlie our transformational work as a living laboratory, and systemic challenges that we have faced at LGL.

Figure 4.1 LGL partners

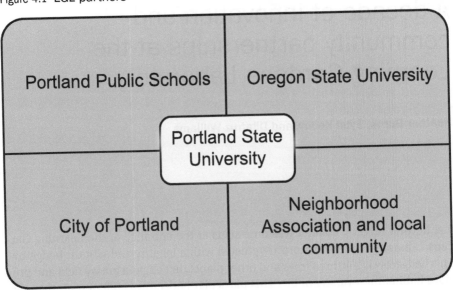

Creation of the Learning Gardens Laboratory

In 2001, the Graduate School of Education at Portland State University (PSU) launched a new Masters-level program known as Leadership in Ecology, Culture, and Learning (Williams, 2012), subsequently renamed Leadership for Sustainability Education (LSE). This initiative was guided by a conceptual framework of a Partnership Model of Sustainability (Parajuli, 2006) that brought together four levels of partnerships: (1) Intra- and Inter-generational partnership: social class, gender, caste, race, ethnicity, and other human-created constructs, institutions, and practices of social inequities; (2) Inter-species partnership: ecological, philosophical, and ethical aspects of humanity's relationship with the more-than-human world; (3) Inter-cultural partnership: an examination of the field of biological, cultural, and linguistic diversity, diversity of knowledge systems and ways of knowing, teaching, and learning; and (4) Inter-economic partnership: social and economic institutions, arrangements of exchanges and surplus, fair trade and free trade between global North and global South, rural and urban relationships, agriculture and industry, and producers and consumers. Portland was becoming nationally recognized as a leader for innovative work that supported local food systems at a time when awareness was increasing about the detriments of large-scale industrial food production. Garden- and food-based education were critical to the understanding of sustainability at PSU and provided a hub for a partnership framework to coalesce as "sustainability" began to be broadly embraced across disciplines.

A successful grant from the Environmental Protection Agency in 2003 for Food-based Ecological Education Design (FEED) enabled the start-up of the Learning Gardens Laboratory partnership with schools in the Portland Public School (PPS) District; the time was ripe for PSU to launch this new partnership project with PPS and the City of Portland, as all three institutions had been in conversation about teaching youth how to grow food in ways that were linked to health promotion and academic success. As a result of intensive year-long negotiations led by Dr Dilafruz Williams (co-founder of the LSE program and an elected PPS School Board member at the time), a proposal was accepted for a partnership project among all three entities—PSU, PPS, and the City of Portland—entitled 60th Avenue Learning Gardens Laboratory: Health, Multiculturalism, and Academic Achievement. There was tremendous impetus in the community to address issues related to food systems, and to support locally grown food that could be brought to school cafeterias. In June 2005, with the passage of the PPS School Board resolution to develop a School Health and Wellness Policy, a tipping point was reached in terms of possibilities for establishing and institutionalizing food policy that enhanced sustainable, local, and organic food choices in schools.

In 2005, with the City of Portland and the Portland Public School District as partners, PSU officially launched the Learning Gardens Laboratory (LGL) at a location where PPS previously housed Green Thumb—a horticulture education program for high school students that had been in existence for many decades but had been shut down due to a lack of funding. The nearly 13-acre property, in joint ownership between the District and the City, was mostly vacant. Since this was historically the site of Zwald Dairy, and later a place for horticultural education, a Portland State University proposal for a learning garden was attractive. It took nearly two years to establish LGL formally, to come to an agreement for a lease on approximately four acres of the property, and to develop a relationship with Lane Middle School as a key partner. This speaks to the complexity of public land ownership and the leasing of that land. There was no template for how a lease could be written among three entities; hence the various staff worked diligently to look at models elsewhere in order to address commitments, liability issues, and long-term financial feasibility.

Subsequently, an interinstitutional agreement was developed with Oregon State University Extension in 2008, to co-manage the site. Currently, a more expanded number of organizations are playing significant roles in offering education and training, and serving both professional communities and neighborhood communities at the Learning Gardens Lab. Like the hedgerow, these partners and programs have grown up around the foundational partnership that was planted with Lane Middle School, rooted in the local neighborhood.

Location of the Learning Gardens Laboratory: diversity of the neighborhood and Lane Middle School

The Learning Gardens Laboratory is located in the Brentwood–Darlington neighborhood of southeast Portland, Oregon, which historically has had a high concentration of immigrant and refugee families from various countries. The neighborhood has three elementary schools that feed into Lane Middle School, a key partner at the LGL. Lane serves approximately 500 students in grades six to eight. The school has significant cultural diversity (60% ethnic and racial minority), and many students come from low-income families: 57% of students qualify for free or reduced lunch (PPS, 2015). Students' lives often include family instability due to unemployment, violence, substance abuse, or incarceration. This has contributed to generally low attendance and academic achievement and high rates of dropout and involvement in problem behavior. Since the LGL is located across the street from Lane, PSU's partnership has been critical in engaging PPS adolescents in hands-on garden-based learning with a focus on science. Middle-school students and their science teachers participate directly in the gardens each week, where PSU graduate students serve as garden educators. These garden educators offer an integrated, seasonally based curriculum that features hands-on learning experiences in designing, planting, tending, growing, and harvesting a variety of seasonal vegetables, fruits, herbs, and flowers. The sixth-grade garden-based education program consists of 30 weeks of programming organized around a full academic year of science. Each week of the program includes a lesson lasting 60–90 minutes; lessons are organized sequentially by seasonal themes. In 2014, with funding from the National Science Foundation, a three-year project entitled Science in the Learning Gardens was started with the aim of supporting the academic success of ethnic and racial minority students at Lane. PSU graduate students work in partnership with PPS teachers to design and offer curricula integrated with Next Generation Science Standards. This project builds on a previous research study at LGL led by faculty in PSU's Psychology department that investigated the impact of garden-based education on motivational engagement and learning among middle-school students (Skinner *et al.*, 2012). This team found that middle-school students who were more engaged at the Learning Gardens Lab performed better in school and that students' engagement at the LGL was connected to more engagement in science and in school in general (Skinner *et al.*, 2012). Through curriculum development, Science in the Learning Gardens seeks to further increase the impact of garden-based education for Lane Middle School students, who are at risk for poor school performance due to their socioeconomic, minority, and/or immigrant status, as well as other factors like family instability. While this research and strong ongoing partnership with Lane Middle School has been the foundation of the garden-based education programs at LGL, ten years after the creation of the partnership there are a wide variety of educational programs taking place on-site.

Programs and partners at the Learning Gardens Lab

Programs at LGL bring a wide variety of participants to the site. Each year, around 200 middle-school students, and hundreds of university students learn at LGL on a weekly basis. Thousands of volunteer hours are logged each year. On a typical late spring day, one might arrive at the Learning Gardens Lab and be greeted by a group of OSU Extension Master Gardeners, working diligently in their demonstration garden where they educate the public about horticulture, offer workshops, and provide volunteer opportunities. Past the demonstration garden, LGL's "farmers in residence," a family who lives in the neighborhood, are harvesting greens for members of their Community Supported Agriculture (CSA), in which families pre-purchase a seasonal weekly share of fresh vegetables. Beyond the family's farm plot, a group of Portland State University students, who are part of the Senior Capstone service-learning course Sustainable Food Systems, are working busily to prepare their tomato patch while another group of Capstone students is having a discussion in the outdoor classroom. Behind the outdoor classroom, one can see small groups of sixth graders from Lane Middle School and garden educators planting cucumbers and squash in their large garden plot as part of their weekly science lessons. OSU Extension participants in the Beginning Urban Farmer Apprenticeship (BUFA) program are weeding leeks and kale in preparation for a farmers' market harvest as part of a season-long training to become urban farmers. A Vietnamese family with two young children and a retired teacher work together in the Lane Family Garden plot, where neighborhood families learn to grow their own vegetables. The LGL volunteer coordinator is giving a tour of the site to students from a local high school, and other LGL staff are harvesting vegetables for the weekly Brentwood–Darlington neighborhood farm stand, a place where neighbors can purchase local affordable produce. In the greenhouse classroom area, the Portland Fruit Tree Project, a local non-profit organization, is holding a workshop for volunteers on managing the orchard that this organization stewards on site.

These are some of the many educational programs taking place at the Learning Gardens Lab on a regular basis. Additionally, graduate students and faculty have been involved in research addressing a variety of interests such as garden-based learning, food security, multicultural family farms, and sustainable gardening. PSU graduate students serve in staff roles (such as Volunteer Coordinator), providing garden education, program coordination, site development, and maintenance at LGL. Like the hedgerow, these programs and relationships continue to grow in depth and complexity each year, creating a mosaic of sustainability learning and change. However, the number of programs and people involved at the Learning Gardens Lab presents an interesting challenge in terms of staffing, funding, and site management. As faculty leaders, we have embraced the idea of the living laboratory, engaging in rich learning at LGL in areas such as organizational development, community building, and sustainability leadership.

A living laboratory

The Learning Gardens Lab has been primarily funded through grants and yearly support from the Graduate School of Education at PSU, mostly in the form of several graduate assistantships. However, the amount of financial support we have received up to this point has not allowed for any regular part-time or full-time staff at LGL during most of its existence. This has been challenging, particularly in managing a four-acre area of cultivated land over the different seasons, in meeting the needs of numerous site partners and providing consistency for teachers at Lane. As a result, we have been forced to be creative in how we manage the site and programs. While challenging, this has been a true opportunity in that we have been able to experiment with participatory and collaborative leadership models, and to create innovative solutions to raising funds. As such, the LGL has been a living laboratory, not only for sustainable food systems and garden-based education, but also for organizational change and sustainability leadership. Sustainability leadership is a key component of LGL's academic parent program, the Leadership for Sustainability Education (LSE) graduate program. LSE graduate students fill the nine staff positions at LGL (see Figure 4.2), and other LSE graduate courses are also linked to the Learning Gardens Lab for community-based learning opportunities. As such, LGL has become a laboratory for practicing what we learn in our graduate program, including sustainability leadership and sustainability pedagogy. At LGL we have created a leadership team, which includes a faculty Coordinator with three credits of course release time for work at LGL, and nine graduate student staff positions. These staff positions are primarily offered as unpaid internships; however, PSU has typically supported at least two students each year with Graduate Assistantships. While each person on the team has specific roles, we work together to coordinate programs at LGL, to learn how to model sustainable systems, and to practice sustainability leadership.

Figure 4.2 Staff team and positions

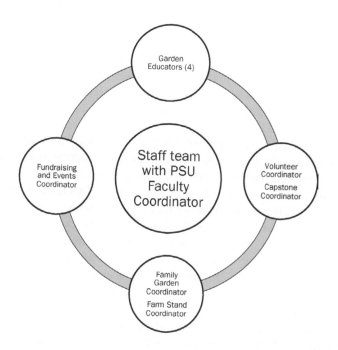

Sustainability leadership refers to a process that includes acting from our values, rooting our work in an understanding of a living systems paradigm and being inclusive, collaborative, and reflective (Burns *et al.*, 2015). At LGL, we identify and work from our values, recognizing that as leaders we must commit to taking action to create the world we want (Ferdig, 2007; Wheatley and Frieze, 2011). Our shared values include justice, equity, love, balance, creativity, relationships, learning, flexibility, accountability, diversity, humility, and participation. Clarifying values and aligning actions with values is key to leadership work (Kouzes and Posner, 2012). Additionally, we seek to model our leadership and our systems at LGL on a living systems paradigm—one that is rooted in the discoveries of quantum science, recognizing that all life is connected and conscious, and is continuously creating and changing (Capra, 2002). We seek to root our work in a living systems paradigm because complex living systems demonstrate sustainable properties and patterns and can suggest important strategies for leadership (Barlow and Stone, 2011). Qualities of living systems include resiliency, adaptivity, awareness, creativity, and relationships (Wheatley, 2006). Since the world is constantly changing, uncertain, emergent, and exists as interconnected webs of relationships (Capra, 2002), sustainability leadership must therefore model this reality by being "adaptive, flexible, self-renewing, and resilient" (Wheatley, 2006, p. 32). For example, we recognize LGL as a complex and responsive living system with the capacity to self-organize to sustain itself, to respond intelligently, and to change accordingly. This view of an organization as creative and self-organizing changes the focus of leadership from control, to leadership with strong confidence in the intelligence of the organization (Wheatley, 2006). We see leadership as something that can be demonstrated by people and teams throughout the organization in emergent relationships and complex responsive processes. This often means that solutions to challenges at LGL are discovered through deepening our relationships with one another, and developing trust. In this process, creative ideas and discussions can emerge, and may be developed through collaborative response.

At LGL, we also treat leadership as an inclusive, collaborative, and reflective process. Sustainability leadership empowers the leader that inherently exists in each person, and fosters strong, healthy, sustainable, and just change through collaborative and creative means (Ferdig, 2007). This means that everyone has the capacity for leadership; that a leader's role is to lead with others. Thus leaders, rather than providing a solution, "create opportunities for people to come together and generate their own answers" (Ferdig, 2007, p. 31). As leaders at LGL, we seek to bring people together and encourage creative participation, but also help people to embrace a relationship with uncertainty and emergence, understanding that although we often don't have answers to the challenges we face, solutions and new developments will emerge from strong relationships and the right conditions.

Working together to solve problems, even when values are shared, can be a challenging process. We have come to understand that the tension, conflict and uncertainty that come from differences provide great potential for the creative emergence of viable solutions (Ferdig, 2007). In a dynamic system such as the Learning Gardens Lab, change is always present, and new challenges pop up like weeds on a regular basis. We don't always know what to do, or how to proceed, but we trust that with strong relationships, regular communication, and room for creative ideas to be shared, appropriate solutions can emerge.

With this understanding, we also see sustainability not as a goal to be achieved, but as a dynamic living process. Like the hedgerow, LGL is constantly changing, growing, maturing, and creatively self-organizing. Like the hedgerow we need weeding and maintenance: focused time for team building, partnership tending, and reflection. We spend time together so that our roots may intertwine, but also so that our individual branches have room to grow. We grow as a team, supporting and nurturing each other, while at the same time individual interests and talents grow and develop. This is the process of learning how to be sustainable, in our own lives, in our organization, and in our community partnerships. As a living laboratory, the Learning Gardens Lab provides a wonderful context for practicing and modeling sustainability, not as an outcome, but as an ongoing process.

Partnerships: challenges and opportunities

The impacts of strong partnerships generally result in synergistic outcomes that are far greater than the sum of any individual contribution. Nonetheless, the vibrant process of partnership work also carries significant challenges. In alignment with a living systems paradigm, "functional redundancy" is a sign of health and resilience—for ecosystems as well as institutions and partnerships. For example, in ecosystems, functional redundancy means that roles or functions are distributed so that disturbances can be absorbed and managed within a healthy system (Odum, 1993). In other words, if one organism moves or becomes extinct, other organisms provide the functionality for the overall system. On the other hand, if too many organisms fill the same role, or, conversely, if other functions are absent completely, then competition and instability result. This same concept of functional redundancy is relevant to partnerships, particularly those involving large institutions and organizations. Broadly speaking, institutions tend to create silos across their organizations, while at the same time, they tend to have complex processes (bureaucracy) that, together, provide stability and structure for decision-making, but can also impede adaptive response to timely issues. In our experience, siloed information and leadership, as well as structures and processes that hinder connections and feedback, are often at the root of partnership challenges, sometimes overshadowing the benefits and positive outcomes.

Not unlike other partnerships, the work at LGL has been non-linear, emergent, and often uncertain. Additionally, as with any actions within a system, there are generally time delays between activities and outcomes. Though short-term, tangible results are seen almost daily through the on-the-ground activities, the less direct, long-term outcomes can be harder to identify immediately. For example, the Garden Educators routinely make personal connections with students that result in "aha" moments and shared experiences, but longer-term academic outcomes take longer to measure, as well as resources and expertise. Fortunately, one element of the partnership has been collaborative research with the Psychology Department at PSU, so positive connections between participation in garden-based education and academic outcomes have been evaluated. Nonetheless, documenting and sharing the benefits of the partnership requires ongoing energy and feedback.

Over the long term, investment in partnerships allows for far greater, synergistic impacts, as well as shared responsibility amongst partners. For example, the middle-school component of the Learning Gardens Laboratory partnership has included Graduate Assistants (GA) to lead the educational programming at the site. For more than a decade, PSU has supported at least two of these GA positions, which include a modest stipend and tuition remission for nine graduate-level credits. Although at the surface level, GA positions may appear to be a fairly substantial investment on the part of the department and institution, the return on investment far outweighs the financial costs. For example, in the short term, this investment in human resources not only contributes to the professional learning and development of the graduate students who gain direct educational and leadership experience, but they in turn provide authentic, hands-on learning for nearly 200 middle school students each week by engaging them in real-world problem solving and exploration. These experiences at LGL increase many low-income students' access to healthful foods, which often carries over to their families, as demonstrated by participation in community events and the family gardening program at LGL. Additionally, these students gain academic skills and agency as they develop leadership skills and practical knowledge of how to grow food (Skinner *et al.*, 2012). In the long term, students' growing awareness of sustainable agricultural practices and science may have further ripple effects that could lead to cleaner water, reduced exposure to toxic chemicals, and renewal of urban soils over time. This aspect of the partnership work at LGL, combined with other programs including the family garden program, PSU Capstone courses, and the LGL Farm Stand, results in synergistic impacts that continue to grow and spread.

Even though this work benefits all the partners and the local community in a variety of ways, trying to establish and maintain partnership work can sometimes feel like trying to turn a supertanker with a rowboat oar. The siloed nature of many institutions, with strong organizational boundaries, often pushes collaborative partnership work to the fringe (Wheatley, 2006). Portland State University has created a culture of partnership and connection with the city we serve; however, relationships often exist at the individual level, rather than becoming embedded in system structures and processes. At LGL, the key partners are all large institutions. One of our greatest challenges has been embedding the system structures and processes of LGL into the larger institutional systems. As a result, we often feel that problem solving and navigating the policies and processes of individual institutions take far too much of our limited time and energy. For example, despite the essential role of LGL staff, funding for our Graduate Assistants has been tenuous nearly every year. Another example: as we currently renegotiate the LGL lease with Portland Public Schools, we do so with the real-estate managers in the real estate department, whose work is completely separate from the instructional aspects of the district. Recently, we have been left explaining our program, justifying its value, and negotiating terms in the face of steep proposed lease fee increases. We must often renegotiate scheduling logistics with school staff and facilities requirements with district staff, making it seem that with every change in personnel, far too much time is spent persuading new people that partnership is important, rather than focusing our time on the work that is having positive benefits to students and the community. These examples highlight again the importance of modeling the partnership after living systems. The relationships, roles, and responsibilities shared among individuals from each partner organization also need to be embedded into the very fabric of those institutions. Communication systems can provide important, timely feedback necessary to keep things functioning well, but likewise the shared vision and values need to be conveyed throughout the organizations. With limited staffing resources, it has been challenging to establish and maintain these information flows. Related to this, it has even been challenging to convey the larger significance of the Learning Gardens Laboratory to administration within our own institution. Again, the concepts of system structures and functional redundancy are relevant. We need to identify the structures that could strengthen interconnections and feedback, or the gaps if these resources do not currently exist. Additionally, there needs to be several pathways (redundancies) to convey messages and provide feedback so that information flow does not stop every time a key staff person leaves a support position at the institution.

Fortunately, due in large part to the grassroots value of our work with the local community, we have gained traction at PSU and with our partners. Both internally and externally, people are recognizing the critical role that LGL plays in the local community, as well as educationally for students at PSU and PPS. We are learning that to support partnerships, we must be adaptive and resilient to change. We are also learning how to nurture the roots of relationships, watering and adding compost to the soil that supports our partnership work. At LGL, several key strategies have been instrumental in supporting partnerships.

Nearly anyone who does community-based work would concur that everything starts with relationships. People connecting with other people at individual and group levels are how good ideas emerge, how ideas are put into action, and how as a species we feel connected (Capra, 2002). Even so, in organizations and institutions, people come and go over time. The work initiated by individuals, through their relationships with others, needs to become embedded in the structures and processes of the organization(s) if it is to last beyond the individuals involved. Individual relationships need to be connected to organizational relationships to build a more networked, interconnected structure.

Increasing connectivity alone is not enough. The individuals making up the relationships and networks need be able to work together to identify opportunities and leverage points, as well as barriers and bottlenecks. Leverage points are the places in a system where small changes have ripple effect throughout the system, resulting in the greatest impacts (Meadows, 2008). For this to happen, organizations need to provide a level of transparency so people see how the system works, and need systems-thinkers who can identify those leverage points. Effective communication—within organizations and across the partnership—is another key component of a strong, resilient partnership. Furthermore, individuals and relationships need to be based on trust, which happens when a shared vision and goals are articulated and clear. Communication, along with transparency and trust, ensures that individuals know how to navigate processes and procedures, and how to find the right person or unit to address various needs or concerns. Individuals also need to know if and how their work is supporting the goals and mission of the institution, which happens when lines of communication provide meaningful, real-time feedback. With transparency, understanding of system structures and processes, and solid communication, people can work together when problems arise and make adjustments to continually improve the processes. At LGL, one of the ways we have worked to increase connectivity, transparency, and communication is by increasing the number of partner meetings on-site, to which participants from all our partnerships are invited. We have also created email lists for the partners to increase communication, and have created an online space for sharing and updating LGL documents and an organizational calendar. Most importantly, we work to build strong relationships with our partners. Because time is limited for both faculty and students involved at LGL, it is important that we share this responsibility and create lateral networks of relationships that can strengthen our partnerships. Similar to a spider web, lateral networks provide interconnections, direct lines of communication and feedback, and intentional patterns and structures that provide functionality of the system.

Conclusion

For over a decade, the work at the Learning Gardens Laboratory has exemplified PSU's mission: "Let knowledge serve the city," and is very well aligned with PSU's commitment to sustainability and community-engaged research and teaching. Each year, hundreds of public-school students, university students and community members regularly learn and participate at the Learning Gardens Laboratory. Spanning a variety of academic disciplines, across colleges and professional schools, PSU students engage in experiential community-based learning with specific focus on leadership and sustainability. Like our hedgerow, the work at LGL is multi-layered, diverse, and challenging, attracting beneficial partners and producing incredible learning yields. The richness of PSU's Learning Gardens Laboratory comes from the diversity and strength of its shared leadership and the community partnerships that have connected PSU to K-12 schools, governmental agencies, non-profit agencies and community organizations in the region. Although there are challenges, a focus on relationships, creativity, and emergence has supported LGL as it continues to ripen and mature as an organization. Through successful partnerships, The Learning Gardens Laboratory is finding success in educating a wide range of learners in ways that cultivate a sustainable future through garden-based education.

References

Barlow, Z., & Stone, M.K. (2011). Living systems and leadership: Cultivating conditions for institutional change. *Journal of Sustainability Education*, 2, 1-23.

Burns, H., Vaught, H., & Bauman, C. (2015). Leadership for sustainability: Theoretical foundations and pedagogical practices that foster change. *International Journal of Leadership Studies*, 9(1), 88-100.

Capra, F. (2002). *The hidden connections: A Science for Sustainable Living*. New York: Anchor.

Ferdig, M.A. (2007). Sustainability leadership: Co-creating a sustainable future. *Journal of Change Management,* 7(1), 25-35.

Kouzes, J., & Posner, B. (2012). *The Leadership Challenge* (5th edition). San Francisco: Jossey Bass.

Meadows, D. (2008). *Thinking in Systems.* White River Junction: Chelsea Green.

Odum, E.P. (1993). *Ecology and Our Endangered Life-Support Systems* (2nd ed.). Sunderland: Sinauer Associates.

Parajuli, P. (2006). Learning suitable to life and livability: Innovations through Learning Gardens. *Connections: The Journal of the Coalition for Livable Future,* 8(1), 6-7.

PPS (Portland Public School District). (2015). Lane. Retrieved from http://www.pps.k12. or.us/schools-c/profiles/enrollment/enroll_out.php?rpt=1044

Skinner, E.A., Chi, U., & The Learning-Gardens Educational Assessment Group. (2012). Intrinsic motivation and engagement as "active ingredients" in garden-based education Examining models and measures derived from self-determination theory. *Journal of Environmental Education,* 43(1), 16-36.

Wheatley, M.J. (2006). *Leadership and the New Science: Discovering Order in a Chaotic World.* San Francisco: Berrett-Koehler.

Wheatley, M.J., & Frieze D. (2011). *Walk Out Walk On: A Learning Journey into Communities Daring to Live The Future Now.* San Francisco: Berrett-Koehler.

Williams, D.R. (2012). Multiculturalism and sustainability education: Engagement with Urban school communities via food and Learning Gardens. In T. McDonald (Ed.), *Social Responsibility and Sustainability: Multidisciplinary Perspectives Through Service Learning,* (pp. 146-161). Sterling: Stylus.

5

Building capacity
Sustainability through student leadership

Amy Spring and Rachel Samuelson

Partnerships between colleges/universities and community organizations have become the dynamic core of higher education's engagement strategy. Faculty, staff, and students with energy, resources, passion, disciplinary expertise, and commitment have embraced these partnerships, but there is strong indication that the efforts often lack an understanding of the complexity of partnership arrangements (Driscoll, 2008). Partnerships are a complex interplay between the individuals and organizations involved. Students, faculty, and community partners bring their personal knowledge and motivations into their relationships, which play out in how the activities are conceived and facilitated, making each partnership unique and difficult to replicate. Couched within this lack of understanding is limited knowledge regarding the essential leadership roles that college students can play in partnership initiation, facilitation, and sustainability. Much of the community–university partnership literature uncovers the role that faculty play in initiating and supporting community–university partnerships and the ways these educational experiences affect student learning. Yet there is little exploration of the impact that student leadership has on supporting community–university partnerships and the importance of this work in sustaining the relationships between communities and institutions.

Portland State University (PSU), in particular, has effectively utilized student leaders to support and deepen its partnership infrastructure for more than 16 years by using students to help facilitate and maintain partnerships that the wider campus community is able to access. The Student Leaders for Service (SLS) program has consistently partnered with 15–20 community partners by placing well-trained student leaders in community organizations to provide nine months of direct service, while also recruiting students and faculty from the wider PSU community to work with the organization. The SLS program model provides students with essential organizational, teaching and research skills, while also providing community organizations with a consistent and sustained student "workforce" that is responsive to their organizational needs. The American Association of Colleges and Universities' Liberal Education and America's Promise (LEAP) report identifies employer priorities for the most important college learning outcomes by surveying 400 employers made up of for-profit and not-for-profit organizations (Hart, 2013). The intellectual and practical skills identified here as well as the personal and social responsibility and applied learning outcomes are all present in the experiences of the SLS program, helping SLS members gain the skills that are widely considered essential in today's workplace. These learning outcomes are consistent with prior community engagement research that affirms the importance of intellectual, social, and civic development (Simonet, 2008; Keen and Hall, 2009; Bamber and Hankin, 2011) and encompass enhanced skills in leadership, critical thinking, and communication (Colby *et al.*, 2003; Zlotkowski *et al.*, 2006). Additional studies (Flores *et al.*, 2007; Swaner, 2007) have shown mental and emotional health benefits associated with student engagement in community projects. Findings from the SLS program reverse the trend in service-learning literature—which focuses primarily on the impact of community engagement on students—by instead focusing on the impact of students on community–university partnerships and sustainability, specifically. This chapter elucidates the factors that make the SLS program successful. The authors of this chapter believe that in the resource-constrained environments of higher education, and those of many of our community partners, this program model will have a wide audience appeal and utility for replication.

Student Leaders for Service program history and accomplishments

Student Leaders for Service (SLS) was founded in 1999 in order to support student civic engagement and community-based learning experiences, and to strengthen PSU's community partnerships. Since its humble beginnings, the program has grown out of the academic office responsible for expanding and supporting the growth of service-learning and expanded beyond four students with a small closet for a workspace. The vision in 1999 was to develop a student leadership team to respond to the growing campus interest in incorporating service-learning projects into courses. The SLS member's primary role was to provide nine months of direct service within their assigned community organization. Through understanding the current needs of the organization, SLS members were then well equipped to work with students and faculty on embedding service-learning projects with the organization into other PSU courses. Initial success with this program model inspired the 2008 expansion of the program through support of an Americorps VISTA member. The Americorps VISTA member worked to increase the capacity of the program and expand the number of SLS members from four to twenty. It was during this same time that the first full-time professional Coordinator of Student Leaders for Service was hired. With this added support, SLS began running additional community service programming that catered to PSU students, such as nationally recognized service days like MLK Jr. Day and Earth Day, developing alternative spring break programming, and more.

In 2011, the program moved from being housed in the Office of Academic Affairs to the Enrollment Management and Student Affairs (EMSA) division due to the size, depth, and breadth of SLS programming, and its distinctive feature of working primarily with students in co-curricular leadership roles and settings. This organizational move allowed for strategic partnerships across the EMSA division that enhanced community engagement and further embedded leadership development programming for SLS members by better networking them with other student leaders across campus. Strategic partnerships within EMSA have included a partnership with Residence Life to support community engagement themed floors, as well as supporting departmental-wide community engagement initiatives such as "Campus Recreation for a Cause." Additional support for SLS members has consisted of shared leadership development opportunities, such as a leadership retreat and opportunities to connect and network with other student leaders. In this environment SLS continued to expand, increasing its offering of programs and services to include, for example, a mentoring program with a local elementary school, student volunteer consultations, and placement for students at large. At this point the SLS program had clearly developed into multiple programs. Through a strategic planning process in 2013, Student Leaders for Service changed its name to the Student Community Engagement Center, strengthening its role as the student volunteer center for the entire PSU campus. Despite the name change, Student Leaders for Service is a signature program within the Student Community Engagement Center and continues to serve as an anchor for sustainable community partnerships for the university.

Over the course of SLS's 16-year history, student members have performed more than 100,000 hours of community service in the Portland metropolitan region, contributing approximately $2,307,000 worth of volunteer service.[1] Since its inception, SLS members have recruited more than 10,000 PSU student volunteers and 3,000 volunteers from the community at large for a total of 76 community organizations.

---

1 This monetary calculation is based on the Independent Sector's 2015 valuation of a volunteer hour at $23.07/hour. For more info: https://www.independentsector.org/volunteer_time

Approximately 150 day-long service projects have been completed. These day-long service projects range from taking a group of college students out to a local elementary school to participate as classroom assistants for the day, to leading multi-project volunteer events for hundreds of college students. These accomplishments have contributed to the development of student leaders, facilitated applied learning through community-based learning, and substantially contributed to the quality of life for communities throughout the Portland metropolitan region.

Building capacity for sustainability

The concept of sustainability is based on the idea that people, and the communities in which they form a part, interact to shape economic, environmental, and social concerns. Working toward sustainability means that individuals interacting in communities are working toward creating a balance between economic, environmental, and social concerns (Roseland, 2000; Wals, 2007). SLS is a program that brings sustainability concepts alive in several important ways.

First, the program recognizes that community organizations are severely under resourced and that expanding their access to resources allows them to more effectively fulfill their mission (Points of Light Foundation, 2004). The SLS program model responds to limited community resources by providing community organizations with a student leader who is able to expand the organization's staffing capacity by working on discrete projects and recruiting and training additional volunteers from the university to work on projects with the organization. This model redistributes an abundant resource (students) and makes this resource available to organizations with limited staff capacity, resulting in making some substantial steps toward the balance of resources.

Second, the SLS program works with a variety of community organizations throughout the region, including non-profits that serve low-income communities, public schools, and governmental organizations like the City of Portland's Office of Neighborhood Involvement. These organizations are pursuing missions that embrace livability and equity issues by addressing economic, environmental, and social community concerns. The students in the program work directly on community sustainability issues because all of the partners are maintaining and enhancing quality of life and equity for both current and future community members.

Third, sustained relationships are the foundation of how SLS works with its community partners. Knowing that volunteers come and go within communities and recognizing the temporary and short-term nature of how university students often work with organizations, the SLS program interrupts this trend by placing an SLS member in a community organization for a nine month academic year. This long-term placement allows the community organization and the student to build a strong and productive relationship that facilitates capacity building for the community organization. For the purpose of SLS, a strong and productive community partnership is one that is reciprocal in nature. Students are both engaged in learning and acquiring skills at the site, while simultaneously meeting community partner goals. These goals often include increased visibility at Portland State and, in the city at large, increased numbers of college student volunteers, and increased or more effective service to the community, among other specific community partner identified goals. The SLS program recognizes the compounded benefits of these community partner relationships continuing beyond the initial nine-month SLS placement, making every effort to sustain community partner relationships year after year through continued placements of student leaders. Each year the majority of SLS community partners are retained to the next year. Occasionally there is a partnership that lasts only one academic year due to extenuating circumstances, but many partnerships have lasted for three to five years, and some have even surpassed ten years of existence.

Program structure

The Student Community Engagement Center is currently staffed by one full-time professional coordinator and three paid graduate interns who work ten hours a week, and jointly manage the SLS program. SLS has continually evolved to improve program components to better serve students and community members. The overarching goals of the SLS program are:

1. Develop and retain socially responsible student leaders throughout the program year

2. Increase the number of opportunities for Portland State students at large to engage in meaningful service opportunities that meet community identified needs

3. Decrease the challenges community partners face in navigating access to Portland State resources

4. Increase the benefits to community partner organizations and the community(ies) that SLS serves, and

5. Sustain most, if not all, of the community partnerships for two or more years

Through years of experience, combined with continually evolving student leadership development theory, there are some program hallmarks that have been found to contribute to the success of SLS meeting the program goals identified above: weekly service at community partner sites, weekly team meetings that include educational modules to promote leadership development, student members developing engagement opportunities between their partner site and PSU, leadership in nationally recognized service days, and, finally, providing opportunities for advancement within the program. The following section outlines the hallmark elements that deliver on SLS goals, and provides examples of the students' program requirements in italics, as well as the rationale for each component:

A. Weekly service requirement: *Student members are required to serve a minimum of five to ten hours per week for the nine-month academic year at the community organization with a focus area or mission relevant to the academic, career, and personal goals of the student.* The first essential component of the Student Leaders for Service program is a long-term service experience in which students become quasi-staff members at community organizations across the Portland metropolitan region. While the work varies between organizations, it is always directly related to the organization's mission and goals. The service requirement has a range of five to ten hours per week to allow the partner and student flexibility in scheduling based on need. If students serve less than five hours per week, they risk not getting sufficiently immersed in the community partner's work to be effective. If the students serve over ten hours, program staff have noticed that students can experience burnout and/or their studies may become less of a priority. Consistent service allows the student to develop the knowledge and ability to create additional engagement opportunities with the organization for the broader PSU community. Consistent service also allows the student more opportunity to meet their learning goals and gain experience and professional development.

B. Weekly meetings with leadership development curriculum: *Each Student Leader for Service is expected to attend a weekly meeting.* These meetings are an essential program element that allow the students to build a team, and to utilize their fellow team members to help them fulfill SLS program goals and the goals they have at their community organization. A portion of the time during these weekly meetings is dedicated to event planning, program planning, and logistics. Another portion of the meeting is dedicated to instructional modules that are meant to assist students in gaining leadership and civic engagement skills. The program draws on the Social Change Model of Leadership Development (Higher Education Research Institute, 1996) as the primary source for this curricular element. Additional materials are used to facilitate students' learning related to social justice, civic engagement, project planning, and volunteer management. The program also uses some process elements to facilitate students' learning. These include generative interviewing—a method of dialogue that surfaces an individual's tacit knowledge (Peet *et al.*, 2010)—a variety of reflective learning practices, and a culminating electronic portfolio that allows student to articulate their learning in an integrative format. The portfolio also serves as an essential program assessment tool. While students are not compensated for their work in the community, SLS members are awarded a leadership scholarship of $1,200 each year for their commitment to the weekly meetings and reflection assignments.

C. Community partner liaisons: *Act as a volunteer recruitment liaison between Portland State and community organizations.* While the individual work of each SLS member varies widely based on the nature of their community partner organization, all members are expected to serve as conduits for connecting their partner organization to university resources, including recruiting additional PSU students, faculty, and staff to work on projects that serve the mission of their community organization. This program element is fundamental to the SLS program model. This role is fulfilled in a variety of ways, including posting community partner projects on an electronic bulletin board that is accessed by students looking for volunteer opportunities, hosting on-campus awareness events, and tabling and outreach for their community organization. In more targeted efforts, SLS members act as a volunteer recruitment liaison by planning and coordinating service projects at the community partner site for individual groups of students and staff. SLS members are often asked by their community partner to connect the partner to professors and academic programs that are from fields of study relevant to a specific project. The success of this program element hinges on the leadership development curriculum and weekly meeting conversations as well as the community partner having a solid understanding of this community partner liaison role.

D. Campus-wide service days: *Coordinate service projects and participate in nationally recognized service days.* Each year, SLS members help plan and implement a minimum of three campus-wide service events in which PSU students, faculty, and staff collaborate to perform community service projects at sites across the Portland metropolitan region. Annual service takes place during New Student Week Service Day, Make a Difference Day, Martin Luther King, Jr. Service Day, and Earth Day of Service. This is an important component to the SLS experience because it provides students with large-scale event planning and team building skills, as well as an opportunity for students to be exposed to local community needs and organizations.

E. Leadership advancement: *Through a separate application process, returning SLS members may apply to become an SLS Mentor.* Students who have successfully completed at least one year in the SLS program are eligible to apply to become an SLS Mentor. SLS Mentors play key roles in orienting the new members, are responsible for regular check-ins with fellow members, and serve as role models for how to engage the PSU community at their community partner sites. Their leadership award is increased to $1,500 per year due to the increase in their responsibilities.

Community partner benefits

Over the years, program coordinators for SLS have compiled feedback from community partners that highlight the benefits specific to the program. Kaleen Boyle, the Outreach Coordinator for SOLVE, a statewide non-profit whose mission is to "bring Oregonians together to improve our environment and build a legacy of stewardship" (SOLVE, 2015), describes:

> This year's partnership has been very beneficial for SOLVE, opening several new doors to a variety of departments to help us connect with students and faculty alike. Likely the best connection to date has been the relationship built with the Freshman and Sophomore Inquiry faculty, a partnership that will likely result in introducing SOLVE projects and environmental enhancement opportunities to a much larger number of PSU students than we've been able to reach in the past.[2]

Across the city in Southeast Portland, SLS members have also worked at Rose Community Development, an organization dedicated to "Revitalizing Outer South East Portland neighborhoods, through the development of good homes & economic opportunities" (Rose Community Development, 2015). Kristian Hochreiter, Communications and Development Coordinator for Rose Community Development reports that, "[The SLS member] has helped to support our efforts, so that we can do more connecting with the community. She has helped connect ROSE with PSU volunteers, as well as other interested partners. She has genuine interest and passion for ROSE's mission."[3]

A final example highlights the work of a Student Leader for Service member at Portland Community Reinvestment Initiatives (PCRI), a non-profit in Northeast Portland whose mission is to "reserve, expand and manage affordable housing in the City of Portland and provide access to, and advocacy for, services for our residents" (PCRI, 2015). The SLS member's supervisor, Kirk Rea, works as the Garden Program Specialist for several of the low-income housing apartments, and is a recent PSU graduate himself. He states:

> [The SLS member] brings a good nature and presence that helps produce a friendly and welcoming environment for our residents and staff. Before, some of our organization's work has been completed by one person, so to have [the SLS member] here helping allows some work to be done at double-speed, or work can be divided so more can be accomplished. For PCRI's advocacy component, we need to connect with partners and people outside our network to share and teach about the work we're doing, so the SLS relationship extends our reach. Lastly, much of our work requires volunteer help, especially big projects like a community garden, so having [the SLS member] get Portland State volunteers is fantastic.[4]

2 Personal communication with K. Boyle, March 21, 2015.
3 Personal communication with L. Hochreiter, March 21, 2015.
4 Personal communication with K. Rea, March 21, 2015.

The unparalleled benefit that all three of these examples mention, and dozens more would likely attest, is that working with an SLS member allows the community partner "insider" access to the institution in order to more readily accomplish their organization's goals. SLS members are trained on how to identify and navigate access to institutional resources and how to connect community partners to different programs and services such as the volunteer database, service days, classes, and students. The students take on the role of facilitating the connection to the University, saving the community partner valuable hours to devote to other work.

As mentioned previously, one of the goals of the SLS Program is to retain community partners from year to year. Many of the community partners involved with the program have participated for multiple years. For example, the I Have a Dream Foundation, which "empower[s] students from low-income communities to thrive in school, college and career," has partnered with PSU through SLS for over ten years (I Have A Dream, 2013). The range of work has been varied over these years; in recent years this sustained partnership has enabled Portland State to commit resources beyond an SLS member to I Have a Dream at Alder Elementary including the "adoption" of the kindergarten grade level, T-shirt sponsorship for students, field trips to PSU and two years of AmeriCorps VISTA member placement to work on the development of a sustainable college student mentoring program with third grade students. The Macdonald Center, an organization that "nurtures the body, mind and spirit of the forgotten poor in Old Town-Downtown Portland by building connections and community," has also partnered with SLS for ten years (Macdonald Center mission, 2014). Although the goal is always to sustain partnerships for consecutive years, there are organizations that will partner for a few years, take a break due to changes in leadership, capacity, or other circumstance, and then return to partner with SLS when their organizational situation allows.

Student benefits

Arguably, the students benefit as much, if not more from the partnership. The introduction to this chapter outlined the many benefits that community engagement has for students. Effective and focused leadership development programs benefit students as well (Kuh, 2009). The Council for the Advancement of Standards in Higher Education's (CAS) "Student Leadership Programs Standards and Guidelines," highlight three main categories of student experience which should be present in leadership development programs: training, education, and development (CAS, 2003). According to the CAS standards, the purpose of training activities is to provide skill development that is immediate and for use in real-world situations. We are to use leadership models and theories as a way to examine and understand what students are doing in their college leadership experiences. The praxis between studying and doing creates an environment where, over a period of time, students increase leadership capabilities and deepen their personal awareness. The SLS program incorporates this developmental process throughout the year. Students receive training on topics like event planning, volunteer management, marketing, organizing, conflict resolution, and problem solving. Leadership education components are incorporated through workshops on identity development, civic engagement practices, systems of oppression, social justice, and social change, to name a few. The development activities combine the experiential component of the weekly service along with the educational activities and reflection, which then builds on itself over the course of the year. One of the main tools used to foster this type of development is the creation of an electronic portfolio with guided reflection questions. Cress *et al* (2001) present a compelling case for benefits of leadership development programs in higher education. By exploring longitudinal data from 875 students at ten universities, the authors found that students who participated in leadership activities scored higher in ten out of fourteen developmental outcome measures, which can be divided into three categories: skills, values and cognitive understanding. Even after controlling for variables such as academic major, the authors found that leadership programs make important impacts on student learning and development.

Perhaps the most meaningful benefit to students is development of a community on campus. Swail (2004) emphasizes the role of peer relations, mentors, and role models on undergraduate students, which leads to campus integration, a key component of student persistence in college. When asked for anonymous feedback on the SLS program from current SLS participants, one SLS member noted, "Making some of my best friends in the world who are also passionate about social justice has been the greatest experience this year."[5] Another student expressed, "I think the curriculum and e-portfolio were great. I had so many opportunities to learn about myself. Weekly meetings were great and I have formed lasting relationships with SLS members."[6]

A recent graduate of the program, Alexandra Bursheim, had this to say of the experience:

> Throughout my SLS experience I had many memorable experiences and learned a great deal about my community... I was inspired to connect PSU community to my service sight in a deeper way, in hopes [sic] of working on the systemic issue of food insecurity in our communities. To do this I connected a PSU capstone at the Learning Garden Labs [see Chapter 4, this volume] to home gardens at my site, Rose Community Development Center (RCDC). I worked with community members, teachers and students to establish an ongoing project that would change each term, yet support the home gardeners at RCDC properties with resources already existing in the community. I can confidently put this experience on my resume, and say that I have made many friends and relationships in the community. After SLS, I plan to continue serving my community, and am

5 Personal communication, May 29, 2015.
6 Personal communication, May 29, 2015.

more aware and able to creatively and collaboratively work to solve social justice issues that face my community.[7]

Lessons learned

Over its 16 years of existence, SLS has weathered many storms, evolving and adapting to institutional and community constraints and needs. This is due largely to the continued efforts of program coordinators, engaged students, and campus stakeholders who have continued to assess strengths, weaknesses, and areas for growth, continually integrating new research and adapting to change. Sharing some of the most salient lessons learned throughout the program's history can provide those who wish to replicate elements of the SLS program model.

Primarily, students are students first! The responsibilities that an SLS member has are large and can be consuming; if not monitored appropriately, the student may become overwhelmed and, over time, disengage. Since its inception, the program has yet to have a year with 100% retention. In any given year, up to 20% of the SLS members do not complete the program. With no compensation for their service work and minimal compensation for their professional development and learning, the Student Leaders for Service program requires a substantial commitment from students. Compromised grades and personal life issues have been the most common reasons that a student leaves the program. To forestall attrition, students should be monitored throughout the year and have regular check-ins with program facilitators.

Second, accountability and reward are key motivating factors for student success in the program. For several years the SLS program functioned on an honor system; hours were tracked at the community partner site but students did not submit them to the program coordinator. The lack of accountability contributed to flagging motivation. Through the PSU's service management system, students now track their hours and community partners verify them so the program staff can maintain a system of accountability. The additional benefit to tracking hours is that students can use them toward applying for awards and scholarship that require them to document the hours they have served in the community. Students are also able to use these numbers to provide concrete evidence when justifying their skills and experience to future potential employers. In addition, many SLS members are often nominated for university-wide and national community engagement awards based on their investment in community partnership work. This documentation provides a level of credibility and impact for these nominees.

Students can connect faculty to community partners, but not without support from professional staff and with organizational alignment. Given the SLS program

---

7 Personal communication with A. Bursheim, July 27, 2015.

is now located in Enrollment Management and Student Affairs, it is an inherent challenge that the professional staff person responsible for supporting community-based learning partnerships for faculty no longer has the direct supervision role of the members. There must be a solid and collaborative working relationship between the person(s) responsible to support faculty community-based learning connections and the coordinator of the SLS program. Without this relationship, the SLS program does not have as effective access to the faculty and their community-based learning courses. If the goal is to support the engagement mission of the campus and create a sustainable and consistent means of supporting community partner needs through both co-curricular and curricular engagement, then this strong relationship with others who coordinate community-based learning is essential.

Student class schedules are constantly fluctuating, making team meetings and schedules for students at community partner sites difficult to stabilize. The higher education system operates on a different annual calendar than community organizations, which often causes scheduling difficulties. For example, Portland State runs on the quarter system and the SLS program begins typically in the first week of October, which makes it difficult for community partners at public schools that operate on a school calendar that begins in early September. For a semester institution, this would cause problems at the end of the year when the college finishes in May and the public school system still functions until mid-June. To help mitigate issues between different organizations' annual cycles, the SLS program coordinator makes an effort to place PSU students at community partner sites who are willing to begin serving at their community organization prior to the official start of fall classes. The higher education calendar also presents problems when midterms, finals, and holiday breaks occur. Finally, some community partners require a regular volunteer schedule, which can be difficult when a student's schedule changes with the beginning of each new term. Students are encouraged to work with their academic programs and plan classes as early as possible so as to have the most flexibility in creating a schedule that works for both the student and the community partner.

In order to maximize institutional sustainability, partnerships across campus allow us to share resources and help achieve mutual goals. The SLS program has been able to do just that through a variety of university partnerships. In 2013, the Institute for Sustainable Solutions launched the Sustainable Neighborhood Initiative which "connects students and faculty with groups of community organizations in long-term partnerships to advance sustainability at the neighborhood scale" (Sustainable Neighborhoods Initiative, 2015). Currently, PSU is focusing on four neighborhoods, also described as ecodistricts. In the inaugural year of the initiative, SLS placed two student members with organizations in the identified ecodistricts. Through their partner site, these students helped plan a large-scale community event that engaged nearly 100 youth and local residents in environmental education activities. Building on this success, in 2015 the SLS program was able to recruit six more community organizations located in the ecodistricts, greatly contributing to this campus-wide initiative. Similar partnerships with other organizations across campus exist. In 2013, the Office of Residence Life at PSU was looking to increase retention in on-campus housing through the creation of themed flooring that would incorporate a community engagement component. These floors were titled after the PSU mascot of a Viking and the goal was to create a living-learning community focused on being a member of the PSU community and the Portland community at-large. SLS members paired with a specific Viking Floor living-learning community and developed relationships with the residents, inviting them to large days of service and developing smaller, short-term days of service for students living on-campus. Partnerships like these have been mutually beneficial, resulting in more efficient use of resources and more student community engagement.

Relationships remain key. Although the one year placement of Student Leaders for Service members in their community organization seems long, it is a relatively short commitment from the partner perspective. The relationship between the community partner staff and the SLS program coordinator is of utmost importance. The program coordinator visits every community partner site in the program at least once a year. These meetings help facilitate the initial meeting between the community partner and the SLS member, as well as check in with the staff to discuss changes and developments for both the community partner site and the SLS program. As the relationship grows over multiple years, better and stronger partnerships are made between the community partner and the institution.

Finally, the need for flexibility shows up in the SLS program in multiple ways. Not every connection between the student and community partner ends up being a good fit. The initial meeting between a community partner and student is essentially an informal interview, where the community partner is interviewing the student and the student is interviewing the community partner. There have been times when one or both parties decides that it will not be a good fit for them for the year and the program coordinator accommodates that request by placing the student at a site that better fits their interests and skills and, when possible, finding a new SLS member to work with the community site. Flexibility in working with community partners is also key. The program coordinator will check in via email or phone call with each community partner once per term. Half way through the year there is a seven question survey that is meant to give the partner an opportunity to provide formative feedback on the partnership and the student working with them at their site. Even being flexible in how the program coordinator collects the feedback (i.e., phone call, email or survey) has been appreciated by community partners. Additionally, the assessment data is used to make program adjustments as needed through the year.

Conclusion

Over its 16-year history, SLS has grown and changed each year to better incorporate student and community partner feedback and improve community–university partnerships at PSU. Through this program, PSU has leveraged sustainability-focused partnerships as a means to achieve student leadership and civic engagement learning outcomes while also increasing the capacity of community organizations around Portland. It is the convergence of these mutual interests that have allowed the once small student leadership program to grow in institutional stature over the years, transforming into the Student Community Engagement Center and contributing to the sustainability initiatives at Portland State University.

References

Bamber, P., & Hankin, L. (2011). Transformative learning through service-learning: No passport required. *Education + Training*, 53(2/3), 190-206.

Colby, A., Ehrlich, T., Beaumont, E., & Stephens, J. (2003). *Educating Citizens: Preparing America's Undergraduates for Lives of Moral and Civic Responsibility.* John Wiley & Sons.

Council for the Advancement of Standards (CAS). (2003). *Student leadership program standards. Accessed 8 April 2009.* Retrieved from forms.naca.org/NR/rdonlyres7F231B57-2A7E-4E15-82DCF7026244AB88/0/StudentLeadershipProgramsStandard.pdf

Cress, C., Astin, H., Zimmerman-Oster, K., & Burkhardt, J. (2001). Developmental outcomes of college students' involvement in leadership activities. *Journal of College Student Development*, 42(1), 15-27.

Driscoll, A. (2008). Carnegie's community-engagement classification: Intentions and insights. *Change: The Magazine of Higher Learning*, 40(1), 38-41.

Flores, R.J., Crosby-Currie, C., & Zimmerman, C. (2007). Engaged pedagogies, civic development, and student well-being within a liberal learning context. *Peer Review*, 9(3), 11-13.

Hart Research Associates (2013). *It takes more than a major: employer priorities for college learning and student success.* Washington, DC: The Association of American Colleges and Universities.

Higher Education Research Institute (1996). *A Social Change Model of Leadership Development: Guidebook Version III.* College Park, MD: National Clearinghouse for Leadership Programs.

I Have A Dream (2013). *Mission and vision.* Retrieved from: http://www.dreamoregon.org/mission-and-vision.html

Keen, C., & Hall, K. (2009). Engaging with difference matters: Longitudinal student outcomes of co-curricular service-learning programs. *The Journal of Higher Education* 80(1), 59-79.

Kuh, G.D. (2009). What student affairs professionals need to know about student engagement. *Journal of College Student Development* 50(6), 683-706.

Macdonald Center (2014). *Mission.* Retrieved from: http://www.macdcenter.org/mission

PCRI. (2015). *Mission.* Retrieved from: http://www.pcrihome.org/about/mission

Peet, M.R, Walsh, K., Sober, R., & Rawak, C.S. (2010). Generative Knowledge Interviewing: A method for knowledge transfer and talent management at the University of Michigan. *International Journal of Educational Advancement*, 10, 71-85.

Rose Community Development (2015). *About us.* Retrieved from http://rosecdc.org/about-rose

Roseland, M. (2000). Sustainable community development: Integrating environmental, economic, and social objectives. *Progress in Planning* 54(2), 73-132.

Shrestha, B., & Cihlar, C. (2004). Volunteering in under-resourced rural communities: Final report. Points of Light Foundation.

Simonet, D. (2008). *Service-learning and academic success: The links to retention research.* Minnesota Campus Compact, May, 1-13.

SOLVE (2015). Retrieved from http://www.solveoregon.org/about-us/solves-mission

Sustainable Neighborhood Initiatives (2015). *The right scale for impact.* Retrieved from http://www.pdx.edu/sustainability/sustainable-neighborhoods

Swail, W.S. (2004). *The art of student retention: A handbook for practitioners and administrators.* Austin, TX: Educational Policy Institute.

Swaner, L.E. (2007). Linking engaged learning, student mental health and well-being, and civic development: A review of the literature. *Liberal Education*, 93(1), 16-25.

Wals, A.E.J. (Ed.) (2007). Social Learning Towards a Sustainable World: Principles, *Perspectives, and Praxis.* Wageningen: Wageningen Academic Publishers.

Zlotkowski, E., Longo, N., & Williams, J. (2006). Students as colleagues. *Providence: Campus Compact.*

6

Creating a campus culture of sustainability through partnerships with enrollment management and student affairs

Heather E. Spalding and Vicki L. Wise

The role of EMSA in the higher education sustainability movement

The Division of Enrollment Management and Student Affairs (EMSA) at Portland State University (PSU) houses departments responsible for supporting student success and engagement from the time students make their first campus visit until they graduate. Departments such as the Disability Resource Center, The Learning Center, Admissions and New Student Programs, Financial Aid and Scholarships, Campus Recreation, and Student Activities and Leadership Programs are but a sampling of units student affairs divisions around the country offer to support student success. Depending on the institution, Enrollment Management may be either separate or connected with Student Affairs. This article refers to PSU-specific EMSA programs as such while using the term "student affairs" when speaking of the profession more generally.

Sustainability educators can utilize the knowledge and expertise held within EMSA to support students as they cultivate the understanding, motivation, and skills necessary to address complex environmental, social, and economic challenges (ACPA, 2014). By utilizing the entire campus as a classroom, collaborations with EMSA can create interdisciplinary, place-based applications of learning and foster deep connections between students and their local environments and communities. EMSA can also model departmental practices that support universities in achieving their sustainability goals.

Increasing student recruitment, retention, and success through sustainability

Many students are entering universities with a strong interest in sustainability, and many learners aspire to develop the competencies and skills that are needed to solve the world's most pressing environmental, social, and economic issues. How can higher education institutions design a student experience that meets the needs of sustainability-focused learners with diverse backgrounds, interests, skills, and professional goals?

PSU's Orientation and Campus Visits Office determined that, between 2013 and 2015, 23% of incoming students indicated sustainability was one reason they chose to attend the institution.[1] Indeed, some campus sustainability professionals believe sustainability offers one of the highest retention opportunities available in higher education (Devereaux, 2013). Yet research has also shown that knowledge of environmental issues doesn't necessarily lead to action (Burns, 2011; Nolet, 2009), and disconnected learning experiences can cause students to disengage (Evans, 2010; Orr, 1996). Learners may even become overwhelmed if they learn about sustainability issues but are not encouraged to build applicable skill sets or take meaningful action (Burns, 2011). To become well-rounded leaders, students must connect knowledge of sustainability issues with their lives and identities through practical application of classroom learning.

Utilizing the campus as classroom

EMSA impacts the whole campus community through its responsibilities of selecting students; implementing the university brand, image, and culture; creating norms and traditions; helping students navigate the institution; offering engagement and leadership opportunities; and helping students make meaning of their experience as a whole. These and other core functions are carried out in EMSA departments that provide direct student services, including admissions; orientations and campus visits; cultural and resource centers; health and counseling; conduct; student organizations; and campus recreation, among others.

---

1 Personal communication with M. Flores, December 15, 2014.

As a result of this campus-wide scope, EMSA divisions may offer the broadest opportunity to encourage students to incorporate sustainability into their lives (Devereaux, 2013). Research clearly shows that learning outside the classroom has a positive impact on the student experience. According to Ishler and Upcraft (2005), students who participate in campus life also tend to be more engaged and successful in classes, are more connected to the institution, and demonstrate increased learning and retention. Research from the National Survey for Student Engagement (NSSE) also indicates that students who are involved in out-of-class activities are more likely to have diverse experiences (Kuh, 2008), and "students' engagement predicts their learning, grades, achievement, retention, and graduation" (Skinner *et al.*, 2011, 17). Wilhite and Banset (2001) have concluded that students take more responsibility for learning that takes place outside of the classroom and believe that strengthening collaboration between EMSA professionals and faculty might be the best way to improve undergraduate education. Due to decreased funding at both the state and federal levels, the perceived effectiveness and institutional value of EMSA has become more focused on student recruitment and retention. Intentional collaborations could increase these metrics of success while simultaneously cultivating well-rounded and innovative sustainability leaders.

Supporting sustainability education through student development theories

The development of EMSA programs and services are grounded in educational theories and best practices. These theories are all related to how students engage, learn and develop into well-rounded individuals through their experiences in higher education.

The Theory of Identity Development examines identity through seven vectors of development stages which the student experiences: Developing Competence, Managing Emotions, Moving from Autonomy toward Interdependence, Developing Mature Interpersonal Relationships, Establishing Identity, Developing Purpose, and Developing Integrity. Students move through these stages at their own rate and, while there is no implied sequence, these vectors (stages) do overlap. With each stage, students deal with emotions and behaviors such as feeling, thinking, believing, and relating to others. Individuals may progress through the vectors at different rates. As students develop in multiple vectors, they learn to function with greater stability and intellectual complexity (Chickering, 1993).

The Theory of Student Involvement posits that student involvement is essential for student success. Students must be engaged both academically and socially on campus, and particularly through involvement in co-curricular activities such as student organizations, connecting with students and faculty on campus outside the classroom, and spending time on campus outside of classes. The three components of this theory are inputs, environment and outcomes. Inputs are the demographics and background the student brings to the learning environment, including life experiences that have shaped the student. Environment includes each of the experiences students encounter in college, including involvement in and out of the classroom, and relationships. Outcomes are the knowledge, attitudes, and beliefs that exist after a student has graduated college, as shaped by the college experience (Astin, 1984).

The Theory of Student Departure explains why students leave higher education and informs efforts of programs and services to retain students. This theory suggests that the three main reasons students leave are academic difficulties, inability to resolve their educational and occupational goals, and inability to connect or stay connected to the intellectual and social life of the institution. Tinto (1993) posits that student retention increases when students integrate their experiences into their academic studies, build relationships with faculty and staff, engage in extracurricular activities, and interact with and belong to peer groups.

Student development theories are directly relevant to all sustainability educators. Regardless of their academic interests, all college students are navigating the stages of identity and leadership development. With an understanding of these foundational theories, sustainability educators can better support students as they cultivate the understanding, motivation, and skills necessary to address complex environmental, social, and economic challenges (ACPA, 2014).

Modeling a holistic perspective of sustainability

Sustainability has been embedded into professional standards and best practices by leading student affairs professional organizations. In a jointly prepared guiding document, NASPA and the American College Personnel Association (ACPA) recommend that student affairs staff develop skills that include the ability to: "analyze the interconnectedness of societies worldwide and how these global perspectives affect institutional learning"; "explain how the values of the profession contribute to sustainable practices"; "describe environmentally sensitive issues"; "explain how one's work can incorporate elements of sustainability"; "demonstrate an ethical commitment to just and sustainable practices"; "implement divisional strategies that account for ongoing changes in the cultural landscape, political landscape, global perspectives, and sustainability issues"; and "articulate an understanding that wellness is…comprised of emotional, physical, social, environmental, relational, spiritual, and intellectual wellness"; among many others that tie to the work of sustainability (ACPA and NASPA, 2010, pp. 5-27). The North American Student Personnel Association (NASPA) also recommends that staff "promote a sense of community among all areas of the campus by working cooperatively with students, faculty, staff, and others outside the institution to address the common goals of student learning and development" (ACPA and NASPA, 2010, p. 76). These recommendations begin to outline how EMSA can bring sustainability to life on campus.

The Council for the Advancement of Standards in Higher Education (CAS) promotes standards in student affairs, student services, and student development programs that are used to enhance student learning, development, and achievement, and to promote citizenship. CAS has incorporated sustainability into its standards for developing student leadership programs. Educators are encouraged to develop qualities such as altruism, promoting human dignity, promoting connected relationships, fostering community, taking responsibility for actions, promoting positive change, "exercise[ing] role responsibilities...without exploiting or abusing power," eliminating barriers to learning, recognizing diversity, "exercis[ing] good stewardship of resources," and "promot[ing] authenticity, mutual empathy, and engagement within human interactions."

Designing well-rounded sustainability opportunities for students

The complexity and scale of sustainability issues requires emerging sustainability leaders to practice a broad range of skills in order to bring about effective and lasting change within organizations and communities. Co-curricular activities, many of which are offered through student affairs units, are designed to complement classroom studies and are ideal learning environments for cultivating sustainability leadership. These opportunities include peer-to-peer programs, volunteer positions, internships, student groups, celebrations, events, trainings, decision-making committees, and service days. Sustainability learning outcomes can also be integrated into orientations, campus tours, commencement, and many other aspects of the student experience. Co-curricular activities utilize the entire campus as an interdisciplinary classroom by convening diverse undergraduate students, graduate students, staff, faculty, alumni, and community. They also engage multiple senses and utilize high impact practices such as experiential, transformative, and service learning (Kuh, 2008). By navigating and participating in these opportunities, students can build robust portfolios of experiences, knowledge, and skills that will prepare them to create adaptive and resilient communities and organizations. EMSA-related guiding documents can provide inspiration and guidance for sustainability educators of all backgrounds and disciplines as they design intentional learning experiences.

Foundational student leadership models such as the Social Change Model (Wagner, 2006), Relational Leadership Model (Komives *et al.*, 1998), and Leadership Identity Model (Komives *et al.*, 2006) ground sustainability education within the lens of student development. Drawing from these theories, ACPA (2014): developed a set of "change agent skills required to help create a sustainable future." These abilities are nested within the following categories: 1) an understanding of sustainability issues; 2) motivation and values that support the actions of a change agent; and 3) change agent abilities. These skills complement other sustainability competencies and are applicable to a wide variety of educational contexts both inside and outside the classroom. EMSA staff can play a leadership role in higher education by sharing their knowledge of student development with sustainability educators and finding new connections between these two fields of research and application.

PSU's EMSA Sustainability Initiative: a case study in capacity building through education, partnerships, and assessment

The Institute for Sustainable Solutions (ISS), as the umbrella organization that embeds sustainability within education and research at Portland State University (PSU), began funding the Coordinator of Student Sustainability Center (SSC Coordinator) position that reports to EMSA in 2009. This partnership provided an opportunity to integrate sustainability into the student experience as well as all 45 EMSA departments. When the sustainability assessment initiative launched in fall 2012, a variety of sustainability practices and projects were already occurring across the Division. The goal was to catalogue and highlight existing examples, obtain an overall baseline of departmental practices and impact on student learning, and provide opportunities for additional projects to launch and flourish.

Training and development

PSU is committed to the three pillars of sustainability: healthy environments, social justice, and strong economies. Professional development as part of the sustainability assessment initiative focused on moving staff from increased awareness to increased knowledge, skills and abilities. The intended outcome was to better prepare staff to practice sustainable departmental practices and develop programs and services for students. EMSA's sustainability initiative had the foundation necessary for success: strong leadership, a culture of employee learning, and a culture of assessment. Strong leadership reinforced the importance of sustainability, held departments accountable for addressing this initiative and measuring impact, and provided staff with the tools and resources necessary for success. Leadership included the Vice-President, Associate Vice-President, and nine alignment leaders who oversee the Division's 45 departments. A strong employee learning culture provided a necessary backdrop for educating staff about sustainability theory and practice. The SSC Coordinator led efforts to provide educational materials for Division staff with support from the Assessment Director. They also designed an online portfolio that included myriad ways to improve sustainability practices in eight key areas: Reusing, Recycling, and Composting; Healthy Offices; Energy Conservation; Transportation; Water Conservation; Event Planning; Marketing and Promotional Materials; Purchasing; Engaging Students; and Establishing Learning Outcomes (EMSA Sustainability Resource Guide, 2014).

EMSA's assessment culture is based on the idea that effective assessment 1) begins with educational values; 2) reflects an understanding of organizational outcomes as multidimensional, integrated, and revealed in performance over time; 3) only works well when there are clear goals and objectives; 4) addresses outcomes and the processes that lead to them; 5) is ongoing, systemic, and systematic; 6) is a collaborative process and needs to involve representatives from across student affairs and the institution; 7) must be linked to what people care about in order to be useful; 8) is part of a larger set of conditions that promote change; 9) allows us to demonstrate accountability and responsibility; 10) is transparent; and 11) includes feedback (Upcraft and Schuh,1996, pp. 22-24).

Figure 6.1 PSU enrollment management and student affairs assessment cycle
Source: Assessment Planning and Practice, 2014

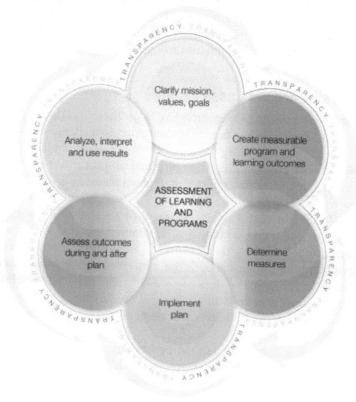

Using these principles, EMSA created the Assessment Cycle model (see Figure 6.1) of how to conduct a transparent, feedback-based assessment process to improve programs and services.

Creating common understanding across the division

EMSA's 2013 winter Division meeting launched the sustainability initiative's education and training component with a conference-style meeting that offered opportunities to increase staff awareness of specific topics and find ways to integrate
best practices into services and programs. Topics included Sustainability and the
Curriculum, Mainstream Sustainability and the Environmental Justice Movement,
Connecting Sustainability and Campus Wellness, Sustainability Advising and
Careers, Sustainability and Service Learning, and Assessing Sustainability Departmental and Programmatic Learning Outcomes.

EMSA culture supports the concept that our programs and services are our
classrooms. They impact the total student experience, including student retention, persistence, learning, development, and engagement. To this end, we recognize the importance of data to measure our impact. Through collected data,
EMSA witnessed the shift in staff knowledge of sustainability theory and practices,
as evidenced in changes in their practices and an increased number of learning
opportunities made available to students through new programs and services.

Designing the benchmark assessment

The Director for Assessment and Research, SSC Coordinator, and EMSA Assessment
Council created a benchmark survey to measure pre-post changes in sustainability practices as a result of professional development. PSU's Campus Sustainability
Office within Finance and Administration provided support and knowledge gained
from a previous initiative that supported staff green teams in departments across
the university.

DeVellis' (2012) eight-step scale development process allowed the assessment
team to produce a scale that accurately and reliably measured the constructs of
interest, and included defining the construct(s) to measure; creating draft questions; determining the format for both the items and the response scale; seeking expert opinion for item and response scale review; reducing social desirable
responding; pilot-testing items with a sample of the target population; analyzing
pilot test results to determine item and scale quality; and determining items to
keep for the final scale.

EMSA departments participated in the benchmark assessment in spring 2013.
After establishing a baseline, departments set goals for themselves in the areas
they could improve their practices. Departments then articulated their goals in
their annual report for 2013 with the expectation to provide evidence of meeting
those goals in their 2014 annual report. They were also informed that they would
complete the post-test benchmark again in 2014 to determine how their practices
improved in their goal areas, and specifically the outcomes they achieved.

A staff member in each department rated their sustainability practices using
the following scale: performed almost all the time, sometimes, not at all, or not
applicable. In analyzing the data, the standard for performance was set at performs

"sometimes." To this end, we combined responses for "almost all the time" and "sometimes" and calculated the percentage of this combined response. Combined response data were then rank-ordered to easily see the items for which we performed well and those where performance could be improved. We set a key performance indicator at 75% (combined response), so that any practice that fell below the 75% indicator was an area for potential improvement. The post-assessment was conducted one year later to determine how our practices had improved in the identified areas. This assessment provided both Division- and departmental-level comparisons of practice.

Evidence of change in departmental practices

So, how did EMSA sustainability practices improve? EMSA made strong improvements with almost all measured areas rising above the 75% threshold, and all 45 departments showed overall evidence of improvement. For areas of improvement but still below the threshold and areas of no improvement, we reviewed findings to determine possible causes and institutional leverage points that might support improvement. For example, most areas in the Energy Conservation category were improved above the threshold, but we realized departments had little to no control over items below the threshold because of university policies (or a lack thereof). These areas included switching to energy-efficient light bulbs; purchasing Energy Star certified electronics; and installing motion sensor lights. In the Event Planning category, we improved in many areas. However, university contracts do not encourage many of the sustainability practices measured. For example, use of local caterers that offer local, fresh, and organic options is ideal but limited under contract agreements.

Evidence of departmental leadership and innovation

The benchmark provided open-ended questions that allowed departments to identify additional sustainability practices that were not included in the quantitative questions. These qualitative data yielded insights about how EMSA departments can incorporate sustainability into their unique professional contexts and allowed Division staff to self-identify their work's contributions to the sustainability movement. For example, Student Health and Counseling shared that they have switched to washable patient gowns and stainless steel medical instruments when feasible. The Disability Resource Center shared how they have created philosophical and building design-related intellectual connections between sustainability and accessibility at the university. Other examples of advanced leadership in sustainability at the departmental level include the following:

In addition to managing PSU's Leadership in Energy and Environmental Design (LEED) Gold certified Academic and Student Recreation Center (ASRC), Campus Recreation (CREC) purchases environmentally friendly promotional items and displays building signage that encourages students to make connections between personal wellness and care for the Earth. In 2015, 16,926 unique individuals, including 14,777 students, visited the ASRC. The director of CREC also participates in the National Intramural Recreation Student Association's (NIRSA) sustainability committee and helped develop a sustainability model that is being used in campus recreation departments across the United States. As part of their annual Healthy Wellness Challenge, CREC has hosted events about local, sustainable food and stress management, and offers discussion courses with the Northwest Earth Institute, a non-profit organization with the mission to inspire people to take responsibility for Earth through community and education. At this annual Wellness Fair, students who filled a stamp card by visiting interactive tables were able to pick up fresh fruits and vegetables as prizes.

Commencement provides all students with the opportunity to take PSU's graduation sustainability pledge and receive a green ribbon for their gowns. Commencement coordinators also seek to reduce the impact of this large event through purchasing materials with at least 30% post-consumer recycled paper and gowns made from recycled plastic bottles. Flowers and plants from the ceremony are planted on campus through a partnership with PSU's Landscaping department.

The Student Community Engagement Center (SCEC) offers activities that include Student Leaders for Service, Alternative Spring Break, mentoring opportunities, and the Earth Day of Service. SCEC has incorporated sustainability into its work by partnering with community organizations to host neighborhood cleanups, organizing Alternative Spring Break site trips focused on food justice, and by including sustainability staff on their advisory board.

Diversity and Multicultural Student Services (DMSS) has built programmatic and departmental connections between social justice and environmental issues. For example, the director of Cultural Resource Centers encourages student participation in the Oregon's Environmental Justice Task Force. In addition, the Upward Bound and TRIO program chose "human sustainability" as the theme for its summer programs in 2014; 90 students participated. Their research posters dissected the compounds in cosmetics and discussed possible health dangers, studied invasive species, researched food resources and access in a variety of countries, and more. The Native American Student and Community Center (NASCC) manages a living rooftop garden and partnered with the Institute for Sustainable Solutions to host a visit to campus by Winona LaDuke, a well-known indigenous environmental activist.

Evidence of interdepartmental collaboration

Social Sustainability Month (SSM) is a month-long series of events that builds connections between ecological and environmental justice, economic, political and human rights, and cultural dimensions of sustainability. Started in 2010 by the Women's Resource Center's (WRC) EcoFemmes Action Team and organized by students with departmental support, the event series is sponsored by the Student Sustainability Center, WRC, DMSS, and Campus Recreation, as well as a variety of student organizations. SSM explores ways to dismantle positions of power and privilege within the sustainability movement. In 2013–14, attendance at SSM events was more than 600, and 34 departments and organizations have been involved with the initiative over the last five years, including the Coalition for Asian Pacific American Studies, the Graduate School of Education, and community organizations such as the Center for Diversity and the Environment and the Oregon Museum of Science and Industry.

Evidence of student learning

All EMSA departments submit their annual reports to an online Briefing Book. The SSC Coordinator and Director for Assessment and Research qualitatively reviewed the 2012, 2013, and 2014 portfolios to capture the sustainability learning activities being facilitated by EMSA departments. In the 2012 Briefing Book, four programs in five departments addressed learning and development. In the 2013 Briefing Book, staff reported 48 programming activities across 20 departments, with at least 18 designed to impact student learning directly. Examples that measured student learning around sustainability include the following:

The Sustainability Internship Program placed 11 graduate students pursuing degrees in the fields of urban planning, public health, urban studies, business, and public administration, and 8 undergraduate students pursuing majors in Economics, Environmental Studies, Communication Studies, Geology, Russian, and Architecture. Qualitative data showed the impact of this program on student participants. They reported gaining significant knowledge of the local food system, how organizations work to promote sustainability, operations of professional bureaus, how to communicate governmental actions to the public, real-world business experience, grant processes, project management, communication skills, confidence, software skills, and much more.

The Student Sustainability Center demonstrated evidence of significant learning by PSU students. Students reported ease with plugging into the sustainability community and augmenting their classroom experience as soon as they step on campus. Participants in the SSC's programs reported overall increased confidence as role models for sustainability, knowledge of sustainability issues, ability to channel their knowledge into action, engagement and connection with the campus, support network and community, and clarity about career and life purpose, among other outcomes.

The EMSA sustainability assessment initiative showed increased sustainability practices within all 45 departments. The results also showed an increase in departmental innovation and leadership, sustainability learning activities offered to the campus, student learning, and inter-departmental collaboration. Analysis made it clear that the Division was willing to make significant efforts and changes to support sustainability efforts as long as the implementation barriers were not too high. The study also provided opportunities to envision future possibilities to build sustainability leadership at PSU and within the EMSA profession as a whole.

Next steps: sustaining a sustainability initiative

Change is an ongoing process

Sustaining any large-scale initiative requires an ongoing investment of time and resources. John Kotter's (1996) eight-step model for organizational change offers guidance for institutions trying to create a culture of sustainability (or any other large-scale initiative). Change is much more likely when it is embedded into the larger organizational culture, and shifts in behaviors are the focus, rather than trying to change culture directly. Kotter recommends that change agents: 1) establish a sense of urgency; 2) form a guiding coalition; 3) form a task force to move from vision to action; 4) seek team members that represent the community as well as individuals with positional authority to enact change and are knowledgeable about the larger context in which the initiative sits; 5) create a vision and action plan; 6) communicate the vision and make modifications; 7) empower others to act on the vision and to carry out plans; 8) provide tools, resources, education, incentives, and recognition needed for success; 9) create short term wins; 10) build on progress; and 11) institutionalize new approaches into institutional culture.

In reflecting on the progress to date of EMSA's sustainability initiative, the authors have identified a variety of opportunities to further develop innovative practice within EMSA departments.

Measure student learning across the division

While a few departments are assessing the impact of their sustainability activities on students' attitudes, behaviors, knowledge and skills, most measure only activities offered and participation. EMSA should identify broadly applicable and relevant sustainability learning outcomes for students who participate in EMSA programs and activities. This learning could be tracked across various student experiences, and potentially with curriculum, to observe changes in student learning and engagement as a result of attending the institution.

Support implementation of PSU's climate action plan.

PSU's Campus Sustainability Office is extending the work of the EMSA benchmark by surveying academic units to learn about their sustainability practices. The authors have shared the successes and challenges of this project so that a PSU-wide survey can be effective and tailored to the unique cultures of various divisions. Practices that did not meet the threshold for success will be considered as opportunities for policy change and further discussion with university leadership in order to remove barriers to sustainable actions.

Maintain leadership

The SSC Coordinator will work with departments to review the results of their assessment results and envision next steps that are professionally relevant and contextual to each department's individual needs. They will also continue to research best practices and participate in relevant professional organizations in order to stay updated about best practices and trends within higher education sustainability.

Advocate for sustainability leadership in EMSA and higher education

The authors hope this case study will inspire EMSA professionals and their colleagues to consider possibilities for innovation in their work, as well as in their departments, divisions, and campuses. This assessment framework can be replicated or used as a starting point for other sustainability and assessment-related initiatives. We believe that higher education can simultaneously cultivate well-prepared sustainability leaders while increasing student recruitment, retention, and success through partnerships with Enrollment Management and Student Affairs divisions.

References

ACPA (American College Personnel Association) (2014). Change agent abilities required to help create a sustainable future. Retrieved from: http://www.myacpa.org/sites/default/files/Change_Agent_Skills.pdf

ACPA (American College Personnel Association) and NASPA (National Association Student Personnel Administration) (2010). Professional competency areas for student affairs practitioners. Retrieved from: http://www.naspa.org/images/uploads/main/ACPA_NASPA_Professional_Competencies_FINAL.pdf

Assessment Planning and Practice (2014). *Portland State Enrollment Management & Student Affairs*. Retrieved from: http://www.pdx.edu/studentaffairs/assessment-planning-and-practice

Astin, A.W. (1984). Student involvement: A developmental theory for higher education. *Journal of College Student Development*, 25, 297-308.

Burns, H. (2011). Teaching for transformation: (Re)designing sustainability courses based on ecological principles. *Journal of Sustainability Education*, 2.

Chickering, A.W. (1993). *Education and identity* (2nd ed.). San Francisco, CA: Jossey-Bass.

DeVellis, R.F. (2012). Scale Development: Theory and Application. *Applied Social Research Methods Series* (3rd ed.). Thousand Oaks, CA: Sage.

Devereaux, J. (2013). Student affairs and the future of sustainability. *Sustainability: The Journal of Record*, 6(5), 265-270.

EMSA Sustainability Resource Guide (2014). *Enrollment Management and Student Affairs*. Retrieved from: https://sites.google.com/a/pdx.du/enrollment-management-and-student-affairs-emsa-sustainability-resource-guide

Evans, T.L. (2010). Critical social theory and sustainability education at the college level: Why it's critical to be critical. *Journal of Sustainability Education*, 1.

Ishler, J.L., & Upcraft, M.L. (2005). The keys to first-year student persistence. In M.L. Upcraft, J.N. Gardner, & B.O. Barefoot (Eds.), *Challenging and Supporting the First-Year Student* (pp. 27-46). San Francisco, CA: Jossey-Bass.

Komives, S.R., Longerbeam, S.D., Owen, J.E., Mainella, F.C., & Osteen, L. (2006). A leadership identity development model: Applications from a grounded theory. *Journal of College Student Development*, 47(4), 4,001-4,418.

Komives, S.R., Lucas, N., & McMahon, T.R. (1998). *Exploring Leadership: For College Students Who Want to Make a Difference* (3rd ed.). San Francisco: Jossey-Bass.

Kotter, J.P. (1996). *Leading Change*. Cambridge, MA: Harvard Business School Press.

Kuh, J.D. (2008). *High impact educational practices: A brief overview.* Association of American Colleges and Universities. Retrieved from: http://leap.aacu.org/toolkit/high-impact-practices/2011/high-impact-educational-practices-what-they-are-who-has-access-to-them-and-why-they-matter

Nolet, V. (2009). Preparing sustainability-literate teachers. *Teachers College Record*, 111(2), 409–442.

Orr, D. (1996). *What is education for? Six myths about the foundations of modern education, and six new principles to replace them.* Context Institute. Retrieved from: http://www.context.org/iclib/ic27/orr

Skinner, E.A., & Chi, U. (2011). Intrinsic motivation and engagement as "active ingredients" in garden-based education: Examining models and measures derived from self-determination theory. *The Journal of Environmental Education*, 43(1), 16-36.

Tinto, V. (1993). *Leaving college: Rethinking the Causes and Cures of Student Attrition.* (2nd ed.). Chicago: University of Chicago Press.

Upcraft, M.L., & Schuh, J.H. (1996). *Assessment in Student Affairs: A Guide for Practitioners.* San Francisco: Jossey-Bass.

Wagner, W. (2006). The social change model of leadership: A brief overview. *Concepts & Connections: A Publication for Leadership Educators*, 15(1), 8-10. Retrieved from: http://web.trinity.edu/Documents/student_affairs_docs/Assessments/Social%20Change%20Model%20of%20Leadership%20-%20A%20Brief%20Overview%20%28Wagner%29.pdf

Wilhite, M., & Banset, L. (2001). Learning outside the box: Making connections between co-curricular activities and the curriculum. *Essays on Teaching Excellence: Toward the Best in the Academy.* Retrieved from: http://www.asa.mnscu.edu/facultydevelopment/resources/pod/Packet1/learningoutsidethebox.htm

7

Integrating aging and sustainability through university–community partnerships

Alan DeLaTorre and Margaret Neal

If we are to afford future generations an equitable and sustainable future, we must do so in a manner that addresses the future composition of those generations. Population aging has global implications, and the disciplines of gerontology and sustainability are logical partners in addressing both the opportunities and challenges that accompany this significant demographic change. Scant attention has been paid to population aging in the field of sustainability however and approaches to sustainable development are seldom used in gerontological teaching and research.

Some universities are well positioned to work with communities to address population aging in a manner that advances quality of life and well-being for older adults, their families, and others. University–community partnerships focused on achieving sustainable outcomes must strive to balance environment, social equity, economy, and cultural issues of current and future generations. Regardless of the positive and negative possibilities that accompany population aging, the phenomenon itself represents a demographic imperative that challenges sustainable planning, and one which has not, to date, been adequately addressed in research, policy, or practice.

This chapter details how faculty members at one university have emphasized sustainable community development principles in their approaches to teaching and research in the field of gerontology. This has occurred by carrying out translational research—i.e., basic and population-based research with the long-term aim of improving the health of the public (Rubio *et al.*, 2010), integrating aging in local policy and practice, and by offering service-learning opportunities for students and citizens that incorporate sustainable development principles into projects aimed at preparing communities for population aging.

Population aging: the biggest demographic change in the coming decades

Portland, like communities around the world, is aging in a rapid and unprecedented manner. As the US population grows older with respect to the number and proportion of older adults—largely due to the baby boomers turning 65 and over—we must pay attention to several age-related trends (Ortman *et al.*, 2014). The "oldest-old" cohort in the US (i.e., those aged 85 and older) is projected to double from 4.7 million in 2003 to 9.6 million in 2030; by 2050 it is predicted to have more than doubled, again, to 20.9 million (He *et al.*, 2005).

From a health perspective, population aging represents a human success story; longevity has increased since the mid-1800s due to improvements in medicine, sanitation, and public health (Kinsella and He, 2009). However, although life expectancy has increased, health status and functional ability have declined. The Federal Interagency Forum on Aging-Related Statistics (FIFARS, 2010) reported that from 2006–2008 self-assessed health status of the 65 and older population in the US showed increases in the "fair" or "poor" health categories and decreases in the "good" or "excellent" categories across all age categories over 65 and across all gender and race categories, despite more years of life. Although there is evidence that rates of physical and cognitive impairment have decreased over the past several decades, the rapid increase in the number of older adults has affected the absolute number of older adults living with some sort of impairment (National Institute on Health, 2013).

The US population, including older adults, is also growing more diverse. From 2010–2050, the proportion of non-Hispanic whites aged 65 and older is projected to drop from 80% to 58%, while all other race categories will increase, including Black alone (from 9% to 12%), Asian alone (from 3% to 9%), Hispanic of any race (from 7% to 20%), and all other races (from 2% to 3%) (FIFARS, 2012). This diversification is expected to affect U.S. families, businesses, and the health care industry (Vincent and Velkoff, 2010), and greater flexibility in program and service delivery will be needed.

Finally, the economic well-being of older adults is important to overall economic sustainability, as issues such as the national debt, federal entitlements, and health care costs are all affected by population aging (Wright and Lund, 2000). Although the economic status of many older Americans has improved as a result of Social Security and private pension systems over the past 50+ years (Schulz, 2001), economic deprivation and insecurity still exist, especially among the oldest old, ethnic minorities, older women, and extremely vulnerable older adults with incomes just above the poverty level (Administration on Aging, 2014).

Aging and sustainability: strange bedfellows?

Sustainability is derived from the word sustain, which means "to endure without giving way or yielding…to keep up or keep going, as an action or process" (Random House, 1992, p. 1,347). An Internet search of the terms "sustainability" or "sustainable development" yields millions of results, ranging from urban planning and design to food systems and recycling. The Oregon Sustainability Act (State of Oregon, 2001) defined sustainability as "using, developing and protecting resources in a manner that enables people to meet current needs and provides that future generations can also meet future needs, from the joint perspective of environmental, economic and community objectives." Oregon's definition is similar to that in the widely embraced origin of the concept of sustainable development (Williams and Millington, 2004), the Report of the World Commission on Environment and Development (United Nations, 1987, p. 16), commonly referred to as the "Brundtland Report," which stated, "Humanity has the ability to make development sustainable to ensure that it meets the needs of the present without compromising the ability of future generations to meet their own needs."

In the 1990s, discourse on sustainable development moved beyond environmental and economic applications into the areas of human settlements, urban areas, and housing (Choguill, 1999). Social equity issues within sustainability studies and practice have been seen as largely peripheral issues compared to economic and environmental concerns, but increasingly they are being considered, as "social sustainability is the only bedrock on which meaningful environmental sustainability can be grounded" (Dillard *et al.*, 2009, p. 1).

Several policies of the State of Oregon and the City of Portland have focused on sustainable development practices. For example, Oregon's Department of Land Conservation and Development (2012) has aimed to foster sustainable, vibrant communities, and Portland has made a push to become the nation's "sustainability capital" (Giegerich, 2008). In addition, in 2009, the mayor combined the Bureau of Planning and the Office of Sustainable Development to create the Bureau of Planning and Sustainability to better align the complementary efforts of the two agencies, to improve sustainable practices, and to increase public engagement (City of Portland, 2009).

So how does aging align with the sustainability discourse? A goal of sustainable development is intergenerational equity, which implies fairness to present and future generations (Berke, 2002; Meadowcroft, 2000). This perspective of looking toward future generations is also seen in Native American considerations of the impact of decisions seven generations into the future with respect to revitalization, restoration, preservation, planning, and development projects (Seventh Generation Fund for Indian Development, 2015). As our population ages and public resources dwindle, there is the potential for intergenerational conflict. However, as Wright and Lund (2000) explained, most commentary on the impact of population aging has focused on problems associated with increased federal entitlements and health care costs. The benefits of an aging population, including the social capital older adults represent, have been overlooked.

Scholarly discussions around aging and sustainability can be found as early as 1995. At a conference at the University of North Texas, scholars examined the relationship between population aging and ecological development in order to explore the ways in which older people could help societies meet ecological and social challenges (Ingman *et al.*, 2005). According to Ekstrom, Ingman, and Benjamin (1999) older adults represent a talented pool of resources for the creation and maintenance of sustainable communities; their available skills, time, and enthusiasm were seen as a potential opportunity for intergenerational mentoring and for empowered citizens to engage in public policy issues. Other scholars have examined how transportation for older adults can be facilitated in an environmentally responsible way (e.g., reducing carbon footprints) (e.g., Rosenbloom, 2001), and Landorf *et al.* (2008, p. 512) argued that the "disabling impact of the urban environment on older people should be an essential consideration in the urban sustainability debate."

More recently, the World Health Organization (WHO, 2007, p. 4) stated that in order to create "sustainable communities [cities must provide] structures and services to support their residents' wellbeing," and that "older people in particular require supportive and enabling living environments." These environments must compensate for the normal physical and social changes that are associated with the aging process. In 2011, policy experts issued a call to action to urban and regional planners and policy-makers to prepare for population aging through thoughtful, intentional planning and development of housing that is affordable, well-designed, close in proximity to essential services and infrastructure, and intended to integrate a diversifying population while fostering social well-being (Farber *et al.*, 2011). The American Planning Association (2014, p. 1) also recently developed a set of multi-generational policy recommendations that support the creation and integration of "housing, land-use, transportation, economic, social service, and health systems that support a high quality of life for people of all ages and abilities... [ensuring] that older members of our communities are not at risk of social isolation, poverty, declining health, and poor economic well-being."

Despite the overlap in the fields of aging and sustainable development, few efforts have emerged to combine the two. The remainder of this chapter will describe various university–community partnerships which have been initiated at one university that have integrated aging and sustainable development in an effort to sustainably plan for our aging society.

University–community partnerships: addressing population aging by integrating sustainable development into teaching and research

Since 1969, faculty at Portland State University's (PSU) Institute on Aging (IOA) have contributed to the local, statewide, and national aging networks and have strived to fulfill the IOA's mission to enhance understanding of aging and to facilitate opportunities for elders, families, and communities to thrive. PSU's motto, "Let Knowledge Serve the City," has been honored through the translation of research findings into policy and practice pertaining to issues of urban planning and population aging.

In 1989, IOA and School of Urban Studies and Planning faculty developed training materials for urban planners in Oregon in order to foster more livable environments for older adults; an American Planning Association publication titled Planning for an Aging Society was one result of the PSU project (Howe et al., 1994), which laid a foundation for urban gerontology nationally. IOA faculty have been involved in numerous subsequent efforts focused on improving the health and well-being of older adults in the region, including a 2006 project with Metro, Portland's regional government (Neal et al., 2006), an ongoing project with the WHO focused on urban aging, efforts of other governmental partners in the region (DeLaTorre et al., 2012), and an Environmental Protection Agency-funded project.

In 2006, the WHO approached the IOA to become a part of its Global Age-friendly Cities research project, which included 33 cities in 22 countries. Portland's selection as the only US city involved in the initial project stemmed from the city's reputation for good planning, the IOA's research reputation, and previous work in global and urban aging issues (DeLaTorre and Neal, 2015). Despite the lack of funding for the project, faculty in the IOA viewed the WHO project as an excellent opportunity to build on interests in global aging, urban studies and planning, and gerontology.

Initially, the WHO's age-friendly research protocol called for a qualitative inquiry into Portland's age friendliness. Once the WHO research was completed in 2007, IOA researchers widely disseminated the findings while attempting to engage students, older adults, and community members in learning about and moving toward becoming a more age-friendly community. Those findings advanced understanding about older Portlanders' day-to-day experiences and the city's age-friendly features and barriers pertaining to physical, social, and service environments. Additionally, suggestions for improvement garnered from older adults, caregivers, and services providers in the government, business, and non-profit sectors have been integral to advancing age-friendly and sustainable development efforts.

In 2010, the WHO initiated its Global Network of Age-friendly Cities and Communities for the purpose of sharing best practices; communities from around the world were invited to join. Requirements for membership included a letter of commitment from the top government official of the community and a pledge to develop an action plan for the community to become more age friendly and then to implement the plan and monitor progress. The IOA approached Portland Mayor Sam Adams with a membership proposal, and the Mayor and the Portland City Council voted unanimously to join the WHO Global Network; Portland was one of the first nine inaugural members of the Global Network.

In 2012, the AARP Public Policy Institute joined the push to foster age-friendly communities and became the US affiliate program to the WHO's Global Network; AARP now convenes the US-based AARP Network of Age-Friendly Communities (AARP, 2015). The Mayor and the City Council approved joining the AARP Network as well, when it was initiated. As part of another IOA-coordinated effort, Multnomah County's Board of Commissioners voted unanimously to join the WHO and AARP Networks in 2014.

Currently, an Age-friendly Portland and Multnomah County Advisory Council is composed of community stakeholders representing government, business, community services and older adults themselves; it is coordinated by the IOA, which also advises the initiative. In October, 2013, the Action Plan for an Age-friendly Portland (Age-friendly Portland Advisory Council, 2013), developed by the IOA with feedback from the Advisory Council, was unanimously approved by City Council resolution and implementation efforts are underway. A Multnomah County-specific action plan is under development for launch in 2016.

The following sections describe the various ways that PSU faculty and students have been involved in preparing communities for population aging through the integration of sustainable development approaches in research and teaching.

Agenda setting: placing aging into the local policy agenda

In Portland, the age-friendly policy efforts have involved collaboration among IOA researchers and students, local advocates, community stakeholders, planning agency staff, special interest groups, city commissions, and elected officials. Kingdon's (1984) theory of agenda setting provides a way of understanding how age-friendly community concepts have been adopted as planning principles in Portland. The theory posits that a policy can be adopted or changed when a window of opportunity opens, permitting policy participants to connect at least two of the following three streams associated with the policy process: (1) problem streams (i.e., defining and placing an issue on the agenda), (2) policy streams (i.e., knowledge and solutions that can be considered by decision makers), and/or (3) political streams (i.e., political climate and will to place the issue on the agenda). It is important to note that policy participants do not only reside in government, but include others such as university faculty who can provide research findings and expert testimony during policy processes.

Neal *et al.* (2014) explained how each stream presented in the evolution of Portland's age-friendly efforts. First, the phenomenon of population aging and the need for local responses were recognized and highlighted by IOA faculty, who acted as policy entrepreneurs in collaboration with regional government staff. Second, two formal planning processes/policy documents in the City of Portland were open to public comment: the Portland Plan and the Comprehensive Plan. These planning processes occurred on a scheduled, anticipated, and predictable basis, which Kingdon (1984) identified as a reliable opportunity for moving an agenda forward. Finally, the correct political climate existed as several elected officials supported the age-friendly Portland effort, meeting with IOA faculty, providing access to City bureaus and staff, and granting researchers legitimate roles as advisors to the policy process while also committing in writing to meet the criteria required for membership in the WHO Global Network (e.g., conducting a baseline assessment, involving older adults in the process, and developing an action plan).

As a result of IOA faculty and Advisory Council involvement in the Portland and Comprehensive Plans, age-friendly policies were proposed, and some were adopted. In particular, the Portland Plan included a two-page insert titled Portland is a Place for All Generations, which detailed ten action steps. Among these were: developing and implementing an age-friendly action plan; developing policies and programs to increase the supply of housing accessible to older and disabled persons; and completing a citywide housing strategy that included exploring opportunities to create housing for older adults and mobility-impaired residents in service-rich, accessible locations (City of Portland, 2012, pp. 24-25).

The intersection between sustainable and age-friendly development

Sustainable and age-friendly development have corresponding elements in their respective conceptualizations and approaches to practice. Sustainability's three main tenets— environment, social equity, and economy—are also integral to WHO's age-friendly domains, the 287 global communities in 33 countries participating in WHO's Global Network of Age-Friendly Cities and Communities (WHO, 2014), and the local applications in Portland and Multnomah County. Looking beyond the WHO's eight age-friendly domains—housing, transportation, outdoor spaces and buildings, respect and social inclusion, social participation, communication and information, civic participation and employment, and community support and health services—age-friendly efforts are intended to lead to well-designed communities with amenities and infrastructure that enable and engage older adults, rather than disabling and isolating them. These features are seen as necessary if we are to tap into the vast resource that is an older adult population, one of the few growing resources in the world.

Comparing the age-friendly and sustainability domains elucidates where the two approaches to development coincide. Table 7.1 shows the three sustainability domains as they correspond to the age-friendly domains. It should be noted that in Table 7.1, as well as in the Portland and Multnomah County age-friendly efforts (e.g., action plans, committee structure), volunteering and economic development have been added to the original WHO domains.

Table 7.1 Corresponding elements of sustainable development and age-friendly communities

Sustainability domains	Age-friendly domains
Environmental equity	· Housing · Transportation · Outdoor spaces and buildings
Social equity	· Respect and social inclusion · Social participation · Civic participation and volunteering · Communication and information · Community support · Health services
Economic equity	· Employment · Economic development

Collaboration with the Portland Commission on Disability

In 2009, one IOA faculty member joined the Portland Commission on Disability (PCoD) as a charter member based on their expertise in environmental gerontology and experience in working with community partners on urban aging issues. PCoD has collaborated on projects with IOA faculty, including a 2011 Solutions Generator project funded by PSU's Institute for Sustainable Solutions. That project focused on enhancing social equity by identifying and mitigating barriers to accessibility for all campus users. The project, Designing a PSU for Everyone, was successful in meeting its proposed goals by hosting two events: (1) a campus-wide aging and disability forum, and (2) a design charrette focused on an area of campus that shared facilities with public spaces (e.g., food carts, public transit infrastructure).

Several equitable design-related solutions were proposed by project participants, including integrating technology (e.g., "apps" for smart phones, tactile maps) and design approaches that were universal and more "intuitive" to all users (e.g., blind/low-vision and deaf/hard-of-hearing communities were similar, in some ways, to students and others who were "plugged into" their phones, music devices, etc.). As a result of the design charrette, specific conceptual designs were created that proposed integrating visual and audible warnings for a proposed streetcar crossing.

PCoD, in collaboration with IOA faculty, has also provided written and verbal testimony on the Portland and Comprehensive Plans. During public testimony for the Portland Plan, advocates coordinated an effort to raise awareness that aging and disability issues were being overlooked by the Bureau of Planning and Sustainability. Advocates attending a Planning and Sustainability Commission meeting placed paper grocery bags over their heads (with eye holes) while speakers explained that, despite numerous advocacy efforts, older adults and people with disabilities "remained an invisible community" (Neal *et al.*, 2014). Eventually, planners called a special meeting with the advocates which led to specific age- and disability-friendly policies in the final version of the Portland Plan.

International education: sustainable community development in Nicaragua

Gerontology is recognized as a multidisciplinary field of study that draws upon expertise from many disciplines (Grabinsky, 2015). This allows for integration of myriad perspectives and areas of research, including sustainability. Faculty members from PSU's IOA have incorporated aspects of sustainability and sustainable community development, into lectures, projects, and collaborations.

The first and longest-standing example of sustainable development being integrated into IOA's gerontology program is a program begun in 2003 titled Global Aging and Health: Enhancing Communities in Nicaragua. The program was created in partnership with the Jessie F. Richardson Foundation, a non-profit organization focused on helping indigent elders live their best lives in the U.S. and around the globe. Approximately 10–12 students take a service-learning course in spring term and then travel to Nicaragua for two weeks to carry out service projects that range from intergenerational education to environmental interventions (e.g., installing hand rails, planting trees). Faculty have approached the preparation for the course with a sustainable community development model adapted from Kretzmann and McKnight's (1993) holistic approach to asset-based community development; this approach requires actively engaging with community stakeholders with an aim to achieve positive, sustainable community development. In Nicaragua, this approach has led to collaboration with a broad range of organizations, including those serving youth (e.g., sports teams and schools), businesses (e.g., through assistance with microenterprise development), and older persons (e.g., government-supported senior clubs, lifelong learning groups).

One example of a project that aimed for sustainable economic and environmental impact involved building a home for an older Nicaraguan woman. Using a model developed for a Peace Corps project in Guatemala, PSU students built part of the home using traditional Nicaraguan building practices—e.g., concrete reinforced steel foundation, galvanized steel roof—to create a building skeleton that then allowed for the walls to be built with recycled 1.5 liter plastic bottles filled with dry, inorganic garbage; poultry wire encased the bottles before cement was applied (Neal *et al.*, 2010). In retrospect, the cost of the project was higher than a traditional Nicaraguan home and, due to the difficulty in obtaining dry, inorganic materials, the project was not repeated during subsequent trips. Other sustainability-oriented projects that have been undertaken include building raised bed gardens, working with environmental advocacy groups, and providing public health education aimed at preventing illness and disability for older adults who lack regular access to medical services.

Service learning: capstones designed with community partners

The majority of students who have participated in the Nicaragua program described above have been PSU University Studies Capstone students; the Capstone program aims to build cooperative learning communities by taking students out of the classroom and into the field (Portland State University, 2015). By creating Capstone projects in response to community requests and guidance, students learn to serve in a manner that is better tailored to local, contextual issues. The PSU Nicaragua service-learning program has benefited since 2003 from its collaboration with the non-profit partner organization. Students are able to contribute incrementally to a long-term program that has achieved sustained change, such as: national recognition of Nicaraguan population aging, establishment of a national council on aging, and the opening of a national training center on gerontology and geriatrics.

The age-friendly initiatives in the Portland area have also led to service-learning opportunities, both as a part of PSU's Capstone program, and with older adults from the community as the service learners. In summer 2009, Creating Livable Communities for an Aging Society was offered to 13 students who worked in two Portland neighborhoods: Hollywood and Overlook. The students ranged in age from 21–70 and came from a variety of majors including Community Health, English, Psychology, Philosophy, and Business.

Although the course was only offered once, the pilot Capstone course was considered by many to be a successful endeavor. The course instructor, students, community partners, and neighborhood stakeholders learned important lessons about service learning, in general, and about the Hollywood and Overlook communities, in particular. After nine months of preparation, the eight-week course came and went very quickly, and many of the activities that were desired by community members were accomplished, including: examining social isolation in affordable public housing, conducting a "roll and stroll" to determine mobility barriers and possible improvements, and presenting policy and program recommendations to government and non-profit partners.

In addition to PSU service-learning courses, IOA faculty have collaborated with numerous community partners with the intent of facilitating sustained community benefits. In 2012, the IOA worked with AARP Oregon, Elders in Action, and Hands on Greater Portland (now a part of United Way) to offer introductory training to volunteers on age-friendly approaches that culminated in four age-friendly community volunteer projects: a walkability audit along a main street that was awarded a sustainable development grant from the City of Portland; grocery shopping and delivery for older adults; a cooking event with residents of an intergenerational housing community; and garden maintenance at a dementia-friendly memory garden. The service-learning course was repeated again in Clackamas County the following year with new community-based projects.

Demonstrating the benefits of green streets for active aging in partnership with a neighborhood association

This project, funded by the US Environmental Protection Agency, examined how sustainable ("green") streets contribute to the well-being of a community, including the physical and mental health of older and younger adults, along with the environment and economy (Dill *et al.*, 2010). Green streets incorporate natural, landscape-based features that reduce storm water runoff in a buffer between the sidewalk and the street and accommodate multiple travel modes, particularly walking and bicycling. The project involved conducting a survey of households in the Lents neighborhood in Portland (divided into four quadrants—two with green streets and two without) and conducting a walkability audit of the four quadrants. The study was done in partnership with the Lents Neighborhood Association, whose members advised the project team with respect to the survey and its administration and also provided feedback concerning the findings of the study.

The survey found generally positive views of the green street features, with 50% of older adults reporting that the green streets made walking in their neighborhood more pleasant (although 78% of adults under 65 felt this way). At the same time, more older adults than younger adults felt that the green streets made parking on the street more difficult (34% versus 21%) and driving more difficult (25% versus 13%) (Dill *et al.*, 2010, p. 4). These findings may be due to the fact that green streets tend to be located along streets with wider arterial streets with higher speed limits and greater traffic volumes (Adkins *et al.*, 2012).

The walkability audits were conducted by both older adult volunteers and graduate students, all of whom underwent two half-day trainings, one in the classroom and the other in the field. The audit tool was adapted from two existing instruments: the Pedestrian Environmental Data Scan (Clifton *et al.*, 2007) and the Senior Walking Environment Audit Tool—Revised (Michael *et al.*, 2008). A total of 380 street segments were audited across the four study areas. Adkins *et al.* (2012) found that, in this predominantly single-family residential area, well-designed green street facilities, parks, separation from traffic, and sidewalk connectivity significantly contributed to the attractiveness of the walking environment.

Conclusion

The intersection of age-friendly and sustainable development has been evident in the university–community partnerships, research, and teaching carried out by faculty within PSU's IOA. In addition to the corresponding elements of age-friendly and sustainable development, they also share one common, critically important goal: intergenerational equity. At the heart of the efforts carried out by IOA faculty are strong university–community partnerships, evidenced by the Age-friendly Portland and Multnomah County initiatives, service-learning programs, and collaboration with Portland's Commission on Disability and other community-based organizations. In fact, a key factor in the success of aging and sustainability efforts is the active and meaningful participation of citizens, government, elected leaders, the business community, and non-profits. The translational research and service-learning projects provide fertile ground for testing ideas around aging and sustainable development.

It seems important to note that although the Portland-area age-friendly initiative has become nationally and even internationally known, little funding has been received to date. Unfunded research efforts are not highly regarded by university administrators, government officials have endorsed the program yet failed to provide funding, and local charitable funding has become youth-focused, despite our rapidly aging population. The lack of funding can slow progress and discourage faculty involvement in community-engaged work, even if worthwhile. Thus, the issue of funding is one that is important to consider for university-community partnerships focused on aging, as well as other disciplines.

Somewhat surprisingly, although academic and community efforts around sustainable and age-friendly development have coincided from 2006 to the present, there seems to be a disconnect between the two. This chapter has provided examples of strategies for blending the two fields. Moving forward, aging represents a demographic imperative that must be considered by scholars, policymakers, and practitioners who are engaged in sustainability-related research and action. The university has, and must continue to, translate research into policy and practice. Although advocacy and politics are not core skills of academicians, sustainable and age-friendly development requires thinking outside of the silos that have defined the academy, government, the private sector, and citizens.

References

AARP (2015). The AARP network of age-friendly communities: An introduction. *AARP Livable Communities*. Retrieved from: http://www.aarp.org/livable-communities/network-age-friendly-communities/info-2014/an-introduction.html

Adkins, A., Dill, J., Luhr, G., & Neal, M. (2012). Unpacking walkability: Testing the influence of urban design features on perceptions of walking environment attractiveness. *Journal of Urban Design*, 17(4), 493-505. doi:10.1080/13574809.2012.706365

Administration on Aging (2014). *A profile of older Americans: 2014*. Administration on Aging, Administration for Community Living, US Department of Health and Human Services. Retrieved from: http://www.aoa.acl.gov/Aging_Statistics/Profile/2014/docs/2014-Profile.pdf

Age-friendly Portland Advisory Council (2013). *Action plan for an Age-friendly Portland*. Portland, OR: Portland State University. Retrieved from: http://agefriendlyportland.org/article/age-friendly-portland-action-plan

American Planning Association (2014). *Aging in community policy guide*. American Planning Association. Retrieved from: https://www.planning.org/policy/guides/pdf/agingincommunity.pdf

Berke, P. (2002). Does sustainable development offer a new direction for planning? Challenges for the Twenty-First Century. *Journal of Planning Literature*, 17(1), 21-36. doi: 10.1177/088122017001002

City of Portland (2009). *Bureau of Planning merges with Office of Sustainable Development*. Portland, OR: City of Portland. Retrieved from: http://www.portlandonline.com/portlandplan/index.cfm?a=225850&c=50730

City of Portland (2012). *The Portland plan*. Portland, OR: City of Portland. Retrieved from: http://www.portlandonline.com/portlandplan/index.cfm?c=56527

Choguill. (1999). Sustainable human settlements: Some second thoughts. In A.F. Foo, & B. Yuen (Eds.), *Sustainable Cities in the 21st Century* (pp. 131-144). Singapore: Singapore University Press.

Clifton, K.J., Livi Smith, A.D., & Rodriguez, D. (2007). The development and testing of an audit for the pedestrian environment. *Landscape and Urban Planning*, 80(1-2), 95-110. doi:10.1016/j.landurbplan.2006.06.008

DeLaTorre, A., DeLaTorre, T., Neal, M., Carder, P., Weinstein, J., DeShane, M., & Wilson, K. (2012). *Periodic atlas of the metroscape: Planning for our aging society*. Metroscape. Portland, OR: Portland State University, Institute of Portland Metropolitan Studies. Retrieved from: https://www.pdx.edu/sites/www.pdx.edu.ims/files/mscapewin12atlas.pdf

DeLaTorre. A., & Neal, M.B. (2015). Portland, Oregon: A case study of efforts to become more age friendly. In F.G. Caro & K.G. Fitzgerald (Eds.), *International perspectives on age-friendly cities*. New York, NY: Routledge.

Department of Land Conservation and Development (2012). *Oregon Department of Land Conservation and Development*. State of Oregon. Retrieved from: http://www.oregon.gov/LCD/Pages/about_us.aspx

Dill, J., Neal, M., Shandas, V., Luhr, G., Adkins, A., & Lund, D. (2010). *Demonstrating the benefits of green streets for active aging: Initial findings.* Portland, OR: Portland State University, College of Urban and Public Affairs. Retrieved from: http://www.cts.pdx.edu/research/pdf/GreenStreetsActiveAging_PSU_InitialFindings.pdf

Dillard, J.F., Dujon, V., & King, M.C. (2009). Introduction. In J.F. Dillard, V. Dujon, & M.C. King. (Eds.). *Understanding the social dimension of sustainability* (pp. 1-14). New York, NY: Routledge.

Ekstrom, C.D., Ingman, S.R., & Benjamin, T. (1999). Gerontology/environmental links in aging education: Toward an intergenerational view of sustainability. *Educational Gerontology,* 25(6), 613-621. doi: 10.1080/036012799267666

Farber, N., Shinkle, D., Lynott, J., Fox-Grage, W., & Harrell, R. (2011). *Aging in place: A state survey of livability policies and practices.* National Conference of State Legislators, AARP Public Policy Institute. Retrieved from: https://assets.aarp.org/rgcenter/ppi/liv-com/aging-in-place-2011-full.pdf

FIFARS. (Federal Interagency Forum on Aging-Related Statistics) (2010). *Older Americans 2010: Key indicators of well-being.* Washington DC: US Government Printing Office. Retrieved from: http://www.agingstats.gov/main_site/data/2010_Documents/docs/OA_2010.pdf

FIFARS. (Federal Interagency Forum on Aging-Related Statistics) (2012). *Older Americans 2012: Key indicators of well-being.* Washington DC: US Government Printing Office. Retrieved from: www.agingstats.gov/main_site/data/2012_documents/docs/entire-chartbook.pdf

Giegerich, A. (2008, April 27). World class sustainability. *Portland Business Journal.* Retrieved from: http://www.bizjournals.com/portland/stories/2008/04/28/story1.html

Grabinsky, C.J. (2015). *101+ Careers in Gerontology* (2nd ed.). New York, NY: Springer.

He, W., Sengupta, M., Velkoff, V.A., & DeBarros, K.A. (2005). *65+ in the United States: 2005* (Report P23-209). US Department of Health and Human Services. Retrieved from: http://www.census.gov/prod/2006pubs/p23-209.pdf

Howe, D.A., Chapman, N.J., & Baggett, S.A. (1994). *Planning for an aging society* (Planning Advisory Service Report No. 451). Chicago, IL: American Planning Association.

Ingman, S.R., Pei, X., Ekstrom, C.D., Friedsam, H.J., & Bartlett, K. (2005). *An aging population, an aging planet and a sustainable future conference.* Denton, TX: University of North Texas Press.

Kingdon, J.W. (1984). *Agendas, alternatives, and public policies* (2nd ed.). New York, NY: Harper Collins College.

Kinsella, K., & He, W. (2009). *An aging world: 2008.* US Census Bureau. Retrieved from: http://www.census.gov/prod/2009pubs/p95-09-1.pdf

Kretzmann, J.P., & McKnight, J.L. (1993). *Building Communities From the Inside Out: A Path Toward Finding and Mobilizing a Community's Assets.* Chicago, IL: ACTA Publications.

Landorf, C., Brewer, G., & Sheppard, L.A. (2008). The urban environment and sustainable ageing: Critical issues and assessment indicators. *Local Environment: The International Journal of Justice and Sustainability,* 13(6), 497-514. doi: 10.1080/13549830802259896

Meadowcroft, J. (2000). Sustainable development: A new(ish) idea for a new century? *Political Studies,* 48, 370-397. doi: 10.1111/1467-9248.00265

Michael, Y.L., Keast, E.M., Chaudhury, H., Day, K., Mahmood, A., & Sarte, A.F.I. (2008). Revising the senior walking environmental assessment tool. *Preventive Medicine,* 48(3), 247-249. doi: 10.1016/j.ypmed.2008.12.008

National Institute on Health (2013). *Disability in older adults.* US Department of Health and Human Services: Research Portfolio Online Reporting Tools. Retrieved from: http://report.nih.gov/nihfactsheets/ViewFactSheet.aspx?csid=37

Neal, M.B., Chapman, N., Dill, J., Sharkova, I., DeLaTorre, A., Sullivan, K., Kanai, T., & Martin, S. (2006). *Age-related shifts in housing and transportation demand: A multidisciplinary study conducted for Metro by Portland State University's College of Urban and Public Affairs.* Portland State University. Retrieved from http://archives.pdx.edu/ds/psu/7989

Neal, M.B., DeLaTorre, A. & Carder, P.C. (2014). Age-friendly Portland: A university–city–community partnership. *Journal of Aging & Social Policy*, 26(1/2), 88-101. doi: 10.1080/08959420.2014.854651

Neal, M.B., Wilson, K.B., DeLaTorre, A, & Lopez, M. (2010). *A service-learning program in Nicaragua: Aging, environment, and health.* International Federation on Ageing: Global Aging, 6(2), 19-28. Retrieved from: http://www.ifa-fiv.org/wp-content/uploads/global-ageing/6.2/6.2.neal.wilson.delatorre.lopez.pdf

Ortman, J.M., Velkoff, V.A., & Hogan, H. (2014). *An aging nation: The older population in the United States.* US Census Bureau, Current Population Reports. Retrieved from: https://www.census.gov/prod/2014pubs/p25-1140.pdf

Portland State University (2015). *University Studies: Senior Capstone.* Portland, OR: Portland State University. Retrieved from: http://capstone.unst.pdx.edu

Random House (1992). *Webster's College Dictionary.* New York, NY: Random House.

Rosenbloom, S. (2001). Sustainability and automobility among the elderly: An international assessment. *Transportation*, 28, 375-408. doi: 10.1023/A:1011802707259

Rubio, D.M., Schoenbaum, E.E., Lee, L.S., Schteingart, D.E., Marantz, P.R., Anderson, K.E., & Espositio, K. (2010). Defining translational research: Implications for training. *Academic Medicine*, 85(3), 470-475. doi: 10.1097/ACM.0b013e3181ccd618

Schulz, J.H. (2001). *The Economics of Aging* (7th ed.). Westport, CN: Auburn House.

Seventh Generation Fund for Indian Development (2015). *Our mission.* Seventh Generation Fund for Indigenous Peoples, Inc. Retrieved from: http://www.7genfund.org

State of Oregon (2001). *Oregon sustainability act* (Oregon Revised Statute 184.421). Salem, OR: State of Oregon. Retrieved from: http://www.co.jefferson.or.us/portals/17/A-Z/ORS/BAK_05252010/ORS184.421-423.html

United Nations (1987). *Report of the World Commission on Environment and Development. United Nations General Assembly.* Retrieved from: http://www.un-documents.net/our-common-future.pdf

Vincent, G.K., & Velkoff, V.A. (2010). *The next four decades: The older population in the United States, 2010 to 2050.* US Census Bureau. Retrieved from: http://www.census.gov/prod/2010pubs/p25-1138.pdf

Williams, C.C., & Millington, A.C. (2004). The diverse and contested meanings of sustainable development. *The Geographic Journal*, 170(2), 99-104. doi: 10.1111/j.0016-7398.2004.00111.x

WHO (World Health Organization) (2007). *Global Age-Friendly Cities: A Guide.* Geneva, Switzerland. Retrieved from: http://www.who.int/ageing/age_friendly_cities_guide/en

WHO (World Health Organization) (2014). *Age-friendly world: Adding years to life: About the network.* Retrieved from: http://agefriendlyworld.org/en/who-network

Wright, S.D., & Lund, D.A. (2000). Gray and green? Stewardship in an aging society. *Journal of Aging Studies*, 14(3), 229-249. doi:10.1016/S0890-4065(00)08020-8

8

Who is at the table?

Fostering anti-oppression practice through a food justice dialogue series

Jen Turner, Nathan McClintock, Monica Cuneo, Alex Novie, and Sally Eck

With its abundant farmers' markets and CSAs, a vibrant urban agriculture scene, food carts, and farm-to-table restaurants, many consider Portland to be a heaven for "foodies" and sustainable food system advocates alike. Most participants in this alternative network of food production, processing, distribution, and consumption situate their activities squarely in opposition to the dominant industrial agrifood system and its deleterious impacts on the environment and public health. But despite such an ostensibly progressive orientation, many participants and supporters of local and sustainable food may be blind to the ways in which systems of oppression are potentially reproduced from within. A brief anecdote illustrates this point. At a community event in March 2012 organized by Portland State University (PSU) and People's Food Co-op to promote the release of the Cultivating Food Justice reader (Alkon and Agyeman, 2011), the first comment from the audience was: "I'll say what I know we all are thinking... poor people are just ignorant about good food!" This comment unfortunately set the tone for a long discussion dominated by calls for missionary-style strategies to educate low-income populations assumed to be disinterested in or ignorant of the virtues of eating well. Ultimately, the tone of the discussion suggested a peculiar disconnect between the good intentions behind the vision of "good food for all," and the thinking and action involved in implementing this vision.

As a group of PSU student and faculty scholar-activists committed to justice-oriented community engagement, we were concerned with this disconnect. Drawing on our diverse disciplinary backgrounds—geography, urban studies, planning, community health, education, and gender studies—we conceived a community dialogue series that would draw on anti-oppression theories and critical pedagogy to help elevate social justice concerns within the city's alternative food movement. We felt that creating such a space could help food systems and social justice activists develop a common language and shared understanding of food justice, while fostering trust and the relationships needed to work toward a more just food system. Our hope was that such a dialogue series would offer participants the opportunity to individually and collectively learn, reflect, and develop visions and practices that might take on a life of their own after the eight-week series.

We were also interested in documenting the process of fostering consciousness of power, privilege, and difference within the context of participants' understandings of the dominant food system and its sustainable alternatives, and reflecting on the challenges and opportunities emerging from this kind of facilitated process. We were drawn to action research as a scholarly framework that would allow us to complement—and even spur—the community-building processes that we believe are necessary to effectively foster momentum around food justice. Broadly, action research is a methodology that emphasizes "doing with" rather than "doing for" participating communities (Greenwood and Levin, 2007, p. 1; Reason and Bradbury, 2008). Like other processes of community organizing, successful action research hinges on a collaborative process of sharing knowledge, ideas, best practices, and visions (Stoecker, 2012). The researcher therefore "must be in the action, be finite and dirty, not transcendent and clean" (Haraway, 1997, p. 36, cited in Clarke, 2005, p. 74). Both the researcher and participant are valued in the production of knowledge and the resolution of social problems, and the researcher is not regarded as a privileged source of expert knowledge (Greenwood and Levin, 2007).

Action research thus demands that the researcher be reflexive and cognizant not to fall into hierarchical roles common to conventional top-down research. In this regard, action research acts as a mechanism for inclusive, transparent knowledge production and problem solving, one that recognizes the complexity of the social environments containing the problems at hand. It can therefore be transformative both in terms of helping to foster social change as well as democratize the production of knowledge (McTaggart, 1994; Reason and Bradbury, 2008). Methodologically, action research does not follow a prescribed outline of appropriate tools and techniques. It is neither an inherently qualitative or quantitative approach, but rather one based on values of reflexivity, diversity, and participation (ibid.). From our perspective, such an approach enables critical food scholars not only to critique dominant sustainable food discourse and practice, but also to participate alongside community members as they build awareness of oppression within the food system and develop ways to challenge it.

In this chapter, we reflect on our own action research. We begin the chapter with a brief overview of the critical food scholarship and anti-oppression theories that guided our work, before describing the planning and implementation of the eight-week food justice dialogue series (hereafter, the FJD) that we facilitated on the PSU campus in February and March 2013. We then discuss the immediate outcomes of the FJD and explore the limitations, barriers, and challenges involved in creating such a space.

Problematizing sustainable food systems

The sustainable food movement emerged as a form of resistance to a global-industrial food system responsible for environmental degradation, the proliferation of cheap, unhealthy food, and disproportionate power in the hands of a select few corporations. Central to its efforts to transform—or secede from—the dominant agri-food system, the food movement prioritizes particular forms of food production and consumption, such as local and organic agriculture, farm-to-table relationships, home and community gardening, and in some cases, vegetarian, vegan, or whole grain diets (Allen, 2004; Fairfax *et al.*, 2012; Kloppenberg *et al.*, 1996; Lyson, 2004).

In emphasizing these values, however, many well-intentioned advocates of agri-food sustainability rely on an overly simplistic analysis of the food system, cleaving stark dichotomies between the conventional and the alternative. They see the former as fast, consumptive, impulsive, and destructive, and the latter as slow, intimate, intentional, and virtuous (Guthman, 2003). But this lens, in turn, can blind food systems advocates to the often contradictory social and political implications of prioritizing these ostensibly eco-friendly practices (Born and Purcell 2006; DuPuis and Goodman, 2005; Hinrichs, 2003). That the sustainable food movement mostly resonates with a privileged white, middle-class population—one that engages with sustainable food largely as consumers rather than as activists—both emerges from and contributes to these blind spots (Alkon and Agyeman, 2011; Guthman, 2008b; Johnston and Szabo, 2010; Slocum, 2007). Critical food scholars have highlighted a few key areas of concern.

First, the sustainable food movement values localism as a sacrosanct way to close the gap and strengthen the bond between farms and consumers (DuPuis and Goodman, 2005; Hinrichs, 2003), reinvigorating a "civic agriculture" lost to global-scale agri-food industrialization. Despite appeals for community-level change and alternatives to the corporate food system, localist discourse frequently lacks an explicit social justice framework, and therefore risks reproducing inequities found within the dominant agri-food system. There is nothing inherently just about the local scale; local farms, for example, do not necessarily treat workers more fairly than large-scale corporate farms (Allen, 2008; Born and Purcell 2006; DuPuis and Goodman, 2005).

Second, scholars have critiqued the sustainable food movement for being elitist and inaccessible. Alternative food activists possess a specific and enlightened understanding of good food and eating, and there is an implication—at times implicit, but often explicit—that everyone else simply lacks such enlightenment. As the People's Food Co-op anecdote illustrates, many within the sustainable food movement believe that those who consume the cheap, processed foods simply lack the knowledge to eat "good" food, and that a behavior shift will naturally occur through proper education (Guthman, 2008b). "If they only knew..." becomes an organizing refrain rallying a missionary-style approach of "bringing good food to others" (Guthman, 2008b).

The preferences and values of a privileged—and mostly white—population are thus elevated and then normalized as the "right" way to engage with the food system (Alkon and Agyeman, 2011; Guthman, 2008a; Slocum, 2006). Values such as "good, proximate, wholesome and local" are fraught with the race and class privilege of those invoking them. Consuming local, organic food becomes a marker of class distinction separating those "in the know" from those who—in the words of the People's Food Co-op audience member—are "ignorant" (Bourdieu, 1984; Johnston and Baumann, 2014), and thus demonizes those low-income people who have no choice but to consume the cheap food produced by the corporate agri-food system (Slocum, 2007, p. 527). This dynamic contributes to an oppressive form of "healthism" in which the embodiment of healthy or "perfect" eating becomes conflated with expressions of virtue, value, and citizenship (Cheek, 2008; Guthman, 2011; LeBesco, 2011). Those who deviate from this perfect embodiment of health, through dietary choices or body size, may be perceived as weak, uneducated, or undeserving (Evans, 2006; Guthman, 2009; Saguy and Riley, 2005).

Third (and very much intertwined with the previous point), scholars have also demonstrated how the alternative food movement espouses a problematic "colorblindness", in that Euro-American cultural values dominate and go unquestioned (Guthman, 2008a; Slocum, 2006). The spaces in which the sustainable food movement operates and the discourse it employs are thus "coded" or seen from the outside as white spaces. This is due not only to the sheer number of white people moving through spaces such as farmers' markets and community gardens, but also to the values celebrated therein—of an agrarian past, of getting one's hands dirty in the soil, of romanticizing rural landscapes. This can in turn produce a chilling effect on people of color, who may not feel welcome in such whitened spaces and whose relationships to the land and to rural life have been defined in part by violent histories of plantation slavery, lynching, Jim Crow, and/or the oppressive conditions of working as sharecroppers or migrant laborers (Alkon, 2012; Carlisle 2014; Guthman, 2008a; Slocum, 2007).

Finally, critics challenge the sustainable food movement's reliance on advocating the importance of individual behavioral change over organized political mobilization. Inherent to the prized notion, the sustainable consumer places emphasis on personal responsibility and individual choice to engage in healthy, sustainable eating habits. Framing activism this way, however, ignores the structural and institutional factors that contribute to negative food- and diet-related outcomes (Alkon and Mares 2012; Allen, 2004; Guthman, 2011; Slocum, 2006). Moreover, consumer-oriented slogans like "buy local" and "vote with your fork" emphasize consumer choice and other market-based solutions as the primary mechanisms for effecting systemic change (Lockie, 2008), but such tactics are relatively apolitical and do little to challenge the deeply entrenched political economic structures that make up the global agri-food system (DeLind, 2002; DuPuis and Goodman, 2005; Guthman, 2003).

Food justice scholar Patricia Allen (2008, p. 158) writes, "our food system does not meet the fundamental criteria of social justice such as freedom from want, freedom from oppression, and access to equal opportunity." To make real change, we must recognize how the conventional food system evolved and continues to survive today through oppressive institutions (Slocum, 2006): from the genocide and dispossession of land (i.e., the systematic "pacification" and removal of Indigenous North Americans) to make way for the westward settlement of homesteaders; to the plantation slavery upon which the agricultural economy was largely built; to the food system's historic and ongoing reliance on racialized migrant labor working under exploitative conditions; to processes of "redlining" that have contributed to the uneven spatial distribution of food retail (Carlisle 2014; Holmes 2013; McClintock, 2011; Post 2003; Walker 2005). The benefits and hazards of the food system are not distributed evenly across race, class, and gender lines nor are they distributed evenly across urban space, as the disproportionate concentration of fast food in black urban neighborhoods illustrates (Block *et al*, 2004).

Taking these critiques seriously, it becomes clear that the alternative food movement's failure to engage explicitly with anti-racism and social justice limits its ability to effect significant change (Slocum, 2006; Sbicca, 2012). Indeed, the values and discourse upon which many well-intentioned people hope to build a sustainable food system may actually buttress or even exacerbate existing race- and class-based disparities. Anti-oppression practice can expose these blind spots while serving as a mechanism to build cross-difference alliances and foster wider participation in building more inclusive sustainable, community-driven food systems (Bradley and Herrera, 2015; Slocum, 2006). Central to the concept of food justice is the belief that access to food on one's individually and culturally specific terms is a human right, and that a more just food system requires "imagining new ecological and social relationships" in food production and provisioning (Alkon and Agyeman, 2011, p. 5). As an organizing concept espoused by scholars and activists alike, food justice bridges theory and practice (Alkon and Norgaard, 2009; Gottlieb and Joshi, 2010) and can help reposition sustainable food systems work within social justice and anti-oppression frameworks. We turn now to our efforts to do just this.

Who is at the table? Food justice dialogues

Participant selection

Determining participants in the FJD was an important component of the process. We distributed applications in late November 2012 across several food systems and social justice online listservs with the request that recipients share widely with their networks. The questions were designed to gauge the applicant's familiarity with both food systems and social justice issues, experience working with diverse viewpoints, as well as questions about age, gender identity, racial identity, primary language spoken, organizational and/or professional affiliation, and schedule availability. For the sake of building trust among future participants, we also asked applicants about their ability to commit to attending at least seven of the eight total sessions.

Over 150 individuals applied to participate. We sent an invitation to 20 of these applicants, 18 of whom accepted. By the final session, a total of 13 participants remained. Our intention in capping the group at 20 was to form a group small enough to encourage informal conversation and the formation of relationships and trust, large enough to ensure that multiple perspectives would be represented within the group, and conducive to discussion in both small and large group formats.

We selected participants with a vision in mind of creating opportunities for both collaborative dialogue and constructive disagreement. Finalizing the participant mix based on our interpretations of the applicants' submissions and our ability to "read into" their characters was certainly fuzzy at best, and we recognize that the final participant mix was the product of our subjective view of the applicants, perceptions shaped by our personal life experiences. Ultimately, the individuals we selected to participate in the dialogue series represented a variety of organizations, experiences, perspectives and familiarity with both food systems and social justice issues. Several individuals had no explicit organizational affiliation, some were unemployed, some worked for non-profits, some worked for businesses, others were retired. In terms of ethnic or racial identity, two of the participants self-identified as Latina, one as Asian-American (Vietnamese), one as Native American, and the rest as white. Only one was male. Ages ranged from 24 to 68.

Timeline and curriculum

We structured the dialogues around exercises and discussion prompts that would guide participants through processes of learning and sharing. Table 8.1 provides an overview of the series structure, timeline, curricular goals, activities, and its broad desired outcome. Sessions 1 through 4 focused on identifying and naming oppression. We first asked participants to brainstorm around the question, "What is oppression?" and followed this with an exercise in mapping one's social identity. Building from the collectively defined understanding of the mechanics of oppression, the focus shifted to how to interrupt moments when oppression is occurring. This activity allowed participants to identify how oppression may operate within a series of food-specific scenarios and brainstorm ways to interrupt oppression in food-related settings.

Table 8.1 FJD overview and timeline

Session content	Intended outcome
Session 1: Check-in: introductions; brainstorm: what is oppression?	Building common language and understanding of anti-oppression
Session 2: Check-in: cultural identity poems; brainstorm: co-creating an ideal learning community; Social Identity Mapping	Co-creating the shared learning environment. Building a common language and understanding of anti-oppression work
Session 3: Interrupting oppression; brainstorm: why interrupt?; interruptions practice: food-specific scenarios	Identifying and interrupting oppression
Session 4: Check-in: reviewing interruptions; more dialogue on interruptions	Identifying and interrupting oppression
Session 5: Concept Mapping: Food in Portland	Conceptualizing and envisioning Portland's food environment
Session 6: Small group discussion: identifying personal collusion with oppression in the food system; distribution of Personal Action Lens	Critical reflection on self-identification and collusion with oppression in the context of food
Session 7: Discussion of Personal Action Lens; brainstorm future visions; creation of action-oriented nodes	Moving forward: co-creating the series' afterlife
Session 8: Potluck; group dialogue on future visions: "Where do we want to go from here?"; creation of actionable next steps	Moving forward: co-creating the series' afterlife

The food systems scenarios in Session 3 provided a useful transition to the content in Sessions 5 and 6, in which participants applied the training to their understanding of food systems. In Session 5, participants formed small groups and created concept maps of Portland's food system. These concept maps illustrated the various nodes of understanding about food in Portland, and provided an interactive method for visualizing urban food issues. We then asked participants to reflect on their individual roles within Portland's food system, and how they might collude with or perpetuate oppression (Hardiman and Jackson, 1997). After honing their understanding of what oppression is, how it operates in the context of food, and personal accountability within systematic and structural oppression, participants then turned to the process of co-creating an "afterlife" for the FJD, i.e., visioning future trajectories that might emerge from our dialogue.

Immediate outcomes

Collaboration and relationships

Social learning—understanding of a topic or concept that emerges via engagement in a group setting—during the FJD centered on recognizing and understanding of difference, oppression, and individual identities, as well as the process of applying these concepts to the context of sustainable food and food justice. Drawing on critical social justice pedagogy, we asked participants to embrace the plurality of experience and opinion present in the room, and apply this lens to their understanding of food systems sustainability (Adams *et al.*, 2007). New relationships formed as participants engaged candidly with each other on these issues, despite the possible differences existing between them. In their final evaluations and reflections on the FJD, nearly all participants indicated that they had formed new relationships and were interested in continued collaboration. Participants also highlighted the conceptual importance of collaboration, and as one participant noted, of creating "a designated time to discuss these issues with people," and ultimately sowing seeds for future collaboration.

Visions for future work

Another significant outcome was the articulation of how the ideas discussed during the FJD might translate into future action. Some participants expressed general excitement at the possibility of applying the concepts learned during the FJD in the future, while others offered suggestions for continued engagement. For example, multiple participants reflected on the immediate application of the dialogue series content at work. One noted, for example, "My current work with elementary school children allows for many more opportunities for interruptions [of oppression] than I would've imagined."

While this desire to move this work forward was promising in many ways, it was also problematic in potentially elevating solutions and action over process and a deeper understanding. Long before we asked them to envision future directions, many participants were quick to move to action, demonstrating a tendency to orient toward solutions and outcomes. But asking "what do we do next?" and "how do we go about resolving this?" before fully understanding the larger context—the complexities of the food system, how oppression works at both structural and individual levels, the lived experiences and needs of the communities of concern, and the ways in which defining these needs may itself be contested within the community—places the proverbial cart before the horse. As many scholars and community development practitioners have lamented, well-meaning proposals are frequently met with resistance in the community because they fail to consider such critical points (Lubitow and Miller, 2013; Stoecker, 2012). In the end we recognized that while many participants may have enhanced their ability to recognize and acknowledge difference at the interpersonal level, there was still considerable room for growth when it came to recognizing difference at an organizational or operational level.

Introduction to new and challenging concepts

Nearly every participant reported that the FJD exposed them to new concepts or ideas. The series was thus effective in challenging participants to think about the manifestation of oppression in a food-specific context and to develop tools to foster an anti-oppression consciousness. During sessions on interrupting oppression in food-specific scenarios, for example, we asked participants to consider how some seemingly neutral sentiments might perpetuate imbalances of power and oppressive perceptions. We provided statements likely familiar to food systems advocates, such as "What this food desert really needs is a farmers' market" and "If people only had the knowledge of what good food is, they would be healthier and more fit." We then asked participants to think through how such statements might recreate oppressive dynamics. There was a palpable sense of discomfort—and even cognitive dissonance—when participants were asked to reflect on statements such as these that many had readily employed at some point.

Indeed, recognizing that food and social justice work requires us to think critically about the language that we sustainable food advocates often use can prove to be uncomfortable. Political theorist Chantal Mouffe (1999) argues that for meaningful social and political change to occur, we must understand and confront the presence of conflict and difference—what she terms agonism—rather than dismiss it. Furthermore, it is important to recognize that engaging with agonism may or may not result in tangible solutions. When a just, sustainable food system is framed not as a series of technical solutions but rather an interrogation of oppression, power, and privilege, the motivation to act may be clear, affirming, and accessible, but the means for acting are not necessarily obvious or intuitive. Rather, meaningful food justice work can only occur by first acknowledging historical trauma, people's anger, pain, and sorrow—as well as the privileges that well-meaning progressives derive from the oppressive structures that have caused these experiences (Bradley and Herrera, 2015). Unlike a colorblind multicultural perspective, that champions universal equality while failing to recognize that the lived experience of oppressed groups is anything but equal, an anti-oppression framework holds recognition of difference and agonism to be core tenets, and allows for a more effective understanding of how and why injustices occur and what might be done to address them.

Wanting more

One of the recurring pieces of feedback we received from participants was that they wanted more time. One participant remarked, "I always leave the group inspired to learn and talk more and develop stronger language around these issues, wishing there was more time." Feelings of rushing through the material were especially prominent during the food-specific sessions: "I think we could have spent more time on looking inward at our place in the [food] systems and how our positions interact with the larger picture."

One of the biggest challenges of the FJD was finding a balance between creating the time and space for casual conversation and reflection central to building relationships, and time and space for deep, self-reflexive and group dialogue on the series content. Breaks would often run long and conversations would become tangential. This compromised the amount of time spent on the "meat" of the dialogue series but substantially contributed to the group's ability to network informally. As a consequence, some activities had to be cut short or omitted, but participants had more time to get to know one another and to forge relationships that might lead to future collaboration.

"Who isn't at this table?" Diversity and representation

A final theme that emerged throughout the dialogue series was an explicit concern for who wasn't represented in the room, and concern over the degree of diversity represented among the participant group. This concern manifested as people wanting to hear the voices of other populations directly affected by food injustice, such as farm workers ("Would have loved to see an actual food grower in here, whether it be a farm worker or small business owner, just for that additional perspective"), as well as reflections on how the project's logistics may have affected participation, such as location and hours. Several participants also commented on the composition of the group, and felt that an important degree of diversity was missing: "The group was predominantly white and female. From that lens, it was very representative of those that work in this field [of food systems] but perhaps not so much of those impacted by systemic food oppression." Many participants also offered that a heightened degree of diversity is a necessary ingredient for moving the food justice movement forward: "I feel that we still have not addressed how we will welcome more diverse voices to the table." These questions of representation in the FJD provide a useful opportunity to reflect on some of the major limitations to the series' design and implementation. We turn to these now.

Lessons learned and future directions

To begin, it became clear that the setting posed a number of challenges for participants and potential applicants. Downtown Portland is expensive to travel to by car, as parking near campus is pricey and limited. Even though public transportation is a viable option for visiting the campus and we provided participants with a stipend for attending, taking transit may have proven challenging for those with children, those who live or work very far from the university, or those with mobility issues. More critically, the university setting may also be intimidating to those who are not comfortable or adept in systems of higher education in the U.S., in which universities could be interpreted as elitist, exclusive, or unwelcoming spaces. Similarly, scheduling the dialogues for a weekday morning likely created barriers for those with children (e.g., access to daycare affecting participation) or those with employment that would not permit taking work time to attend. This is especially relevant in considering the nature of wage labor, in which many workers do not receive personal time off and may have inflexible or unpredictable work schedules.

Another factor that may have limited applications for participation in the FJD was the snowball-style recruitment method and the project's web-based communication. While the application dissemination crossed a number of institutional, organizational, and topical boundaries, we know that the application did not reach people who are not regularly on email. Snowball sampling is limiting in that it is an inherently networked recruitment method, and therefore possibly insular (Morgan, 2008). Disseminating our call for applicants by email, as well as relying on an online application process, were both clearly problematic considering disparities of computer access and literacy. Those without regular computer access and the familiarity needed to complete the application may have been barred from participation from the outset.

A final limitation that affected who was in the room was the requirement of an attendance commitment to seven of the eight sessions. It introduced some challenges involving more nuanced, culturally specific conceptualizations of time, attendance, and participation. One participant expressed extreme dissatisfaction with attendance commitment very early in the series, and appeared to want to drop in and out of the series as available. When this participant missed Sessions 2 and 3, we asked this participant not to return for the remaining sessions. This participant was upset by this request, and felt that the values embedded in the seemingly rigid attendance commitment reflected academic, intellectual, and cultural privilege. This participant's concerns presented a valuable—and humbling—opportunity for us to reflect on how our own understanding of time and commitment are indeed culturally situated, and that different understandings may exist and significantly affect who comes to the table and when.

With these limitations in mind, participants' concern over the lack of diversity raises an important and complex issue related to anti-oppression consciousness work. At first glance, the participants' observations were accurate: the people at the table appeared to represent the same identity groups. Many were white, and most were women. As the participant quoted above commented, there is a seemingly disproportionate number of white women working in the fields of sustainable food and food justice (Allen, 2013; Allen and Sachs, 2007), which begs interrogating whether and how the FJD series challenged or reproduced this condition.

Like many of the FJD participants, we were initially concerned by the lack of racial and ethnic diversity at our table, worried that we were perpetuating the very problem we were trying to tackle with a series entitled "Who is At the Table?". This raised some challenging questions: How might project organizers know when the "right" degree of diversity is achieved? Is there a "right" level of diversity to have when engaging with topics of oppression? How might the project organizers better teach and develop curriculum to gain a more nuanced and intersectional understanding of identity and diversity before making any sweeping judgments limited to racial/ethnic diversity alone?

Giving primacy to increasing racial/ethnic representation at the so-called table risks devolving into tokenism, and frequently imposes a burden onto participants of color to "speak for their race" or "figure it all out" for white people (Adams *et al*, 2007). Moreover, it often diverts attention from the need to do deep, personal, interior work to develop an anti-racist consciousness. Describing his frustration at receiving repeated invitations from white-led food justice groups asking him to provide prescriptive "how-to" lists to address the "lack of diversity" in their organizations, food justice activist Marcelo Garzo Montalvo (2015, p. 4) notes that an "overemphasis" within the food justice movement on race has resulted in an "almost complete erasure of other systems of domination that make white supremacy even more durable, not the least of which are analyses of class (neoliberal capitalism) and gender (heteropatriarchy), and how deeply these systems affect our cultural practices as movement organizers." While attention to racial/ethnic diversity is vital—indeed, the FJD emerged in part by our concern with the lack of diversity within Portland's food movement—it is important to move beyond simply striving for a balanced headcount, and to instead prioritize acknowledging various kinds of difference and how these intersect, benefitting some and aggregating additional layers of oppression for others. And importantly, key to anti-oppression work is experiencing and facing the discomfort—indeed, the agonism—of sharing such different lived experiences, for the negative experiences of some may implicate others at the very same table.

As the project organizers, we occupied the privileged position of having read every participant's application, in which several people reflected on their experiences with poverty, hunger, and cultural difference. This experience underscored for us that, while mostly invisible to the eye, there was a significant degree of class and cultural diversity present in the room. Having participants complete the social identity mapping exercise independently was therefore a missed opportunity. Had participants explicitly shared their personal histories and identities, it might have allowed the group to recognize its internal diversity and to develop deeper and more compassionate evaluations of one another. Instead, many FJD participants simply lamented the lack of racial/ethnic diversity, and seemed to overlook the transformative potential of the specific group that was at the table and the important work of recognizing privilege and oppression within sustainable food activism.

Indeed, the challenges involved in fostering the kind of critical, reflexive thinking necessary to develop anti-oppression consciousness became evident both through the participant evaluations as described above, as well as through our own observations of participants' interactions with the materials covered during the eight sessions. The reactions we observed when we asked participants questions regarding "positionality"—how they fit individually into networks of power and systems of oppression—were particularly illustrative. During Session 6 some participants resisted answering questions about how we personally collude in systems of oppression by redirecting the conversation to more macro-scale issues, such as farmworkers' rights and environmental degradation, without explicitly situating themselves within those debates. Other participants resisted by redirecting the conversation to previous discussions regarding diversity and concern for who wasn't represented at the FJD table, implying that by raising these questions, they were tacitly admitting their privileged position of participation. Other participants resisted by making claims to their expert knowledge on food justice issues, invoking their experience with various campaigns and community action programs.

As these different examples of resistance highlight, these questions about collusion likely made the participants feel vulnerable, resulting in a variety of reactions. For some, the concept of collusion resonated and they were able to reflect on their positionality and complicity in oppressive structures. Some also expressed feelings of discomfort, hopelessness, or confusion. But while we anticipated some of the resistance and powerlessness that participants might express, the activities planned for the second half of the FJD were intended to be actionable. We wanted to leave the participants with a sense of hope by providing an opportunity to use their deeper understanding of oppression to impact food justice within their own spheres of influence. While awareness and understanding among participants of how oppression works was perhaps less robust in the end than we would have wished, we do feel that they left the FJD feeling hopeful and at least thinking somewhat more critically. To further promote reflexivity, perhaps we should have engaged more explicitly with the scholarly critiques outlined at the beginning of the chapter rather than anticipating that participants would arrive at similar conclusions on their own. We were wary of playing the traditional role of the academic who imparts knowledge in a top-down manner, but ultimately we might have pushed the conversation along further—and actually been more transparent—by sharing more of the insights that we had gleaned from our engagement with critical food scholarship.

In the end, the FJD provided an opportunity to critically examine how stakeholders in Portland's sustainable food movement might engage with concepts of anti-oppression and social justice. We succeeded in providing these sustainable food advocates with a more nuanced and reflexive understanding of power and privilege that may be more conducive to their work toward more socially equitable outcomes. Using action research to probe the disconnects between the sustainable food movement and food justice, we focused our efforts on creating the space needed to begin to build meaningful relationships and establish individual and communal understandings of how to develop and apply an anti-oppression lens to food systems work. As a movement still in search of its footing, however, food justice is challenged by the need to establish a common ideological and theoretical understanding of anti-oppression theory (Sbicca, 2012). We, too, learned this from the FJD and have reflected here on the growing pains that we experienced in our effort to foster such a common theoretical understanding of anti-oppression. Given the centrality of food systems within the mainstream sustainability agenda, it is clear that a food justice framework grounded in anti-oppression pedagogy offers an important—but not necessarily clear-cut—pathway for reconciling tensions between sustainability efforts and the need for greater reflexivity and equity.

References

Adams, M., Bell, L.A., & Griffin, P. (Eds.). (2007). *Teaching for Diversity and Social Justice* (2nd ed). New York, NY: Routledge.

Alkon, A.H. (2012). *Black, White, and Green: Farmers Markets, Race, and the Greeneconomy.* Athens: University of Georgia Press.

Alkon, A.H., & Agyeman, J. (2011). *Cultivating Food Justice: Race, Class, and Sustainability.* Cambridge, MA: MIT Press.

Alkon, A.H., & Mares, T.M. (2012). Food sovereignty in US food movements: Radical visions and neoliberal constraints. *Agriculture and Human Values*, 29(3), 347-359.

Alkon, A.H., & Norgaard, K.M. (2009). Breaking the food chains: An investigation of food justice activism. *Sociological Inquiry*, 79(3), 289-305.

Allen, P. (2004). *Together at the Table: Sustainability and Sustenance in the American Agrifood System.* University Park, PA: Pennsylvania State University Press.

Allen, P. (2008) Mining for justice in the food system: Perceptions, practices, and possibilities. *Agriculture and Human Values*, 25(2), 157-161.

Allen, P. (2013, June). *Dancing with (not around) the elephants in the room: Building sustainable and equitable food systems for all.* Keynote Address at the Canadian Association for Food Studies 2013 Assembly, University of Victoria, Victoria, BC.

Allen, P., & Sachs, C. (2007). Women and food chains: The gendered politics of food. *International Journal of Sociology of Food and Agriculture*, 15(1), 1-23.

Block, J.P., Scribner, R.A., & DeSalvo, K.B. (2004). Fast food, race/ethnicity, and income: A geographic analysis. *American Journal of Preventive Medicine*, 27(3), 211-217.

Bourdieu, P. (1984). *Distinction: A Social Critique of the Judgement of Taste.* Cambridge, MA: Harvard University Press.

Born, B., & Purcell, M. (2006). Avoiding the local trap: Scale and food systems in planning research. *Journal of Planning Education and Research*, 26(2), 195-207.

Bradley, K., & Herrera, H. (2015). Decolonizing food justice: Naming, resisting, and researching colonizing forces in the movement. *Antipode*, 48(1), 97-114.

Carlisle, L. (2014). Critical agrarianism. *Renewable Agriculture and Food Systems*, 29(2), 135-145.

Cheek, J., (2008). Healthism: A new conservatism? *Qualitative Health Research*, 18(7), 974-982.

Clarke, A. (2005). *Situational Analysis: Grounded Theory after the Postmodern Turn*. Thousand Oaks, CA: Sage Publications.

DeLind, L. (2002). Place, work, and civic agriculture: Common fields for cultivation. *Agriculture and Human Values*, 19(3), 217-224.

DuPuis, E.M., & Goodman, D. (2005). Should we go "home" to eat?: Toward a reflexive politics of localism. *Journal of Rural Studies*, 21(3), 359-371.

Evans, B. (2006). "Gluttony or sloth": Critical geographies of bodies and morality in (anti) obesity policy. *Area*, 38(3), 259-267.

Fairfax, S.K., Dyble, L.N., Guthey, G.T., Gwin, L., Moore, M., & Sokolove, J. (2012). *California Cuisine and Just Food*. Cambridge, MA: The MIT Press.

Garzo Montalvo, M.F. (2015). To the American food justice movements: A critique that is also an offering. *Journal of Agriculture, Food Systems, and Community Development*, 5(4), 125-129.

Gottlieb, R., & Joshi, A. (2010). *Food justice*. Cambridge, MA: MIT Press.

Greenwood, D.J. & Levin, M. (Eds.). (2007). *Introduction to Action Research*. Thousand Oaks, CA: Sage Publications.

Guthman, J. (2003). Fast food/organic food: Reflexive tastes and the making of "yuppie chow". *Social & Cultural Geography*, 4(1), 45-58.

Guthman, J. (2008a). "If they only knew": Color blindness and universalism in California alternative food institutions. *The Professional Geographer*, 60(3), 387-397.

Guthman, J. (2008b). Bringing good food to others: Investigating the subjects of alternative food practice. *Cultural Geographies*, 15(4), 431-447.

Guthman, J. (2009). Teaching the politics of obesity: Insights into neoliberal embodiment and contemporary biopolitics. *Antipode*, 41(5), 1,110-1,133.

Guthman, J. (2011). *Weighing in: Obesity, food justice, and the limits of capitalism*. Berkeley, CA: University of California Press.

Hardiman, R. & Jackson, B.W. (1997). Conceptual foundations for social justice courses. In Adams, M., Bell, L.A., & Griffin, P. (Eds.), *Teaching for Diversity and Social Justice: A Sourcebook* (pp. 16-30). New York, NY: Routledge.

Hinrichs, C. (2003). The practice and politics of food system localization. *Journal of Rural Studies*, 19, 33-45.

Holmes, S. (2013). *Fresh Fruit, Broken Bodies: Migrant Farmworkers in the United States*. Berkeley, CA: University of California Press.

Johnston, J., & Baumann, S. (2014). *Foodies: Democracy and Distinction in the Gourmet Foodscape* (2nd ed). New York, NY: Routledge.

Johnston, J., & Szabo, M. (2010). Reflexivity and the Whole Foods market consumer: The lived experience of shopping for change. *Agriculture and Human Values*, 28(3), 303-319.

Kloppenburg, J., Hendrickson, J., & Stevenson, G.W. (1996). Coming in to the foodshed. *Agriculture and Human Values*, 13(3), 33-42.

LeBesco, K. (2011). Neoliberalism, public health, and the moral perils of fatness. *Critical Public Health*, 21(2), 153-164.

Lockie, S. (2008). Responsibility and agency within alternative food networks: Assembling the "citizen consumer". *Agriculture and Human Values*, 26(3), 193-201.

Lubitow, A., & Miller, T.R. (2013). Contesting sustainability: Bikes, race, and politics in Portlandia. *Environmental Justice*, 6(4), 121-126.

Lyson, T.A. (2004). *Civic Agriculture: Reconnecting Farm, Food, and Community*. Medford, MA: Tufts University Press.

McClintock, N. (2011). From industrial garden to food desert: Demarcated devaluation in flatlands of Oakland, California. In A. H. Alkon, & J. Agyeman (Eds.). *Cultivating Food Justice: Race, Class, and Sustainability*. Cambridge, MA: MIT Press.

McTaggart, R. (1994). Participatory action research: Issues in theory and practice. *Educational Action Research*, 2(3), 313-337.

Morgan, D. (2008). Snowball sampling. In L.M. Given (Ed.). *The SAGE Encyclopedia of Qualitative Research Methods* (pp. 816-817). Los Angeles, CA: Sage Publications.

Mouffe, C. (1999). Deliberative democracy or agonistic pluralism? *Social Research*, 66(3), 745-758.

Post, C. (2003). Plantation slavery and economic development in the antebellum southern United States. *Journal of Agrarian Change*, 3(3), 289-332.

Reason, P., & Bradbury, H. (Eds.). (2008). *The SAGE Handbook of Action Research*. (2008 ed.). Thousand Oaks, CA: Sage Publications.

Saguy, A., & Riley, K. (2005). Weighing both sides: Morality, mortality, and framing contests over obesity. *Journal of Health Politics, Policy and Law*, 30(5), 869-921.

Sbicca, J. (2012). Growing food justice by planting an anti-oppression foundation: opportunities and obstacles for a budding social movement. *Agriculture and Human Values*, 29(4), 455-466.

Slocum, R. (2006). Anti-racist practice and the work of community food organizations. *Antipode*, 38(2), 27-49.

Slocum, R. (2007). Whiteness, space and alternative food practice. *Geoforum*, 38(3), 520-533.

Stoecker, R. (2012). *Research Methods for Community Change: A Project-Based Approach* (2nd ed). Thousand Oaks, CA: Sage Publications.

Walker, R. (2005). *The Conquest of Bread: 150 years of Agribusiness in California*. Berkeley, CA: University of California Press.

9

Research + action

The first two years of the Center for Public Interest Design

R. Todd Ferry and Sergio Palleroni

The Powwow begins

After an intensive period of initial research, design, and fabrication in Portland, Oregon, a team of ten designers from Portland State University's Center for Public Interest Design (CPID) loaded up a large van named Lola (it is usually loaned out to touring bands) with their camping equipment, tools, sketchbooks, and building components for a temporary pavilion they planned to erect at the annual Fourth of July Powwow on the Northern Cheyenne Reservation in Lame Deer, Montana. The group is made up of young design students from throughout the world joining the effort as interns, CPID Student Fellows, or students pursuing the new Graduate Certificate in Public Interest Design. The Reservation suffered devastating wildfires in 2012 and the goal of the week on the Reservation is to use the three days of the powwow to engage the community about issues of resiliency, meet with project partners, and to finish constructing a barn that was begun the previous year for a family that lost their barn and home in the wildfires.[1]

---

1 Resilience is a term increasingly used in design and other fields to encompass issues of sustainability, with a focus on a community and built environment's ability to bounce back after a traumatic event. The position of the American Institute of Architects is that "Architects have a responsibility to design a resilient environment that can more

Figure 9.1 CPID Gateway Pavilion: design-build pavilion project in Portland with children from Gateway community

Photo credit: Therese Graf

This initiative builds on over two decades of work that CPID Director Sergio Palleroni has done with the community along with collaborator Professor David Riley from Penn State University. Their work in straw bale construction through the American Indian Housing Initiative is peppered throughout the Northern Cheyenne Reservation and other First Nations in the region, with a concentration of buildings on the campus of Dull Knife College.

Like this current project, the Center for Public Interest Design itself has grown out of Professor Palleroni's career-long effort to address the challenges of sustainability and health in disadvantaged communities, as well as the work of the Center's four other founding faculty fellows (Travis Bell, Todd Ferry, Margarette Leite, and B.D. Wortham-Galvin). In the two years since its founding, the CPID has become a vibrant place to conduct interdisciplinary research, explore ideas, and train an emerging generation of designers and thinkers in public interest design practices. As the first university center in the country focusing on public interest design, an examination of the first two years of the CPID can offer insight into the trajectory of the emerging field of public interest design, successful strategies for organizations with a shared focus, and challenges that the center and the profession will need to overcome.

successfully adapt to natural conditions and that can more readily absorb and recover from adverse events."

Public interest design

The Center for Public Interest Design is a research and action center at Portland State University's School of Architecture that aims to investigate, promote, and engage in inclusive design practices that address the needs of the increasing number of communities underserved and often in crisis worldwide. It was established in 2013 in response to the critical need for design practices that address issues such as inadequate shelter, disaster preparedness and recovery, and economic well-being.[2] Though the first such institution in the country, it heralds a growing awareness in both education and the profession for research and education into the expanded practices that will make design relevant and central to the 21st century. The CPID fosters opportunities for interdisciplinary collaboration among professionals, faculty, students, and community partners in order to advance engaged design practices and public interest design.

While public interest design has recently become accepted as the overarching term used to identify a socially-driven design practice, terms such as community design, social impact design, and human-centered design have all been used to try and describe the work over the last few decades. Working definitions may vary, but public interest designer Bryan Bell (2015, p. 13) points to research that indicates that a collective consensus of what constitutes public interest design has emerged among design professionals as the practice of design with the goal that "every person should be able to live in a socially, economically, and environmentally healthy community". Helping to create this consensus has been a growing body of design projects, in all design fields, which have demonstrated design and design thinking to be powerful tools by which to address a broad range of community needs, some of which would have been traditionally thought to be outside the concern of designers.[3] These projects are also capturing for the first time, thanks to the quality of their designs, the attention of the mass media and are being recognized by the design establishment as portents of a potential systemic change within the profession.[4] The systemic change is an emphasis on community needs rather than principally client desire, which, until recently, has limited design's social impact. The

2 While officially established in 2013, it took Professors B.D. Wortham-Galvin and Sergio Palleroni two years to get the agreement of other units at the university and navigate official approval for a Center. Getting academic institutions and academics to agree to the benefits of social engagement in professional programs such as architecture continues to be a challenge, as it is in the academy as a whole.

3 Design Thinking is increasingly being emphasized in fields outside of design disciplines like architecture and industrial design to encourage creative problem solving and an iterative approach of investigation to challenge assumptions and yield the best possible solution to a given problem. IDEO and Stanford's D. School have notably promoted the efficacy of this approach.

4 The Curry Stone Design Prize is one noteworthy example of ways in which architects, engineers, social entrepreneurs, and community leaders are recognized for their innovations toward improving a social condition. www.currystonedesignprize.com

shift is essential to the well-being of the society as a whole, as it brings architects and designers into the collaborations and alliances that are necessary to effectively address problems such as the sustainability and public health issues of society as a whole.

For the benefits of design to be available to all people is crucial, as architects and other designers have historically only served a very small percentage of the global population that could afford their services. This disproportionate distribution of services was notably made visible to the greater public with recent exhibits and books highlighting work benefitting traditionally underserved populations, such as Cooper Hewitt, Smithsonian Design Museum's *Design for the Other 90%* exhibit.[5] Increased attention on the strength and impact of this work has led to a growing recognition of the power of design to transform lives, and an opportunity for the design profession to expand its reach. Nowhere is this shift in thinking being felt more powerfully than among young designers and students of design whose concern for the condition of the world has made opportunities to apply their newly developed skills toward a greater purpose a demand and priority. *Wisdom from Field: Public Interest Design in Practice* (Feldman *et al.*, 2013), the first comprehensive survey and study of the field, found more than 80% of students and young professionals interested in both public interest design and demanding more opportunities to engage and learn skills in this field. These young architects reflect a general disenchantment with a profession "known for its thunderous silence" and "complete irrelevance" in regards to social change, as was famously critiqued of architects by American civil rights leader Whitney Young in 1968.[6] Indeed, this critique is widely considered the call to action of the modern public interest design movement (Abendroth & Bell, 2015).

As is the case with many young people today, the students working with the CPID are determined to use their skills and energy to contribute to improving the social, economic, and environmental conditions in communities that could greatly benefit from design services. Building upon social and environmental movements, these students and others across the country are fully responding to the challenge. It is really quite fitting, then, that the Center for Public Interest Design is located just a stone's throw away from where Whitney Young delivered his powerful address to a room full of architects at the national convention for the American Institute of Architects in downtown Portland, Oregon, decades earlier.

5 The Smithsonian's Cooper-Hewitt, National Design Museum, followed up the *Design for the Other 90%* exhibit and publication with *Design with the Other 90%: Cities*. This shift in title from designing for underserved communities to designing with underscores a change in the emphasis of approach of public interest designers toward a more inclusive process.

6 In his powerful speech at the 1968 AIA Convention held in Portland, Oregon, Whitney Young Jr. specifically addressed the lack of African Americans represented in architecture and architectural education, architects' implicit contribution to planned segregation in built environments, and a lack of community involvement by the profession.

Figure 9.2 CPID Students working on a design-build project at the Montesinos
orphanage in Titanyen, Haiti

Photo credit: CPID

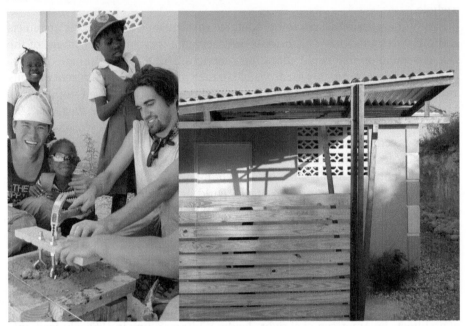

Students driving the movement

For students coming into the architecture field, public interest design is a key issue
nationally according to the AIA (2013), with 82% of incoming students declaring
a strong interest in coursework and certification. These findings are consistent
with trends that PSU's School of Architecture is noting, with many applicants to
the graduate program listing the Center for Public Interest Design as their primary
reason for wanting to study at PSU. Students' interest in public interest design is
helping to accelerate the development of a field that has been steadily growing for
decades among grassroots practitioners and educators.

The shift in architecture and architectural education from modernism's
approach of serving the abstract masses with mixed (often devastating) results to
an approach that sought social engagement in communities with context-specific
work arose parallel to the progressive movements of the 1960s (Schuman, 2012).
Charles Moore's Yale Building Project, begun in the late '60s when he was Chair
of Yale's Department of Architecture, marked a shift in design-build education
where the utility of construction was combined with a social agenda. When Moore
formalized the project with its social mission, it was very much a response to the

social re-engagement and activism that student movements demanded from their colleges and universities (Hayes, 2007). Moore noticed a design-build culture was already emerging in the mid-'60s, beginning with students like David Sellers and Peter Gluck building commissioned work while still in school. While emphasizing the importance of hands-on education at Yale, Pratt took community engagement and design services to poor communities in the New York Metropolitan area as its mandate for social and political re-engagement. These two approaches toward creating more meaningful educational experiences represented two world views that have persisted in the academy until today. Both of these programs are still active, and informed academic programs that have followed. The BASIC Initiative, an international service-learning program founded by Professor Palleroni almost three decades ago, was one of the early followers that would herald the current period of broad social re-engagement that architecture is currently experiencing. The program merged Yale and Pratt's approaches by challenging students and faculty to apply their research, intellectual assets, and coursework to help underserved communities achieve a sustainable and equitable way of life by offering both an immersion in the communities they would serve worldwide, and professional consultancy and research to communities in need (Palleroni and Merkelbach, 2004).

Socially focused design-build projects like those run through the BASIC Initiative and Design Corps, have largely been the primary entry point into public interest design for students before the advent of centers like the CPID were able to provide a broader range of opportunities to engage in the subject field.[7] There is something tremendously powerful about design-build projects in an architectural education, and they remain a significant component of the work of the CPID. They offer a service-learning experience that demands students use a range of skills that include and often surpass those required of the profession of architecture, with an impact on a site and community that is immediately perceptible. They are an extremely effective way to put research into action and expose students to many aspects of public interest design. In addition to elucidating the profound relationship between the lines on a drawing and the real world implications for the building of a structure, students are also able to understand firsthand how a project is the result of complex relations and conditions on site. Working on a site for weeks or months at a time allows ample opportunity to create a deep understanding and relationship with the client and/or community, and to learn the skill set of practices

---

7 Operating for decades outside the academy, these organizations served as essentially non-profit service organizations to overcome the objections to engagement that characterized the intellectual environment of most architecture schools in the decades after the 1960s. In this period, even a suspicion of the merits of design build education was prevalent in the architecture academy, and by the mid-'90s less than half a dozen programs continued to be active in the academy nationally. Looked at through today's perspective, it's somewhat inconceivable that there would be an objection to giving students the educational opportunity to learn by building full scale and from the complexities of real-world conditions, materials, and cultural issues that are difficult, if not impossible, to replicate or reduce to an assignment in a classroom.

and strategies needed to support a successful outcome. This essential mixture of engagement and time allows the designers to make adjustments and adaptations to the project to better serve the needs and desires of the community, an expanded definition of what architects traditionally defined as the 'site' and 'client' that is not possible in the abstraction of a studio environment at school.

Adaptation

Figure 9.3 Our model of working encourages students to discuss and challenge conventional wisdom in a collaborative atmosphere

Photo credit: CPID

The group working at the powwow is having to learn quickly about adaptation and the challenges of design-build projects. The students have to be resourceful. The site that was allotted for use at the powwow has turned out to be of very different dimensions and on a different part of the site than expected. Additionally, and more significantly, the planned methods of community engagement have to be reconsidered. A few of our hosts on the Reservation have expressed concerns that did not come up in the discussions leading up to the event. They worry that directly discussing the wildfires might be too sensitive a topic for a community still reeling in the trauma of the event. Furthermore, there is concern that in spite of a successful track record of working with the group it is likely that this historically disempowered group of people might be understandably distrustful of personal questions from a group they may not be familiar with. The concern and resulting conversation are enlightening and crucial. The point is taken and the students meet to rethink their approach.

Design, and public interest design in particular, requires this type of flexibility. The ability to quickly adapt to new challenges and opportunities and to accommodate students, professionals, and community groups seeking to collaborate has been essential in the development of the CPID itself.

Engaging within and without

The response to the establishment of the CPID has been overwhelming. Architecture, engineering, and urban planning students from within PSU, as well as from places like Tokyo, Rome, Barcelona, and Mexico City, have come to work and study at the Center as its work has gained national and international recognition. It quickly became apparent that we needed to institutionalize a variety of roles to accommodate a range of skills, interests, and experience, such as those represented by the students working with us on the Reservation. We needed more options than simply the student or graduate assistant roles traditionally offered at university centers. These new roles needed to accommodate the student and/or professional and make clear the expectations on both sides.

Interns work with us much like they would at a traditional design firm, only with a greater focus on research and public engagement. CPID interns usually come for three- or six-month periods and are matched with projects that fit their interest and skills. Visiting Scholars join us from other universities and serve as critics and speakers, contributing to projects as their time allows. Faculty from any department can apply to become a Faculty Fellow and conduct their research and projects through the Center. Students can choose to take classes with faculty of the CPID who often incorporate active projects into their studios and seminars.

An obvious challenge with using students for work in a community is that the relationships and trust built during the project can end abruptly with the conclusion of the academic quarter if an approach toward sustaining ongoing engagement is not planned in advance. As Dan Pitera of the Detroit Collaborative Design Center pointed out during a session discussion at the 2015 Structures for Inclusion Conference, there is an important distinction between community participation and community engagement and much of what is being called engagement is really momentary participation in an activity. Community engagement speaks to a deeper relationship forged over time. This can be difficult to do with rotating students working on the quarter system. Two of the most significant ways the CPID has sought to address this challenge is through the development of the CPID Student Fellows program and the Graduate Certificate in Public Interest Design.

The CPID Student Fellows program is designed to give outstanding graduate and upper level undergraduate students at PSU the opportunity to gain valuable experience outside of the classroom through participation in a meaningful public interest design project for a minimum of one year. Student Fellows are each given a leadership role on an active CPID project under the guidance of one of its faculty members, which limits the current number to five. Projects that the inaugural class of student fellows worked on includes the design of a sustainable community center in Inner Mongolia, a design intervention to promote safe transit usage in some of Sacramento, California's most disinvested neighborhoods, and the development of an adaptable school made of affordable modular classrooms that are healthful for both the student and the environment.

This program has proven to be extremely valuable for the students, faculty, and client community. It creates a core group of students to advance work and allows for significant collaboration between students and faculty. The project that the student fellow works on throughout the year is based on his or her interests and abilities, current Center projects, and the focus area of their faculty collaborator. As important as this relationship is for the success of individual projects and consistency with community engagement, this program also fosters the esprit de corps of the organization. The fellowship begins with a one-week intensive trip to one of CPID's project sites to examine broad issues of public interest design and tackle a small project that responds to an issue the group identifies. This trip has proven to be essential for creating camaraderie among the students and faculty, allowing faculty to get to know students before matching their interests to a project, and beginning a working relationship with a foundation of understanding about the strengths and challenges of public interest design work.

The first year of this program was exceptionally successful by all accounts and the applications to the program for the coming year far outnumber available positions. While the fellowship is unpaid (though we hope to change this in the future), students receive IDP credit toward their architecture license, gain valuable work experience, receive funding to cover all expenses for participation in CPID trips and special events, and may fulfill fieldwork/practicum hours toward the Graduate Certificate in Public Interest Design at Portland State University.[8]

---

8 IDP stands for Intern Development Program and is administered by the National Council of Architectural Registration Boards (NCARB). Before becoming licensed as an architect, graduates of an accredited architectural program need to pass their Architectural Record Exams and complete several thousand hours of work in architecture under the supervision of an approved organization. The CPID's ability to help young designers complete these hours toward their professional licensure through participation in real-world projects has been instrumental in its ability to recruit and maintain students and interns.

The First Graduate Certificate in Public Interest Design

The Graduate Certificate in Public Interest Design at PSU is the first of its kind in the country, with several more anticipated at other universities in the next few years. The creation of the certificate has marked a significant moment in public interest design education. It was created as a means to prepare future leaders in architecture, urban planning, sustainability, community development, and other fields to aid currently underserved populations through sustainable, human-centered design methods. The curriculum for the certificate was informed by an in-depth study of the field, as well as successful certificate programs in related fields at PSU, such as the Social Innovation Certificate offered through the Business School and the Graduate Certificate in Sustainability from the Institute for Sustainable Solutions.

The Graduate Certificate in Public Interest Design is offered to both graduate students and professionals in Portland and beyond. It consists of a minimum of 18 credit hours of course options from several disciplines, with a focus on the "triple bottom line" of sustainability (social, environmental, economic), ranging from Social Entrepreneurship to Environmental Sustainability to Creating Collaborative Communities.[9] The coursework is anchored by an Introduction to Public Interest Design seminar and culminates in fieldwork or practicum on a real-world public interest design project. These two courses make up the core requirements of the certificate. The elective courses fall into the categories of Social, Economic, and Environmental options, with five courses in each subject area from a variety of fields, including Urban Planning, Public Administration, and Architecture. The inclusion of multiple disciplines in the certificate has already provided some excellent opportunities for students to be exposed to concepts in other fields, as well as for cross-disciplinary collaboration (with faculty of the CPID co-teaching a course on Design Thinking with the Business School, for example). As the culmination of their certificate, students submit a thorough portfolio of the certificate work, containing a thoughtful reflection of their experience within the realm of public interest design and how it can inform their careers going forward, which will hopefully serve as an open resource for other designers.

9 The elective courses in the Graduate Certificate in Public Interest Design were built around the social, economic, and environmental categories to emphasize the importance of the triple bottom line of sustainability in design. Additionally, the current leading tool, the SEED Metric (Social Economic Environmental Design), is a methodology for mindfully creating and evaluating public interest design projects through a set of goals arrived at and agreed upon by the client community, the designers and other stakeholders. It embodies in both its approach and methodology the founding principles of the CPID and is being taught by faculty to students. Several of the Center faculty members are actively involved in the creation and refinement of the SEED metric and other forms of evaluation.

From student to practitioner

The pressing question of how to turn their passion for using their design skills in the service of the public good into an economically viable career path is on every student's mind when they come to the CPID to discuss the certificate program. What have largely remained side projects for architects in traditional firms—or has been restricted to the work of university programs that can rely on a symbiotic relationship between salaries from a university and an eager student workforce—is no longer sufficient for the sea of young architects insistent on not only making great design, but also making a difference in the world. Perhaps the urgency of this group comes from growing up in a dramatic time in history that has made clear the need to address some of the most pressing issues facing society, such as climate change and economic inequality. In any case, this new generation of designers has a challenging path in front of them, but one that is not without hope.

Recent reports by the professional architecture organization in North America, the American Institute of Architects (AIA), have shown that public interest practices are the fastest growing segment of the field, and the only ones that have shown an expanding market penetration as compared to population-adjusted demand since 2000 (AIA, 2013). In fact, according to this report and the in-depth study of the field funded by the Latrobe Prize, Wisdom From the Field: Public Interest Design in Practice (Feldman *et al.*, 2013), public interest practices have shown an incredible resilience even in conditions such as those of the Great Recession of 2008–12, when such firms only lost an average of 20% of their personnel compared to a much higher percentage in traditional firms. But it is not only market viability that reflects the general interest in this field: in surveys conducted by the AIA as part of the aforementioned studies, 70% of a statistically significant number of firms nationally ranked interest in public interest design as a top priority, ahead of sustainability alone. Some of the largest architecture firms in the country have also acknowledged that to recruit and retain the best students, the firm has had to develop and incorporate a robust public interest agenda. The goal of the CPID is to prepare the students that come through our program to become leaders at these firms, while providing the framework and skills to forge new paths within the profession.

Challenges of a university program

In spite of an eventful and successful first two years, the sustained development of the CPID will require expanding on the elements that are working and finding creative solutions to the obstacles facing both the profession and the Center in particular as a university-based organization. Many of the challenges facing the CPID will likely be familiar to anyone working in academia that has attempted a community-based project. A need for project funding and flexibility in the way a program develops are particularly notable and can be difficult within the bureaucracy of a university, even with an extremely supportive administration. Pioneering an academic certificate in a field, for example, will surely require modifications to improve opportunities for students and accommodate new courses and developments within the profession.

Figure 9.4 Youth sharing about their community at the Northern Cheyenne powwow in Lame Deer, Montana

Photo credit: Tomasz Low

While there is usually a great advantage to being a university-based center in that we can gain trust from the public more quickly, there is also the possibility of entering a community that has had negative experiences with professionals, government officials, or even students and faculty from the same university, all of which make gaining trust and forming partnerships that much more difficult. Practicing within a university also demands ensuring that a project is beneficial to both the student and the client community, which can occasionally seem at odds. At the powwow, the pavilion was made of a series of steel-braced, wood triangles covered in translucent panels, arranged to create a space to have the kind of conversations and interactions that we hoped to have with the tribe. The pavilion served the purpose of attracting and engaging people who otherwise might not have participated, but it also provided a design challenge to the students that encompassed issues of cultural appropriateness, fabrication, methods of engagement, and structural soundness. A space was needed to host a conversation that would help the community come together over a shared need, but for the CPID faculty much of the emphasis on the structure was also led by an opportunity to provide a powerful educational experience to the students. This challenge of serving both the student and project needs, however, contributed to addressing another persistent challenge in public interest design: proving the value of design to those who typically do not receive design services. The positive reaction to this pavilion was in part because it was able to demonstrate tangible evidence of design thinking in action, something that needs to be made evident to the public and that cannot possibly be taught to students with the same effect through a lesson plan in a classroom. Despite the challenges, the students left with a more profound experience, and the sense of achievement and lessons learned that only comes when one realizes that it is not the product, or pavilion in this case, that validates your effort to the community and yourself, but how you are able to make it achieve the agreed-upon goals and learn something significant about yourself in the process.

After the powwow

After three days at the powwow, the students had each had a number of meaningful conversations and gathered together to share anecdotes and overall takeaways. One thing that has become clear is that the Northern Cheyenne have a proud history of managing the land and wildfires themselves. In the recent wildfires, the same community members that had rushed to join in the effort of fighting small fires before they became large fires were turned away due to new government protocols. This has left many frustrated, as they had to helplessly watch their land burn when they felt that they had the skills, experience and desire to participate in fighting the fire. Any resiliency plan that would come forth would have to take advantage of these skills and the strong social asset of a neighbor willing and eager to help neighbor.

Another takeaway is that there is a group of extremely bright and motivated young activists in the tribe that have rallied their community around saving the waterways on their reservation threatened by proposed coal mining activity. The work of this organization has grown and it is clear that the passion and the leaders are present, therefore much of what we might be able to offer would come in the way of support for the ambitious grassroots work already being undertaken.

Finally, the group has agreed that the term resiliency itself was a problem. While it encompasses a strengthening of the community through the process of arriving at common goals and identifying assets by which to prepare them for traumatic events like wildfires and allow them to rebound faster, the word was met uneasily. What the group seemed interested in was disaster prevention and relief, and the students found it difficult to easily and adequately articulate the relationship between disasters and resilience to an audience unfamiliar with the concept. Most difficult was the idea of long-term planning implicit in resilience preparations. Like most communities, the group seemed understandably most interested in addressing the immediate possibility of future fires rather than engaging in the potentially more conflictive and protracted process of community planning and asset mapping. As proven by the success or failure of other social movements, one significant challenge that public interest design will have to face is striving to make the professional language of architecture and design accessible to the greater public (Wilson, 2015). This is not only true of language, but of the tools used during an inclusive design process. Both the term charrette and the act can be alienating if not well considered or explained in everyday terms to a non-professional.[10] One recent strategy that the CPID has found successful in overcoming the reluctance of community partners to participate in the design process, is the creation of physical chalkboard models. While it may be difficult for those not used to looking at plans and other architectural drawings to decode the design implications of lines on a paper and contribute to making changes, three-dimensional models are much more accessible, and the unintimidating use of colored chalk encourages participation. In this case, the medium of chalk prevents a perception that any lines or ideas drawn are intended to be beautiful, and the ability to quickly erase and redraw elements further decreases potential intimidation and allows the conversation to evolve.[11] At the powwow, the activities followed the same logic by engaging people through photography, hands on explorations, and experiential learning which, rather than presenting them with an alienating artifact like a professional drawing, allowed the participants to draw from their knowledge and experiences, bestowing on them the role of expert.

The pavilion itself was intended to serve as one such tool to facilitate a strategic process of exchange between the community and students. As an object, it represents only one step in service of larger goals with the community that will help create the relationships, capture the stories, and foster the understanding necessary for a successful partnership and outcomes. There are elements like this in each of our projects at the CPID that have been powerful mechanisms for both educating students and bringing the community into the process, and the range of projects at the CPID is nearly as broad as the field of public interest design itself. In Inner Mongolia, the CPID is investigating new ways to house the elderly in quickly

10 The term "charrette" is used in design and other professions to describe an intense period of collaborative brainstorming about an idea or design. In the architecture profession, charrettes with community members at the onset of a project are probably the most common form of community involvement in the design process.

11 Models at different scales have always been effective tools of communication in CPID and BASIC Initiative projects as everyone has at some time of their lives had a dollhouse or fort, which grew out of their imagination. Models are also easier to understand since at scale they replicate the human experience of shadows, shade and materiality.

changing rural areas while retaining the community's history and tradition through the design of a community center, gardens, and grounds for an assisted living community created from a Qing dynasty public school. In Sacramento, California, the Center is working to launch a project that partners with disinvested neighborhoods to design new bus stops that can double as programmable community spaces as a way to provide immediate needs while exploring how to access the state's new carbon credit tax for these areas. In these examples, and in each CPID project, the aim is to identify entry points for larger systems of change on pervasive issues facing vulnerable communities through the design process. This is public interest design.

Figure 9.5 Chalkboard model used for design with client on project for a
sustainable community center in Inner Mongolia, China

Photo credit: CPID

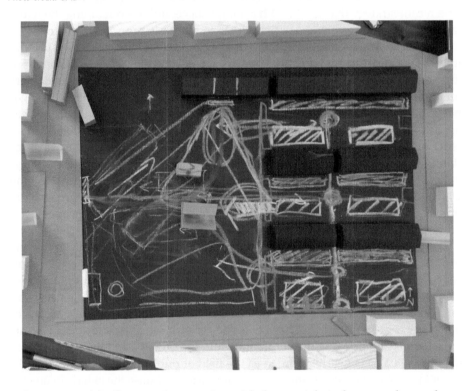

As opportunities for pursuing a project with the group have become clear, so have many of the challenges. Three of the students are CPID Student Fellows and are particularly undaunted by the challenge. They have faced these obstacles before. As part of the Student Fellows program, they participated in a design-build project in Haiti during their week-long orientation trip. The project involved designing two play structures as part of a larger four-year planning and design effort of the CPID at an orphanage and school in a community about 40 minutes outside of Port-au-Prince. On that trip they faced a lack of power, difficulty locating materials, and torrential storms. These three students stand out as leaders among a group of natural leaders, confident in their abilities and clear in the larger goals. These Student Fellows will also be among the first students in the country to receive the Graduate Certificate in Public Interest Design. Regardless of how the field of public interest design specifically develops in the coming years, there is little doubt that these emerging professionals and their peers working passionately to apply their skills toward a better world will lead the way toward a practice that is inclusive, equitable, sustainable, and beautiful.

References

Abendroth, L.M., & Bell, B. (2015). Introduction. In L.M. Abendroth & B. Bell (Eds.), *Public Interest Design Practice Guidebook: SEED Methodology, Case Studies, and Critical Issues* (pp. 1-7). New York, NY: Routledge Press.

AIA (2013). *National Objectives*, AIA National Grassroots Conference. Washington DC.

Bell, B. (2015). The state of public interest design. In L.M. Abendroth & B. Bell (Eds.), *Public Interest Design Practice Guidebook: SEED Methodology, Case Studies, and Critical Issues* (pp. 11-18). New York, NY: Routledge Press.

Feldman, R., Palleroni, S., Perkes, D., & Bell, B. (2013). *Wisdom from the field: Public interest architecture in practice.* 2011 Latrobe Prize Research. Retrieved from www.publicinterest-design.com/wp-content/uploads/2013/07/Wisdom-from-the-Field.pdf

Hayes, R. (2007). *The Yale Building Project: The First 40 Years.* New Haven, CT: Yale School of Architecture.

Palleroni, S, & Merkelbach, C.E. (2004). *Studio at Large: Architecture in Service of Global Communities.* Seattle, WA: University of Washington Press.

Schuman, A.W. (2012). Community engagement: Architecture's evolving social vocation. In J. Ockman (Ed.), *Architecture School: Three Centuries of Educating Architects in North America* (pp. 252-259). Cambridge, MA: MIT Press.

Wilson, B.B. (2015). What social justice movements can teach us about public interest design. In L.M. Abendroth, & B. Bell (Eds.), *Public Interest Design Practice Guidebook: SEED Methodology, Case Studies, and Critical Issues* (pp. 19-33). New York, NY: Routledge Press.

10

Accelerating urban sustainability

Helping cities translate plans and policies into the reality of more sustainable communities

Robert Liberty and Judy Walton

Except for the rugged Organ Mountains towering above the empty parking lots and shuttered commercial businesses, El Paseo Road could be anywhere in the United States. It is a typical auto-oriented commercial strip development, which uses large amounts of land and resources while providing minimal commercial space, employment, or community character. Its vitality has been sapped by more recent, more distant commercial development at a freeway interchange even more inaccessible except by car. The densities of housing and employment are so low that they cannot support transit. Sidewalks are missing in many areas and only people with little regard for their lives would bicycle along it. The road is bordered by acres of heat-reflecting pavement, contributing to storm water disposal and pollution problems. It is also dangerous: a disproportionate number of traffic injuries occur along its 1.7 mile length. Adjoining it is a neighborhood of small homes and apartments where, as of 2011, more than 40% of households were in poverty.

In 2011 Las Cruces completed a *Picturing El Paseo* planning effort funded by a technical assistance grant from the US Environmental Protection Agency (EPA) as part of EPA's 2009–2010 Smart Growth Implementation Assistance program.

Picturing El Paseo engaged over 200 citizens through workshops, interviews and tours. That effort was translated into the *El Paseo Corridor Community Blueprint*—adopted as the city's official policy document in 2012— calling for the redesign of El Paseo Road into a complete street[1] and for the revitalization of the adjoining commercial strip and adjacent residential area.

Two years after adoption of the *Blueprint* the city had still not taken any steps to implement it. There was no redesign for the road; no amendment to the capital improvements budget for construction; and no special programs or incentives for commercial and residential revitalization. While the *El Paseo Corridor Community Blueprint* could not actually gather dust in the city's computers or on a shelf in the gleaming new city hall, it might as well have.

In the U.S. in general, the gap between official plans and policies and their implementation is so well known that virtually every effort to draft or update a city plan begins with a promise that it will not sit on a shelf and collect dust. And yet so many plans often do. That is why the Urban Sustainability Accelerator program was created: to help urban areas in the United States[2]—particularly smaller cities and regions—translate their sustainability plans, policies and goals into the reality of a more sustainable city.

Faculty research identified the need for the program

The concepts and ideas behind the Urban Sustainability Accelerator (USA) resulted from an extensive data gathering effort carried out by Portland State University urban planning professors Jennifer Dill, Connie Ozawa, and Ethan Seltzer (2012).[3] This effort included interviews with prominent leaders in the urban sustainability field and local agency staff across the United States; a web-based search of more than 70 relevant organizations; and a review of meeting agendas from an array of national organizations.

---

1 "Complete street" is not a precise term but refers generally to streets that provide safe travel routes for pedestrian, bicyclists, and transit, with slower car and truck travel speeds, and landscaping and design elements that support a mix of adjacent uses.

2 While the USA program was created to provide assistance to cities in the U.S., some of the expertise it offers has been taken up by small and mid-sized urban areas in China (where "small" and "mid-sized" reference a very different scale). This work was a result of PSU's years of providing trainings and tours for visiting officials from China's Ministry of Housing and Urban and Rural Development and Ministry of Land and Resources. Oregon's 40-year history with urban growth boundaries is of interest to China, which recently adopted a national policy calling for similar boundaries for their major cities.

3 The part of this chapter summarizing the research done by Professors Dill, Ozawa and Seltzer draws heavily on their own report, with their consent, for which the authors are grateful.

The aim of that research—to help cities implement their sustainability plans—embodied the university's motto, "Let Knowledge Serve the City." This motto reflects the strong, collaborative relationships between faculty/students and planners, public managers, politicians, non-profit organizations, and community leaders throughout the Portland region. One goal of the USA program was to tap this network of expertise and knowledge and begin serving cities outside the region.

In the interviews, members and staff from organizations such as the Urban Sustainability Directors Network (USDN), the International Council for Local Environmental Initiatives (ICLEI), and the Institute for Sustainable Cities (ISC) cited an unmet need for assistance among smaller US cities and counties. Larger cities seemed to be getting most of the assistance available.

While periodic conferences held by organizations such as the above serve as a mechanism for disseminating and sharing information, one of the often-repeated shortcomings of these conferences, as cited by the interviewees, was the lack of follow up or any mechanism for continued interaction. Conference sessions may start to open a leader's mind, but rarely provide enough information or follow-up to sustain action, particularly in under-resourced urban areas.

The sum of the interview findings was that a shortage of information is not the problem for cities; but accessing **usable information** is. Research over the years suggests that what makes knowledge usable is its relevance to critical contextual issues.

Interviewees generally agreed on the need for greater support for cities in three areas: technical knowledge, strategy development, and relationship building. Regarding technical knowledge, respondents frequently identified these topics as areas where more assistance is needed:

- Land use and transportation (mixed use, infill development, multi-modal transportation)
- Energy efficiency (energy conservation, building efficiency, reduction in private automobile use)
- Waste management (composting, food scraps, recycling)
- Storm water and water quantity and quality, and
- Tree cover, urban vegetation, and the heat island effect

Innovative solutions in these areas are both highly visible and readily accessible in the Portland region. Moreover, rather than isolated examples in each topic area, Portland offers a unique opportunity for observers to gain technical knowledge in the context of an integrated system of solutions. For example, the region's "Green Streets" program combines transportation safety goals with green storm water management infrastructure development.

In terms of strategy and relationship building, interviewees often cited the following as areas of interest:

- Identifying and creating "usable" information, knowledge that makes a difference

- Promoting interagency and cross-sectoral coordination and collaboration, and

- Generating political support from critical stakeholders and the public

Again, such efforts are amply demonstrated and visible in the Portland region, and the professionals associated with their implementation are available through the USA program to engage in dialogue about not only the successes achieved, but also challenges and failed strategies along the way.

The research by professors Dill, Ozawa, and Seltzer also underscored the importance of engaging political leadership. However, there was clear acknowledgement of the additional need to support government staff (and others) who are focused on the technical aspects of innovation. Providing them with greater access to key information is one way cities can offer such support. A few respondents noted the value of including not just businesses, but small business leaders who might not otherwise be connected into the sustainability discussion. A fourth sector of support identified by respondents—civic leadership among the non-business community—has been shown to be a strong asset in mobilizing for social change.

As a result of this research, the USA program incorporated the distinctive premise that "the problem" is less the lack of green technologies or practices—or even the "how tos" of implementation—than the challenge of generating sufficient political will and confidence among leaders to initiate and steward such change. As Professors Dill, Ozawa and Seltzer (2012) concluded, "True sustainability is made, not bought, and is the product of choices consciously entertained and made over time."

The Urban Sustainability Accelerator program in action

With financial support from The Summit Foundation in Washington, DC, the Institute for Sustainable Solutions at PSU, and the Nohad A. Toulan School of Urban Studies and Planning, the Urban Sustainability Accelerator was initiated in October 2012 and convened its first participants in the summer of 2013. Although the program has evolved slightly over time, it has hewed fairly closely to the original concept as conceived by Professors Dill, Ozawa and Seltzer.

The cohorts and their themes

As the first step in the USA program, a group of places that are working to implement similar sustainability plans or policies is identified and recruited to participate as a cohort that can learn from each other.

The first cohort (2013–14) was made up of cities working to implement plans and policies calling for infill, redevelopment and revitalization of a city center or an inner neighborhood, and incorporating additional sustainability elements in the form of enhanced transportation choices and green storm water infrastructure. The participants in this cohort were El Paso, Texas; Elk Grove, California; Louisville, Kentucky; Portland, Maine; Rancho Cordova, California; Sacramento County, California; Waco, Texas; and Wichita, Kansas.

The second cohort theme (2014–15) was city-university partnerships on urban redevelopment projects, incorporating increased transportation choices and green storm water infrastructure. The participants in this cohort were Auburn and Auburn University in Alabama; Duluth and the University of Minnesota Duluth; and Las Cruces and New Mexico State University.

The focus of the third cohort (2015–16) is the implementation of regional plans to shift from sprawl to compact growth (emphasizing infill and redevelopment) and conservation of rural lands outside the urban areas. These plans also incorporate goals to increase housing and transportation choices and in some cases, geographical boundaries to identify the limits for the extension of urban infrastructure. Participants in the third cohort are the Truckee Meadows region (the cities of Reno and Sparks and Washoe County in Nevada) and the Tri-County region in Mid Michigan, made up of Lansing, East Lansing; Clinton, Eaton, and Ingham Counties and their constituent townships; and a small part of Shiawassee County. The same theme is shared by a separate, two-year cohort organized by the Sacramento Area Council of Governments, which consists of more than a dozen governments in the Sacramento region.

The implementation teams

Based on consultations and a site visit by USA's director, each participating urban area assembles a project implementation team of about 10–20 individuals. Teams typically include people from different sectors whose participation is necessary to translate the policy or plan into reality. Usually this means government staff, elected officials, board members and/or staff from nongovernmental organizations, and private sector developers or business professionals. The multi-sector membership of the implementation team is a key ingredient to success in the implementation of the team's projects.

Las Cruces, New Mexico (2014–15 cohort) offers a good example of a multi-sector implementation team. Its team included representatives from three chambers of commerce (Greater Las Cruces, Hispanic, and Green); senior and mid-level staff from three city departments (Public Works, Community Development, and Transportation); three city councilors; a staff member from the metropolitan planning organization; and the department chair and two PhD students from New Mexico State University's civil engineering department.

The implementation team from the Tri-County region in Mid Michigan (2015–16 cohort) offers another example of a diverse mix of participants. It includes the vice chair of Lansing's city council, a county commissioner, a major developer, staff from the regional planning agency, the director of a county farmland preservation program, a senior planner from a small city in the region, a public health official, and a professor from Michigan State University.

The team's work over the course of the year

The year-long program begins with a July convening of a subset of each team's members in Portland. The convening is not a conference; instead of sessions where participants listen passively to presenters, it offers interactive tours and consultations with experts addressing the specific needs and interests of each team. The experts and tour guides have been individually briefed on the team project and interests. Experts include elected officials, government staff, university faculty, private sector professionals, non-profit staff and board members, and retirees with years of expertise. This diversity of backgrounds reflects the basic premise that implementation requires action by actors from multiple sectors.

The range of sectors represented by participants is also essential to allow peer-to-peer learning, the most effective method of learning due in part to the inherent credibility of someone who shares the same background, role, training and experience. USA's roster of experts is continually expanding, with over 110 individuals at the time of this writing. Most are in the Portland region but a growing number come from other parts of the country, and include a few prior participants in the USA program.

A very important aspect of the convening is what happens during the unstructured periods—the meals, breaks, receptions, free time, and evenings. It is during these times, when relaxation and socializing are encouraged, that team relationships begin to develop and informal education between local experts and team members takes place.

On the last day of the convening, the teams meet for several hours to refine or draw up a work plan for their project year. The work plan consists of outcomes, deliverables, a list of activities by month, and names of participants. The outcomes are both "hard"—such as construction, funding, or adoption of a new regulation or incentive—and "soft," such as new collaborative relationships and new knowledge.

After the convening the implementation teams begin to execute their work plan, including tapping assistance provided by the USA program. Assistance takes many forms, including telephone consultations with USA experts; expert visits to the community; site visits to Portland and other places by team members; commissioned research; scholarships to attend conferences and training programs in Portland (or elsewhere); projects by graduate-level classes or individuals; and help organizing community engagement or planning events in the participating city.

Wichita, Kansas offers a good example of USA providing faculty and student assistance to a project team. The Wichita Downtown Development Corporation (WDDC) asked USA for help in broadening the thinking of local property owners, developers and designers about the kinds of projects that could be built as part of the redevelopment of the area around Union Station (this area is between downtown Wichita and the redeveloping Old Town District). The WDDC specifically asked for designs and concepts that were plausible and feasible, but were beyond the comfort zone of current local thinking about redevelopment.

Figure 10.1   Peer-to-peer learning during the mid-year meeting in San Diego. A green chamber of commerce representative discusses business impacts of complete street redesign with a small business owner while a city councilor, a graduate student, a community activist, and city staff listen and share in the learning

Photo credit: Robert Liberty

PSU Architecture Professor B.D. Wortham-Galvin enlisted several students in her undergraduate studio on Adaptive Reuse to travel to Wichita, where they were given tours and briefing sessions, and were hosted by members of the local design and development community. As their term project, student teams prepared six different videos describing types of potential buildings, their uses, and why they were appropriate. Their videos were presented to a WDDC-assembled audience, who discussed the concepts with the students back in Portland through an internet link. One team member, a prominent local developer, was intrigued enough by some of the student work that he suggested retaining a couple of them (although this opportunity was not pursued by the students).

Each team's work on the implementation plan is supported and kept on track through monthly check-in calls with USA staff. In response to a suggestion from the first cohort, a mid-year gathering was added each February (San Diego was the chosen site in 2015) with a small subset of implementation team members. The purpose of the meeting is to report progress to each other, consult with USA staff about additional assistance opportunities, and learn from local experts and projects through site visits and tours (see Figure 10.1).

At the end of the program, a year after the initial convening, a few members from each team reconvene in Portland for three primary purposes: to report on what they have accomplished, to evaluate the USA program, and to provide advice to the incoming cohort of implementation teams about how best to take advantage of the USA program. In addition, the reconveners can choose to participate in the tours and consultation sessions aimed at the new cohort during their own convening, taking place at the same time. The program also offers its alumni (members of previous teams) the opportunity to participate in USA activities well beyond the end of their program year.

Realizing El Paseo

How did the USA program play out in Las Cruces? In 2014, two years after the adoption of the *El Paseo Corridor Community Blueprint*, a staff member in the city's Community Development Department persuaded the City of Las Cruces to participate in the USA program. Over time, USA staff came to understand the various reasons why the Blueprint was not being implemented: skepticism and opposition from within two city departments, limits on staff time and technical capacity, disengagement by elected officials, and opposition from within parts of the business community. USA staff, working with the Las Cruces implementation team, attempted to overcome each of these barriers in turn.

The Public Works Director, while skeptical at first, became a proponent of complete streets after site visits and discussions with experts during USA's 2014 convening in Portland and mid-year meeting in San Diego. She asked USA for help in adapting a set of complete street guidelines published by NACTO (National Association of City Transportation Officials) into operable standards for her department. This revised set of standards would greatly facilitate the transformation of El Paseo Road.

The new head of the Civil Engineering Department at New Mexico State University, Professor Peter Martin, also attended the convening in July (along with one of his graduate teaching assistants) and developed new or deeper relationships with city staff and other team members. In January, Professor Martin assigned the redesign of El Paseo Road as the senior Civil Engineering students' capstone project. Student teams developed proposals for redesigning El Paseo with different themes—e.g., safety, community revitalization, and reducing traffic congestion.

This kind of real-life project was a novelty for the students; and after some initial resistance they became enthusiastic.

In early February the USA held its first mid-year meeting so teams could report to each other on their progress and learn from each other. As part of the meeting, held in San Diego, Las Cruces team members visited La Jolla Boulevard and heard glowing testimonials from businesses about the benefits of reducing the road from five lanes to two, widening sidewalks, adding landscaping and bike lanes and replacing intersections with roundabouts. The two city councilors on the trip became excited about the possibilities of doing the same for El Paseo Road, and shared what they learned with other city councilors back home.

In late February, the student designs for El Paseo were shared with the public at a workshop opened by Las Cruces Mayor Ken Miyagishima and attended by two city councilors (Image 2). Community members participating in the workshop included nearby residents, business and property owners, a realtor and members of the congregation of a church located on El Paseo Road. The event was used to identify concerns (such as impacts on business during construction) and to educate attendees about how and why a narrower road could achieve multiple objectives (i.e., improved safety, better storm-water management, enhanced retail environment) without causing congestion—for example, through improved signal timing, shorter crossing times, and reduced merging. The engineering students' designs, revised after the workshop to incorporate green storm water features, were completed and shared with the city later in the spring.

The next challenge was to alleviate business and property owner concerns about the project. USA sent its retail revitalization expert to visit Las Cruces in March, meet with business and property owners and city staff, and detail specific paths to local economic success.

USA then identified places where arterials similar to El Paseo had been redesigned to create complete streets as a means of stimulating private reinvestment, and found business owners and operators along each arterial who were willing to share their experience. Using simple technology[4] we plan (at the time of this writing) to have business managers, property owners and realtors from the El Paseo corridor in Las Cruces see and discuss the experience of their counterparts in other communities. These peer insights will be more trustworthy and relevant to most of the Las Cruces businesses than the comments of city staff, no matter how well grounded. As this work has progressed, the City Council has felt confident enough to support making the redesign of El Paseo a priority within the city's modest capital improvements budget. These were the steps the USA program used to help the Las Cruces community move from a "picture" of a redeveloped El Paseo Road to reality.

---

4 Technologies included: Google Earth to view the redesigned street, screen-sharing software that allowed everyone to see the Google Earth tour and other images, and a teleconference system for audio.

Figure 10.2 Civil engineering students from New Mexico State University present their "complete street" redesign proposals for El Paseo Road in Las Cruces to community residents

Photo credit: Robert Liberty

Lessons learned

USA participant evaluations and volunteered comments from the first three years have validated several, although not all of the elements of the program model:[5]

- Providing assistance to smaller and mid-sized urban areas because those places lack the resources of larger urban areas.

    "With limited staff time and dollars the City could not have afforded to pay for the expertise and experience available through the PSU staff and the private sector advisors they made available through the USA. We would have never been able to find them let alone pay for their time and expertise!"
    —Randy Starbuck, Former Economic Development Director, City of Elk Grove, California (from USA Project Report for Elk Grove)

---

5 The evaluations also included many criticisms and suggestions for improvement. For example, several participants felt their teams did not have adequate time to understand and prepare for the program prior to participation in the Convening in Portland. However, most of the criticisms were directed at the way in which the program was administered and not the basic model, which was endorsed.

> *"Overall, our participation in the USA program was well worth it. We were able to substantially complete a planning effort that would have required a six figure contract with a consulting firm at very little cost."*
> —Jeff Levine, AICP, Director, Planning & Urban Development Department, City of Portland, Maine (from USA Project Report for Portland)

- Providing assistance over the course of a year or more.

> *"All through the year, our regular conference calls with USA staff have allowed us to bounce concepts and ideas off professional peers and provided us with referrals and examples in other communities."*
> —Jeff Levine, AICP, Director, Planning & Urban Development Department, City of Portland, Maine (from USA Project Report for Portland)

- The importance of creating multi-sectoral implementation teams, including elected officials, government staff, business and professional associations, nongovernmental organizations and in many cases, a local university or college. This collaborative experience creates new working relationships that enable or accelerate project implementation.

> *"The team is pleased with progress, coordination among partners has been increased dramatically. Relationships between public and private sector partners [are] strong, unity among partners on all sides of the river have [sic] improved. This is a direct result of outreach and teamwork oriented toward implementing the USA project."*
> —Chris McGowan, Director of Urban Development, Greater Waco Chamber of Commerce, Waco, Texas (from USA Project Report for Waco)

> *"One of my strong interests, and part of our mandate as a [university] sustainability office in the sustainability movement, is to engage with our local communities to act in accord with the principle that we are all interconnected and need to work together to innovate and improve with all due speed. This project provided the first structured opportunity for me to do that."*
> —Michael Kensler, Director, Office of Sustainability, Auburn University, Auburn, Alabama

> *"The USA Program helped establish a strong framework to support [the district's] long-term redevelopment through teambuilding and education. The program created and formalized existing relationships through which ideas were generated, information was shared and resources were pooled."*
> —Maria Koetter, Director, Office of Sustainability, Louisville Metro Government, Louisville, Kentucky (from USA Project Report for Louisville)

- A tailored, individualized program of assistance that emphasizes peer-to-peer exchanges.

"The Urban Sustainability Accelerator program was a game-changer in unexpected ways and we encourage other potential cohort cities to exploit USA resources, offered so generously. A key strength of the USA program is the model of expertise matched and available to any project. We have networks that allow us to share information, but the USA program is a prototype for implementation assistance in that an expert multi-disciplinary team with decades of private sector experience is available in many venues."
—Lauren Baldwin, Sustainability Program Specialist, Office of Resilience & Sustainability (ORS), City of El Paso, Texas

"Of particular benefit was a customized two-day tour of several projects representing sustainable practices in both an urban and suburban setting for a small delegation of private developers, public agency staff and elected officials. At each location, the project developers provided a behind-the-scenes tour of their project. The connections with private developers that the PSU Team was able to assemble who could answer questions about the evolution and current performance of on-the-ground examples of built projects was enormously helpful as the Sacramento Group evaluated what could be translated and replicated in Sacramento."
—Leighann Moffitt, Planning Director, Department of Community Development, Planning and Environmental Review, County of Sacramento, California (from USA Project Report for County of Sacramento)

- Drawing on the reservoir of sustainability talent that has been acquired in the Portland, Oregon region over the last 40 years (much of which is volunteered), and sustainability showcase projects.

"Everyone on my team saw that what Portland is doing is paying off big time in terms of community character, enhancing the urban experience, improving environmental conditions, etc. And, just as importantly, that all of it is eminently doable. There is nothing Portland is doing that Auburn could not do in ways that fit our climate, community culture, etc. And part of that story is that Portland wasn't always like that. With community engagement and the right visionary leadership and commitment, Portland made it happen."
—Michael Kensler, Director, Office of Sustainability, Auburn University, Auburn, Alabama

"Our Transportation Planning Manager was inspired by Portland's bike lanes and walkable streets that he experienced while there and it gave him the push he needed to get these high-quality design standards adopted. In addition, he was able to bring a resolution to City Council to create a Bike Advisory Committee to review bike lane design and connectivity around the city and help with other bike matters. This resolution was approved by Council in May 2014. In September 2015, we formed an internal Bike Committee to support the development of a Bike Plan.
—Lauren Baldwin, Sustainability Program Specialist, Office of Resilience + Sustainability (ORS), City of El Paso, Texas

- Creating a peer learning network.

Experience with the first four cohorts has revealed a number of areas where improvement is needed in creating a learning network among the teams.

One challenge has been the difficulty of creating an active learning cohort among people working on different teams. Most government staff members are busy working to implement their own team's project and have little time to spend building professional relationships outside their community. The convening and mid-year gathering are too brief and too agenda-packed to allow team members to develop close professional relationships with members of the other teams. At times the USA program has promoted professional exchanges between members of different teams when it seemed useful, but these have not led to lasting professional relationships.

The USA program plans to convene representatives from the first four cohorts for the purpose of evaluating the longer-term performance in implementing sustainability projects. This will also be an opportunity to determine if there has been any continued contact between team members and advise on how a learning cohort might be created, or whether this is an unrealistic objective.

Another challenge related to building a learning network, as well as to a project's success, has been personnel changes in a community through elections or senior staff transitions (many of which result from elections). Sometimes participants are reluctant to discuss or reveal the risks that political changes may have for the completion of their project. USA program staff have learned to probe and explore these possibilities early on and avoid or alter projects that might be terminated or disrupted by political events.

Another general lesson for the USA program is the recognition that participation may present risks and uncertainties for mid-level government staff. USA is neither an internal agency nor a consulting firm; and the efforts of its staff can be anxiety-inducing—such as speaking freely to elected officials, breaking down barriers between different units of government, and building bridges with businesses and non-profit groups outside government.

There is no easy answer to this challenge. Organizing the teams and creating the cohort well in advance of the program year would provide more opportunities to explain the operation of the program, identify and recruit critical team members (including elected officials), and build relationships between team members and momentum for the project. Starting each cohort earlier would also allow the team members to waste less time getting organized after the initiation of their program year and might help them stay focused.

There is often difficulty in coordinating student projects with the schedules and needs of government staff or private parties. Students do not always understand the pressure of deadlines for partners awaiting the students' work products. Students often delay working on class projects until close to the deadline but then find that people in the organization for whom the work is being prepared are not available. Academic writing and concepts may be poorly understood or received by the client organization, and sometimes the quality of student work is not up to their standards. These are familiar problems for faculty members but USA's non-faculty staff have few opportunities to provide this guidance to students. Increasing the clarity of the assignment and giving examples of work products would help address this problem.

The growth in sustainability professions, programs and research around the US and in other countries creates an important opportunity for USA to attract new volunteer talent to the program to help cities implement their sustainability projects. The accelerating retirement of the Baby Boom generation is another important opportunity for the program, because many of the retirees will be inclined to stay intellectually active and to put their skills in service to their community and the world.

Reflections on the Urban Sustainability Accelerator's Place within the University

The Urban Sustainability Accelerator program differs in certain respects from the other sustainability programs at Portland State University described in this book. For one, it is not focused on serving the local community (i.e., the Portland, Oregon region) but rather communities outside the region. Second, it is not administered by faculty, although its administrators do have connections to both teaching and research at PSU.

What it has in common with other sustainability programs at PSU is the application of faculty and staff knowledge and student enthusiasm to the challenge of sustainability, and the building of connections between PSU faculty, students and staff and various sustainability practitioners in the region. Several PSU faculty members (as well as faculty at other universities) have found that the work of USA implementation teams can make good subjects for class assignments. Over time USA staff expect to find more and more of these class project opportunities across a range of disciplines—from urban design, to real estate finance and development, engineering, and public policy. The program could and should be doing more to draw tighter connections between its expert advisers/practitioners in the Portland region and university faculty, students, and staff (including facilities planners charged with implementing university sustainability plans).

Engagement of faculty with practitioners[6] in the diverse fields of sustainability is often limited to guest lectures by practitioners. The USA program could begin recruiting faculty experts and practitioners to work in tandem in assisting USA implementation teams. This would create opportunities for intellectual exchange around new ideas and practices that would not take place in the setting of a guest

6 Of course, many faculty members are practitioners as well as teachers and scholars..

lecture. The USA program could also enrich the student experience by recruiting practitioners to advise students on USA class projects. This could be accomplished, for example, by having sustainability-oriented redevelopers provide advice to real estate and architecture students creating concepts for redevelopment.

Another important opportunity for the program is as a subject of academic research. A neglected area of scholarship is how and why plans and policies are implemented,[7] and USA offers opportunities to explore answers to that question. The success or failure of plan or policy implementation cannot be explained simply by the presence or absence of political will (especially since so much of a plan's implementation is not government's responsibility). There are many complex factors that influence the implementation process, ranging from how priorities for action are determined, to conflicting institutional missions, to civic support and leadership (separate from government action), to dominant narratives and political framing, to simple endurance and perseverance. Case studies on the whys and hows of plan implementation would supplement and enrich the academic fields of land use planning and sustainability policy.

Conclusion

Judging by its first few years, it is clear that the basic concepts behind the Urban Sustainability Accelerator program are sound and that the program can provide a framework for integrating the intellectual resources of the university with the experience of practitioners in the community in ways that accelerate the implementation of sustainability plans and policies while enriching the educational experience of students.

In the course of the 21st century, sustainability will inevitably continue to evolve from a narrow academic and policy specialty to a source of daily concern for all citizens living in cities. Offering and sharing skills, expertise, and examples of success in creating and operating sustainable cities may provide an ever more important ingredient for success in the transition to urban sustainability, hope, optimism and a sense of community.

---

7 For example, a search of MIT's catalog of courses in urban studies & planning showed only four or five courses that focused on plan or policy implementation (generously defined) out of nearly 200 courses. A search of articles in the Transportation Research Board's journal, *Transportation Research Record*, revealed only a handful of the hundreds of articles since 1996 focused on transportation plan implementation.

References

Dill, J., Ozawa, C., & Seltzer, E. "The Innovative Cities Institute (ICI) at Portland State University." Executive summary of an unpublished grant proposal to The Summit Foundation. July, 2012. Portland State University.

11

Higher education as a driver for urban sustainability outcomes

The role of Portland State University Institute for Sustainable Solutions

Fletcher D. Beaudoin and Jacob D.B. Sherman

Introduction: urban sustainability and the university

Urbanization is a defining characteristic of the 21st century; today, more than 50% of the world's population lives in cities (World Urbanization Prospectus, 2014), which is a remarkable transformation from how humanity lived only a couple of generations ago. The quest for urban sustainability is based on the premise that the benefits of this migration to the city can be harnessed to create a more just society that functions within the world's natural limits, while also finding ways to address and ameliorate the challenges that urbanization has simultaneously introduced. Achieving this vision for urban sustainability is a complex task that will likely require a major social and political transformation, ushering in new levels of infrastructure investments for energy efficiency, affordable housing, and transit expansion; innovative policies that shift major parts of the economy to incorporate sustainable practices; and, among other things, the development of a dynamic and collaborative workforce that can manage complexity. Together, these shifts will require a deeper understanding of how our cities operate; their level of resilience in the face of disaster; the impacts and opportunities they create; the role that technology can play in ushering about new efficiencies; and, how to create a more equitable society in which all can participate and prosper (Policy Link, 2014).

While research is undoubtedly needed to investigate these important questions, knowledge generation alone is not enough. As fundamental questions arise around higher education's value within society, there is an opportunity for universities to play a greater role in enhancing the collective understanding about urban sustainability—generating new knowledge while ensuring that research is connected to the very creation of sustainability policies and programs that address the challenges that cities actually face. This chapter explores this pursuit in depth, looking at not only how universities can take into account advancing research and student learning, but also the "sustainability outcomes" that can result from their teaching, research, and community engagement activities (Melnick, 2015). A sustainability outcome refers to when "a sustainability problem has been reduced, eliminated, or deflected by applying a research-based, practical solution" (Melnick, 2015). It is important to note that sustainability outcomes exist on a continuum, wherein there may be:

1. An immediate impact (s) of applying a solution

2. An intermediate effect of a refined and reapplied solution over time, and

3. A lasting effect, where decision-makers, decision influences and those effected better understand the sustainability problem, solution, and change their perspective and behavior (Melnick 2015)

Significant discussion and experimentation is taking place to identify student and faculty activities that can produce sustainability outcomes. "Solutions-oriented learning" is one of these approaches, where the learning arena is designed for students to engage in "learning while transforming" (Wiek *et al.*, 2015). This approach allows student learning and development to be balanced with the goal of producing products and processes that can have a lasting effect for the project partner (Wiek *et al.*, 2015). This type of learning exposes students directly to the specific challenges being faced by sustainability implementers, providing them with the experiences needed to develop critical communication, problem solving, and collaboration skills. It also provides the practitioners with more time and energy (from students and faculty) to support progress on their sustainability challenge. Therefore, solutions-oriented learning offers a useful framework for thinking about how curricular and co-curricular experiential learning activities can be designed and implemented to have significant benefits for both the students and the community. Special consideration should also be given to how multiple student experiences (such as internships, student research, and service-learning courses) can be sequenced over time, resulting in both deepened student learning and personal growth, and increased opportunities for sustainability outcomes in the community (Vygotsky, 1978). Providing students with access to a diverse set of sustainability experiences also increases their capacity to make meaningful progress on "complex sustainability challenges" during their time at the university and in their post graduation lives and careers (Allen *et al.*, 2014).

Research plays a major role in advancing sustainability outcomes. The "transformative sustainability research" framework aims to produce scientifically rigorous scholarship that results in "actionable knowledge" that can be applied to "transformational action" on sustainability challenges (Lang *et al.*, 2016). Similar to solutions-oriented learning, this type of research values the sustainability outcomes of the project in the community at a similar level as the university outcomes; outcomes such as student learning, student development and training, research grants, and published papers. Admittedly, transformative sustainability research and solutions-oriented learning are not easy. Teaching and research projects that aim to produce sustainability outcomes are often more complex to design and implement; as a result, "adequate institutional structures" must be put in place to support the unique demands of these endeavors (Wiek *et al.*, 2013). Furthermore, for universities to launch academic and research programs that produce sustainability outcomes they must adapt existing institutional structures and approaches —or launch new, innovative ones—that can support long-term and thriving partnerships between important community and university stakeholders.

Building and maintaining a supportive ecosystem within universities that can produce teaching and research programs that create sustainability outcomes is a complex task. One emergent approach for effectively managing this complexity is exemplified by an organization at Portland State University—the Institute for Sustainable Solutions (ISS). There are two important concepts from the literature that help conceptualize the role played by ISS:

1. The boundary organization, and

2. The transacademic interface manager (TIM) (Brundiers *et al.*, 2013)

Boundary organizations manage the ongoing exchange between science and policy and also serve to broker knowledge between scientists and decision makers. (Lemos *et al.*, 2014). ISS has many similarities to a boundary organization, but it exists within the university–community context. As such, ISS has a central aim of building robust partnerships and programs between the university and community stakeholders that can lead to productive projects and outcomes for both sides. Complementing the idea of a boundary organization, significant work has been done to understand the individual role and functions of people who broker community-university sustainability projects that are aimed at producing sustainability outcomes. According to the literature, this individual, also known as TIM, exists within the university and has the task of designing, managing and evaluating the community-university partnerships as they relate to individual projects (Brundiers *et al.*, 2013). By building and maintaining strong communication and collaboration channels, the TIM enables university faculty and students and community stakeholders to focus the bulk of their time energy on executing the goals of the project, which in turn helps increase the usability and success of the project outputs. The

Portland State University (PSU) Institute for Sustainable Solutions (ISS) brings the boundary organization and TIM concepts together, making it composed of multiple TIMs working in unison to build sustainability programs and partnerships that are designed to produce sustainability outcome-oriented projects. Multiple TIMs working together creates added capacity that allows for ISS to operate major programs that support and guide projects. Moving from the project level to the program level offers a variety of benefits. For example, a programmatic approach enables synergies to be identified (and captured) across multiple individual projects, fostering more comprehensive and impactful communication and development campaigns, and developing closer relationships with partners over time. In addition, the programmatic focus helps ISS look at project opportunities within the context of major sustainability challenges in order to identify which projects have the highest likelihood to lead to strong sustainability outcomes at the university and in the community.

This chapter examines the ISS in Portland, Oregon, USA, as a case study of an organization within PSU that supports innovative university programs that deliver on sustainability outcomes. This chapter examines two of these programs at PSU, the Sustainable Neighborhoods Initiative (SNI) and the Portland Climate Action Collaborative (PCAC), and focuses on their programmatic work with community partners to advance the university's teaching and research agendas while also delivering positive sustainability outcomes in the community. In demonstrating how PSU leverages its resources to advance urban sustainability, this chapter outlines the design, success, and challenges that these sustainability programs face, and it places a particular focus on the unique roles played by the ISS in supporting outcome-oriented community–university collaborations.

Growing a community–university broker for sustainability: the Institute for Sustainable Solutions

As detailed by Allen and Ervin in Chapter 1 of this volume, Portland State University's orientation to sustainability has been building for many years and ISS (formerly the Center for Sustainable Processes and Practices) has been at the forefront of this movement since its inception. In 2006, the Center for Sustainable Processes and Practices (CSP2) was formed in response to student and faculty interest in sustainability topics with the intention of providing support for interdisciplinary sustainability education and research. From the start, CSP2—renamed the Institute for Sustainable Solutions (ISS) in 2012—focused its limited resources on fostering interdisciplinary research and teaching and engaging with community partners interested in sustainability issues. In 2008, the James F. and Marion L. Miller Foundation approached the university about making a ten-year, $25 million (USD) investment in PSU to build its capacity to serve the community. PSU's leadership proposed that this investment be made in the university's sustainability programs because this thematic area had already successfully engaged faculty across the university, had a track record of meaningful community engagement, and offered an opportunity to model transformative change within the institution. The Miller Foundation was receptive, and made the $25M award in 2008. This investment—the largest philanthropic gift in PSU's history—is administered by ISS, and much of the early focus was to use the money to build out PSU's capacity to provide exceptional, cutting-edge student and faculty sustainability programs. Over time, these early investments catalyzed significant growth in the sustainability movement at PSU; examples include multiple interdisciplinary faculty receiving successful research and education grants for sustainability topic areas, the development of new student programs for students interested in sustainability topics, and attracting competitive faculty to come to PSU. These investments grew ISS's relationships with, and understanding of, the PSU sustainability community, and also helped establish expertise and reputation as an effective internal grant maker.

As the activity within the PSU sustainability community increased, ISS also began to invest in its own capacity to deliver programs focused on better leveraging and connecting the resources and expertise at PSU to foster sustainability outcomes in the region. Within these programs, ISS pursued internal and external strategies to develop effective programs. Internally, ISS focused on creating collaborations across interdisciplinary teams of students and faculty; externally, ISS aimed to leverage the expertise and capacity of the university to respond to community-identified sustainability needs held by local businesses, non-governmental organizations, and governments agencies. Through these experiences, ISS has developed a core set of functions and capacities, which allowed the unit to operate programs that enhance the student and faculty experience, and facilitate sustainability outcomes in the community. ISS core functions include:

- **Designing projects to deliver strong, mutually identified outcomes**: Catalyzing a connection or conversation between stakeholders about a collaborative project. Facilitating processes to ensure that both parties agree on project scope and outcomes, and recognize mutual value in the project before codifying stakeholder commitments in written form.

- **Storytelling**: Growing broader awareness for the sustainability project and the program, as a means of celebrating success and creating awareness that allows for new partnerships or resources to form.

- **Clear collaboration channels and problem solving**: Ongoing high-level project management to ensure progress on project outcomes, strong communication, and to serve as a third party to help resolve any conflicts.

- **Leveraging new resources**: Identifying financial and human resources that could expand and deepen the impact of a given project or program.

- **Assessment for continuous improvement**: Designing and implementing assessment frameworks to understand the research or student learning outcomes, as well as the impact within the community. Assessment is essential for communicating a program's impact and identifying places where processes can be improved for future projects.

- **Bridging between project phases**: Creating pathways and structures that allow individual projects to complete one phase while working with stakeholders to plan and be ready for implementation in its next phase.

ISS is made up of program managers that work on research, curricular, or extra curricular programs, communications specialists, development personnel, assessment staff and researchers. As a result, some staff have more expertise over certain skillsets or topical areas than others, but this does not mean that these functions exist in silos. In fact, ISS programs are built with the intention to facilitate the integration of multiple staff functions. For example, an individual project could have a project manager who takes the lead on "designing for strong, mutually identified, outcomes" and "clear collaboration channels and problem solving," but they also have some expertise in "storytelling" and "assessment and continuous improvement," meaning that they stay attuned to opportunities for integrating additional functions into the project along the way. The capacity to integrate multiple functions into a single project allows ISS to operate as an ecosystem of support, bringing together a unique set of resources that, together, can greatly expand an individual project's impact. It is important to note that this integrative capacity is something that ISS exhibits currently in some of its programs, but that there is significant room for continued learning and growth, both as it relates to staff abilities to design and implement integrated programs, as well as improving institutional systems to make this work more feasible.

Programmatic examples: modeling what is possible

The following sections highlight two of these integrated programs, the Sustainable Neighborhoods Initiative and the Portland Climate Action Collaborative, which exemplify how ISS functions to leverage the assets of the university and works with community partners to make progress on urban sustainability challenges in the region. In framing these two examples, it is important to note that there are many programs at Portland State University that facilitate strong student experiences and community impacts in the region; these range from internships to consulting contracts to classes working on service-learning projects, and more. However, many of these engagements have the primary goal of enriching student learning, conducting academic research, or publishing scholarly work, and a secondary goal of facilitating positive change in the community. In the authors' perspective, universities expend a significant amount of human capital to build strong educational and research experiences, yet little work is underway to construct these university endeavors in a way that also produces impact in the world. The current value placed on teaching and research greatly limits the potential impact of sustainability research and education advancing sustainability outcomes in the community. In contrast, the intent behind the ISS programs mentioned here are to render a balance between university and community goals from the start, meaning that not all community–university projects will fit into that criteria, and the ones that do, may require more time and energy in the design and implementation processes.

The programs highlighted below offer specific approaches for how to balance student experiences and faculty research goals with community-identified needs. When considering these cases, it is important to recall the sustainability outcomes spectrum outlined at the beginning of this chapter (Melnick, 2015). The program examples discussed are particularly focused on making immediate impacts and having intermediate effects, which are the first two phases in the sustainability outcome spectrum. To date, the Portland Climate Action Collaborative and the Sustainable Neighborhoods Initiative have yet to result in a lasting effect, which is the third phase in the spectrum and is an aspirational goal for the programs. The following sections' examples will outline the history and trajectory of the programs, their core elements, and preliminary impacts occurring in the community and at the university. Finally, both programmatic examples will discuss the role of ISS in supporting teaching and research projects that can enhance the academic and scholarly experience for students and faculty, while also facilitating sustainability outcomes in the community.

Portland climate action collaborative

In 1993, the city of Portland was the first U.S. city to develop a local action plan for cutting carbon (Climate Action Plan 2016) and has since been recognized a national leader in climate action (Portland Mayor Charlie Hales 2015). Over the last decade, PSU has also become a leader in climate action (Williams 2013). As Oregon's largest urban research university, there has been a long history of partnership between PSU and the city of Portland's Bureau of Planning and Sustainability (BPS), with deep collaborations between the city and a variety of university centers, institutes and departments, involving capstone classes, internships, guest speakers and more. In 2013, there were many discussions between BPS and ISS about the existing partnership channels and both parties developed a shared vision to create a focused collaboration aimed at advancing the goals of the city and county's joint Climate Action Plan. Together, this served as the genesis of the Portland Climate Action Collaborative (PCAC), which was formally launched after ISS received a grant from the Bullitt Foundation in late 2013. With matching resources from the James F. Marion Miller Foundation's gift to PSU, this grant provided funding to develop a partnership framework and support an initial round of research projects under the banner of the Portland Climate Action Collaborative.

Through PCAC, the Bureau of Planning and Sustainability identifies potential research needs connected with the city's Climate Action Plan, as well as staff leads willing to work on each potential project. Once a need is identified, ISS reviews the proposed project materials and serves to catalyze a project connection, identifying relevant students or faculty experts at the university and then facilitating initial meetings between city staff and PSU researchers. These initial meetings are based on a co-developed set of principles (see Table 11.1) to ensure projects deliver mutual value to both parties.

Table 11.1 Shared principles that guide the Portland Climate Action Collaborative
Source: F. Beaudoin

Principles of PSU–BPS climate action collaborative
These projects require active engagement between PSU researchers and BPS staff. The principles are intended to create exigency for both partners to participate. The process requires upfront work where project scope, outcomes and outputs emerge through collaborative discussions between major stakeholders.
· Overlapping research need and interest between BPS and PSU: ISS works with BPS to develop a list of needs, and matches that with PSU resources.
· Project helps achieve goals/inform decision making around the Climate Action Plan.
· Project deliverable is immediately applicable and relevant to the city.
· Projects are co-developed between PSU and BPS: Partners work together in planning stages to create the project.

These principles guide a process where BPS staff and PSU faculty researchers co-develop a proposal, which is then reviewed by BPS leadership and ISS staff to ensure the proposal meets the criteria and determine whether or not it is funded. Once a project is funded, ISS works with BPS leadership to monitor progress and adaptively manage the projects to ensure the outputs are delivered. The city and ISS also meet quarterly to review new proposals, discuss the strategy for the program, and ensure projects are on track to deliver scholarly outputs and useful information for making progress on climate goals. As projects are completed or transition into a second phase, an assessment is conducted with the BPS staff lead and the faculty researcher(s) to better understand the impact of the projects on the university, the city, and on the overarching partnership. Any areas for improvement are also identified. Throughout the life of a project, ISS and BPS also work with their respective communications teams to highlight results and share broader findings with interested stakeholders, including the public.

In 2015, there were eight active projects as part of the Portland Climate Action Collaborative. One project from PCAC has focused on urban heat island effects and air quality hot-spot mapping across the city—developing an online map that identifies the hottest places with the worst air quality around the city. This project has resulted in manuscript submissions, grant proposals, stories in the local press, and it also produced a heat island "hot spot" map which was included in the latest revision of the city and county's joint Climate Action Plan (City of Portland and Multnomah County, Climate Action Plan 2015). This individual project is now entering a second phase in 2016, where researchers will take the mapping data and create an interactive online platform for city staff and citizens to use in order to understand heat island and pollution issues at a more localized scale. The aim of this second phase is to empower local communities to use these data to organize around the major strategies needed to combat heat island and air quality risks.[1]

This example highlights how an applied research project contributes to the university's scholarly agenda, while at the same time balancing community needs and perspectives so the research has a high likelihood to have a sustainability outcome. This project therefore demonstrates an initial impact by providing information that is included in a major city policy document and creating an online portal that can be used for better city and community planning. However, this is merely a first step. In order to achieve lasting sustainability outcomes, it would first be necessary to determine the support that communities need to engage with the tool successfully. Other key factors to achieving intermediate and lasting effects will revolve around how the tool will be perceived by city decision-makers, as well as determining the systems for updating the information over time so the online platform can be an ongoing reliable source of data. Achieving the first milestone—of creating a usable and community-informed tool—is a vital step toward these broader goals, but not an end unto itself. Therefore, it is critical that a broader vision is considered at the start of the project—even if project goals could not be fully accomplished in its first phase—in order to make sure that the initial success is framed within the context of the larger sustainability outcomes that need to be achieved.

ISS's functions within the Portland Climate Action Collaborative

ISS has been successful using PCAC to communicate a robust institutional relationship to others at the university and to external partners and funders, making a strong case for supporting participation, catalytic grants, and the administration of the PCAC. In addition, the program's overarching framework has been used to acquire other resources to support the collaboration. For example, in 2015, when ISS received a grant to support sustainability internships from the PSU Bookstore, this resource was directed to PCAC and aimed at advancing climate adaptation and

---

1 More details about the full set of projects can be found at https://www.pdx.edu/sustainability/portland-climate-action-collaborative

mitigation "projects" in the City of Portland and Multnomah County. PCAC has also been a platform for storytelling, specifically as it relates to individual research projects. PCAC's "Local Food Economy" research project got significant attention from multiple news outlets, which resulted in broader awareness of findings, follow-up conversations about replicating the study, and positive press for the university.

ISS's roles in bridging project phases, executing project management and also engaging in program assessment have also been critical to ongoing success. As mentioned in the heat island example, above, ISS has helped bridge the project from one phase to the next, not only supporting the design of a future phase, but also providing financial resources to invest immediately in the implementation of that next phase of work. This "function" helps ensure that momentum on the project is maintained and that there is little turnover within the community partner and university team; maintaining momentum and focus are important factors in producing sustainability outcomes.

Assessment is important to ensure continuous improvement. PCAC's proposal process has evolved over time due to early feedback from project participants and initial project evaluations. Findings from early assessment identified the need for there to be one strong lead from BPS and from the university to ensure there was clarity about responsibility and communications channels. As a result, programmatic changes were made. Now, individuals from both parties serve as the primary point people for the ISS project manager to engage with, schedule major project meetings, and to help diagnose and resolve any collaboration issues that may arise.

Sustainable Neighborhoods Initiative

In 2009, Portland's mayor created the non-profit Portland Oregon Sustainability Institute (POSI) to ensure that the city's sustainability efforts remained at the cutting edge of the field. POSI created and launched the EcoDistrict protocol, which was a process for multi-sector stakeholder engagement to inform the development of rigorous plans and quantifiable metrics to advance sustainability at the neighborhood scale (EcoDistricts Protocol 2016). Stakeholders from across the city were convened to develop a framework for EcoDistrict planning, and five pilot Ecodistricts were launched in different areas of Portland. Together, this effort built significant capacity for collaborative sustainability planning in the five pilot districts, and inspired the creation of other informal EcoDistricts within Portland. During this formative phase between 2009 and 2012, PSU staff and faculty were involved in research, applied teaching and research projects, and planning around Portland's pilot EcoDistricts. In 2013, POSI changed its name to EcoDistricts and refocused its efforts nationally, where it is now "propelling a model of urban regeneration that ensures just, sustainable, and resilient neighborhoods for all" (EcoDistricts About 2016).

PSU's early engagement with EcoDistricts laid the foundation for the development and launch of the Sustainable Neighborhoods Initiative (SNI), which connects PSU students and faculty with groups of community organizations in long-term partnerships that advance sustainability at the neighborhood scale. The SNI is testing a model for how long-term, place-based community–university partnerships could be leveraged for community impact over time, while also enhancing student learning (Holliday *et al.*, 2016). The program is designed to deliver cumulative sustainability impacts, bridging single-term projects into clusters of projects that engage students from various classes, over multiple terms, in order to make measureable progress on sustainability issues identified by community partners. The SNI provides rich learning and research opportunities that engage students in addressing real-world sustainability issues, while adding capacity to help local organizations advance their projects and initiatives (Sustainable Neighborhoods Initiative 2016).

Through the SNI, ISS currently focuses research and engagement efforts on four long-term, place-based partnerships with different non-profit organizations and city agencies that are working to make progress on neighborhood-scale sustainability efforts around the city (Holliday *et al.*, 2016). Figure 11.1, below, visually depicts how ISS and one partner, Living Cully, are connected through the SNI.

Figure 11.1 Illustration of how PSU and one community partner (the Living Cully Ecodistrict, a collection of four non-profit organizations working on sustainability in a single Portland neighborhood) are connected through the ISS's Sustainable Neighborhood Initiative

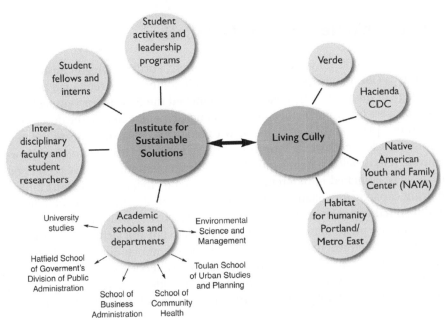

In developing these partnerships, ISS first works closely with community organizations to identify important neighborhood challenges. Next, ISS staff methodically connect faculty experts and motivated students with these partners to co-develop research and applied projects that are designed to not only meet community needs, but also enhance the student experience (Holliday *et al.*, 2016). As Holiday *et al.* explain:

> To ensure these partnerships benefit both the community and faculty and students at the University, ISS staff function as a broker between all parties, working closely with SNI partners to first identify important neighborhood challenges that the University might be able to support through research and applied projects (Brundiers 2013). After understanding local priorities, ISS staff then return to the University and approach faculty who may have research interests that align with community questions, or will be teaching courses that could serve as a platform for community-based learning projects. Increasingly, ISS staff also seek out opportunities to deliver on community-identified needs by connecting with PSU staff who administer student leadership programs, pitching projects directly to student groups, or creating internships or fellowships where students can work one-on-one or in small groups with SNI partners outside the classroom (Holliday 2016).

A core strategy associated with SNI is to create signature projects with partners each year. Signature projects represent sustained engagement from partners, students, and faculty on a single project over several academic terms. ISS plays a critical role in fostering signature projects by sequencing the university's engagement through multiple courses, different faculty, and new groups of students over time. This strategy allows for project success to be built on over time, offers students and faculty greater depth of investigation, and, ultimately, results in collections of projects that, when added up, result in initial sustainability impacts. One example of a signature project is the SoMa parklet project where a course from the School of Architecture was partnered with the South of Market (SoMa) EcoDistrict to design a small park in front of popular food carts near campus. The project achieved the community partner goals for place-making and green building, offered architecture students the opportunity to apply sustainable design principles in an urban setting, and allowed the professor to engage in service through her teaching. The partners were enthusiastic about the project, and sought to advance it toward implementation with help from ISS, the professor, and another architecture class. At the onset of the next course, students were tasked with designing a parklet that would actually be built, requiring them to focus not only on making elegant digital renderings but also on grappling with the added complexity of material costs and the city's design and permitting process too. After the city approved the project, SoMa and a team of PSU students, faculty, and ISS staff worked closely with the PSU Foundation to complete a crowd-funding campaign that successfully raised more than $15,000 for permits and building materials. With the resources and approvals needed to advance the project, another architecture class then finalized the designs and built the parklet for the larger neighborhood to enjoy. ISS coordinated media outreach for the project, resulting in coverage from Portland's major newspapers, the evening news, radio, and more. With ISS maintaining continuity throughout every stage of the process, an emergent idea was able to flourish, growing over time into a rich and comprehensive project with a tangible outcome in the community. Looking forward, signature projects will be a used as central design principle when launching new projects in the hopes of creating additional opportunities that can serve as powerful platforms for faculty research, student learning, and positive change in the community.

ISS's functions within the SNI

As mentioned above, the SNI has focused on cultivating signature projects that bridge from one course-based engagement to the next. One of the structures that has supported this connection across terms is the ISS Sustainability Fellows program. This program works with an existing SNI class to identify one or two talented students who want to receive support to continue working on their project after the course ends; this provides a valuable opportunity for the student to continue to deepen their knowledge of the project and also a key resource for continuing momentum on the project. ISS tracks the evolution of these extra-curricular projects and identifies future opportunities where the student project can then re-integrate to new engagements with future faculty, classes, and students. This level of coordination is made possible by having an individual within ISS who is tracking class projects, managing the communication flow, and looking for talented students and solid projects that, if continued, could result in sustainability outcomes in the community. Another factor that supports the success of this program is the project scoping document. When initiating a project, ISS staff, community partners, and the faculty collaboratively complete this form to outline the proposed project, desired outcomes, and critical background information about the partner. This scoping document not only describes the specific project to students who might work on it, but it also helps frame out the vision and long-term aims of the partner—information that can be used to identify future project phases.

Another mechanism for bridging the term has been to develop clear agreements or memoranda of understanding (MoUs) with SNI partners. These documents play an important role in helping define the complex challenges facing the community, and articulate how the university and community can work together to make measurable progress on sustainability goals. In this way, the MoU provides a platform for proactively framing the scope of work for the larger partnership, and subsequently allows ISS to map out the opportunities where it can pull together different university resources—service-learning courses, faculty experts, student research, internships, and student groups—to effectively meet the partner's needs. This MoU is also helpful for building principles for clear communication and collaboration that the ISS and the partner organization can refer to throughout the partnership cycle. In addition, this document can serve as a platform for identifying processes for joint story telling and also for leveraging additional resources to support the overarching partnership structure. A future area of focus will be to identify how to use these MoUs as a means for assessing the partnership's progress overtime.

Finally, ISS has also developed an assessment process with the SNI program to better understand its impact and to improve the program. An aggregate of the 2014–15 assessment data concluded that 91% of PSU faculty engaged in the SNI agreed or strongly agreed that "the SNI provides more benefits compared to traditional partnerships at PSU" (SNI End of Year, 2015). Traditional partnerships refer to engagements where the faculty member is responsible for facilitating all aspects of a community–university partnership, including locating partners, scoping projects, defining deliverables, managing students working on the project, tracking outcomes, and more. This is a critical piece of information that shows PSU faculty value the role that ISS plays through the SNI.

Expanding the impact

The Sustainable Neighborhoods Initiative (SNI) and Portland Climate Action Collaborative (PCAC) provide insights about what is possible when universities design programs and partnerships that aim to deliver both academic and scholarly value, as well as positive outcomes to the community. In 2014–15, the SNI partnered with 34 faculty teaching 44 courses that engaged nearly 800 students on applied teaching and research projects around neighborhood sustainability. During this time, SNI also supported ten ISS Student Sustainability Fellows who continued working on their projects over time. These student fellows experienced additional professional development opportunities through grant submissions and the development of two academic papers, and they provided significant additional capacity to sustainability projects that community partners were advancing. Meanwhile, during the 2015–16 academic year, PCAC engaged 22 faculty and eight student researchers, and it supports a paid internship program where almost one dozen PSU students are working with a variety of community organizations and the city to address climate mitigation and adaptation challenges in historically under-represented communities.

The current scale of student and faculty engagement, described above, has had an initial impact on urban sustainability in Portland, but this impact is very limited when considering the full capacity of the university. So far these engagements only add up to a small fraction of the more than 1,700 research and instructional faculty at PSU, and the more than 28,000 students attending the university (PSU Profile, 2015). For PSU to play a major role in advancing urban sustainability in Portland, it must engage a much larger portion of the faculty and students at PSU in programs directly addressing our society's complex sustainability challenges. In addition, there will need to be a greater number of community partners that also engage in these types of collaborations to interact with the expanded base of faculty and student interest.

As noted elsewhere throughout this chapter, ISS has focused on building programs that are designed to balance the development of community sustainability outcomes with the university's academic and scholarly agenda; however, this work is taking place within academia which does not place a high value on the production of sustainability outcomes. On the other hand, community partners are also vital to the success of programs like SNI and PCAC, but they do not always place a high value on the research agendas and student learning outcomes that are highly regarded within the university. Therefore, at this stage, ISS not only serves as a translator and a connector for community–university projects, but also spends a great deal of time and energy adapting the internal and external systems so that the university can place a greater value on the sustainability outcomes while it also encourages external partners to place a higher value on the research and student learning outputs. The following section discusses some of these institutional shifts, identifies known challenges, and hypothesizes potential solutions to better promote sustainability outcomes in the world. While some of these challenges may be specific to PSU, others are generalizable to universities working to advance sustainability on their own campus and in their communities.

1. Placing a high value on the broker

Essential to any partnership is the ability to find common interest between parties, define a focus for the partnership, and then embark upon the work together in a way that creates value for each stakeholder. In most partnerships, these responsibilities are traditionally taken on by either an individual faculty member or a community partner, rather than relying on a third party that might hold an understanding of both partners to broker the relationship and assist with the formulation and implementation of teaching and research projects. As described earlier in this chapter, there are a multitude of benefits that ISS offers PSU, but despite their benefits, boundary organizations and TIMs are not common within higher education, more generally. Where this role does exist, the functions (see above) are stretched thin and sometimes not intact at all (due to limited resources or a broad area of focus). Without an investment in the type of integrated ecosystem that ISS offers, it might be possible for an individual to achieve positive outcomes within the university and in the community, but it becomes very difficult to sustain that work over time and also to ensure those outcomes are lasting and institutionalized.

Making the case to invest in an organization like ISS can be challenging. This challenge likely results from the perception that this role requires significant resources and/or because it is new and not fully understood within higher education or the community. Building the case for this role can start by making sure the language used to describe it is clear and supported by examples; this chapter provides some concrete information about how ISS functions and provides examples of similar entities identified in the literature. The functions themselves, and the language to describe them, can be adapted to build a strong value proposition that speaks to the unique needs and context of different higher education institutions committed to achieving sustainability outcomes in their communities. One way to build momentum toward a unit like ISS is to start small by articulating the functions and value of this role within the project context (otherwise known as playing the role of a TIM). This provides the opportunity to demonstrate increased success and provide the value of this function. It is also important to leverage the voice of community partners to educate and influence decision-makers at key places in university leadership. Since community organizations stand to benefit significantly from the university's assistance on achieving sustainability outcomes, they can also be provocative voices for discussing the challenges experienced during some community–university partnership experiences, while also heralding the opportunities that a unit like ISS offers. Many community partners already acknowledge and appreciate ISS's function as a metaphorical "front door" for connecting with the university's depth and breadth of expertise around sustainability projects. However, for university–community collaborations for sustainability to reach their full potential this acknowledgement needs to evolve into a robust culture of support and investment for the role of the broker.

2. Organizing around the problem, not the quarter

When community projects and applied research are integrated into university curricula, academic constraints fundamentally shape the nature of how community–university projects are designed and implemented. This stems from the fact that, traditionally, the primary outcome of these projects is to support students in honing their skills and engaging in a learning endeavor. For the most part universities tend to run on the quarter or semester systems—10- or 15-week spurts of activity followed by finals and then a short break before jumping into the next term. The academic calendar is a engrained timeline within the university, providing a clear structure for when students register, when grades are delivered, when faculty do or do not teach specific courses, and this structure also has implications for how faculty organize their research agendas. The pulse and flow of universities are defined by these periods of time, but society's complex sustainability challenges rarely conform to the relative neatness of the academic calendar. Therefore, a major challenge is how to create a wide array of opportunities for bridging projects across the ebb and flow of the academic calendar in a way that allows momentum and focus on a project to be maintained over time.

As referenced when discussing the Sustainable Neighborhoods Initiative, above, an important mechanism for continuing projects over time has been to offer flexible opportunities for students to continue their project through a post-course, paid fellowship program. Structures like this can better allow the university to respond to challenges in the community by creating strong professional development opportunities for talented students who have a strong likelihood to continue to advance the project toward sustainability outcomes. Furthermore, the ISS Student Sustainability Fellows program has provided additional capacity to partners that has helped underwrite and incentivize their participation in future class projects because they know there is a strong likelihood that a student fellow may be able to continue to work with them on a project after a course ends. This mechanism has proven to be valuable, but it only exists because of ISS's access to limited financial resources to incentivize participation from the students. In order to scale and sustain programs like this, ISS must evaluate the potential for adapting existing mechanisms like independent studies, for-credit internships, or multi-term workshops to serve as platforms for continuing projects that first initiate in a class.

Another shift that could better advance sustainability outcomes has to do with better promoting an understanding of the university's academic cycles with community partners. Community partners operate on much different timelines and are often responding to critical and timely issues. Furthermore, since they are not within the university system they do not track the milestones that signal important moments in the academic year, such as midterms, dead-week, finals, or winter and spring break. This can cause challenges with aligning the course cycle with partner timelines, as well as with faculty-community research collaborations because faculty breaks also tend to follow the course timetables. Developing a deeper understanding of the university timeline within key community partners is an important shift that could support better project design and communication and collaboration channels. One strategy to consider is to engage long-term community partners as instructors or co-instructors in courses. This activity would provide direct experience for the partner about the timelines and dynamics of a course, which has the dual benefit of growing their appreciation of the student learning process and also deepening their understanding of the ebb and flow of the academic calendar. The co-teaching model is particularly interesting because it provides a venue for the community partner to bring their own timelines into the course, influencing the faculty member's understanding of the timelines and unique dynamics within the practitioner world. The shifts discussed in this section offer useful tools that ISS could leverage to deepen community–university projects and to open up new collaborative possibilities to expand partnerships for greater sustainability outcomes in the world.

3. More easily crossing administrative and disciplinary boundaries

As noted by leading sustainability scholars, the complex sustainability challenges society faces require interdisciplinary approaches to establish lasting solutions (Orr, 2004; Cortese, 2003), Addressing complex societal challenges from a disciplinary lens may identify single-issue solutions, but these "solutions" might fail in the longer term to adequately grapple with the complex and systematic costs and benefits (and/or unanticipated consequences) associated with said solutions.

Therefore, positively impacting the sustainability of the city while also advancing scholarly pursuits for students and faculty requires the identification of mechanisms for building interdisciplinary faculty and student teams who can not only effectively collaborate with one another, but also with diverse partners as they grapple with complex societal challenges over time. Numerous faculty at PSU are already engaging in this type of work, where they are co-teaching classes with other disciplines, collaborating across colleges, and also engaging deeply with community; however, in many cases this type of work is done in spite of the barriers to interdisciplinary collaborations as opposed to work that is actively enabled by university structures.

ISS recognizes the importance of interdisciplinary teaching and research when it comes to investigating sustainability challenges or providing training on sustainability topics, and has invested in projects and programs that allow these types of collaborations to occur. Modest financial incentives have been key to this support, but these resources are limiting when looking at the full scale of need and opportunity. In considering a significant expansion of faculty engaged in interdisciplinary teaching and research, it is important to look beyond the resources held by ISS, and into the financial and political levers that exist within the broader institution. At PSU, there are some incentives to support collaborations within individual colleges and departments, and fewer incentives for cross-college collaborations. In order to spark more interdisciplinary collaboration, university leadership and central administration could shift performance metrics and resources to incentivize cross-college project-based learning. This could foster new research and teaching relationships across faculty, providing new combinations of expertise that ISS could utilize when building community partnerships and offering students a greater quantity and spectrum of applied experiences. Team-teaching collaborations could also be a specific by-product of this prioritization of cross-campus collaboration. These courses offer ISS the opportunity to take on more complex projects due to the different faculty expertise and the diverse student body that a co-taught course attracts. Currently there are significant challenges to supporting co-taught courses. Financial and political support can be helpful for incentivizing more team-taught courses, but there is also a need to develop creative university mechanisms that allow these courses to be institutionalized within the university's curriculum. Interdisciplinary student and faculty teams offer a rich set of expertise to address sustainability challenges. Growing these connections expands the ISS's capacity to respond to community sustainability needs, and also creates a nurturing environment for attracting new faculty hires, many of which have a desire to be publicly engaged and possess a collaborative mindset.

Conclusion

Around the world, the migration to cities continues, shining a spotlight on the challenges that urban environments face on our rapidly changing planet. Higher education, in general, and urban-serving universities in particular, have a vital role to play in the urban sustainability movement; in making their campuses models for sustainable design and operation, delivering innovative training to the next generation of urban citizens, and conducting cutting-edge research on the challenges facing cities—and solutions to overcome them. Over 700 universities across the U.S. and North America are already taking up this charge (AASHE, 2016); and, similar to Portland State University (PSU), many universities that are also taking on the challenge to advance sustainability outcomes in urban communities.[2]

This chapter begins by considering the literature around a transacademic interface manager (TIM) and boundaries organizations as it frames out the role and function of the PSU Institute for Sustainable Solutions (ISS). This framing is used as a foundation for exploring the valuable role that the ISS plays in advancing partnerships and projects that can grow academic and scholarly agendas in the university and sustainability outcomes in the community. To articulate this role, two ISS programs are dissected: the Portland Climate Action Collaborative and the Sustainable Neighborhoods Initiative. This chapter also discusses some of the broader institutional shifts that, if made, could increase the impact that units like ISS could have within the university and in their surrounding community. Furthermore, ISS's programs have employed processes for uncovering and documenting lessons learned that may help accelerate progress in university–community partnerships; lessons that could also help inform the development of units like ISS in other institutions that are deepening their commitment to advance urban sustainability.

In conclusion, while making significant progress on urban sustainability in the Portland-metropolitan region is a major aim for PSU, this activity must also be coupled with efforts to inspire action beyond the region. Adequately addressing complex sustainability issues, such as climate change and its cascading effects, must require a movement of cities that catalyze and demand a new way of being. This chapter has attempted to show how urban universities can play an important role in resourcing and accelerating this movement through focused education, a persistent dialogue, and a growing set of inspiring and impactful models that work to advance a just society that functions within the limits of natural systems. As universities question their larger purpose in society, now—perhaps more than ever—it is vital for higher education to further explore its responsibility in making meaningful progress on the most complex sustainability challenges of the 21st century.

2 The authors would like to make note of significant efforts to advance sustainability outcomes at the University of British Columbia's Sustainability Institute; Arizona State University's Julie Ann Wrigley Global Institute for Sustainability; and New York University's Center for Urban Science and Progress, recognizing that this isn't an exhaustive list of activity in this space.

References

AASHE membership directory. (2016). Available from: http://www.aashe.org/membership/member-directory. [February 1, 2016]

Allen, J. Beaudoin, F., Lloyd-Pool, & E., Sherman, J. (2014). Pathways to Sustainability Careers: Building Capacity to Solve Complex Problems. *Sustainability.* 47-53

Brundiers, K., Wiek, A., & Kay, B. (2013). The Role of Transacademic Interface Managers in Transformational Sustainability Research and Education. *Sustainability.* 4,614-4,636 (City of Portland and Multnomah County, Climate Action Plan 2015)

City of Portland and Multnomah County, Climate Action Plan, (2015). *Climate Action Plan* https://www.portlandoregon.gov/bps/article/531984 Page 111. (Climate Action Plan 2016)

Climate Action Plan, A Better Way Forward. (2015). Available from: https://www.portlandoregon.gov/bps/49989. [January 26, 2016].

Cortese, A.D. (2003). The Critical Role of Higher Education in Creating a Sustainable Future. *Planning for Higher Education* 31 (3): 15–22.

EcoDistricts Protocol, (2016). Available from: http://ecodistricts.org/certification/protocol/. [January 26, 2016]. (EcoDistricts About 2016)

EcoDistricts About/Home, (2016). Available from: http://ecodistricts.org/about/. [January 26, 2016].

Holliday, M., DeFalco, T., & Sherman, J. (Forthcoming) Community–University Partnerships to Advance Authentic Neighborhood Sustainability. *Metropolitan Universities: Special Issue entitled Curricular Innovation: Engaged Capstones at Portland State University.* Volume 26.3

Lang, D.J., & Wiek, A. (2013). The role of universities in fostering urban and regional sustainability. In: Mieg, H.A., & Töpfer, K. (Eds.) (2012). *Institutional and Social Innovation for Sustainable Urban Development.* Earthscan: London, pp. 393-411.

Lemos, M., Kirchhhodd, C., Kalafatis, S., Scavia, D., & Rood, R. (2014). *Moving Climate Information off the Shelf: Boundary Chains and the role of RISAs as Adaptive Organizations.* American Meteorological Society. 273-285.

Melnick, R. (2015). *A Strategy for Scaling Sustainability Solutions: The Global Network for Sustainability Outcomes* (GCSO). 1-11

Orr, D. (2004). *Earth in Mind: On Education, Environment, and the Human Prospect.* Washington, DC: Island Press.

Policy Link About, (2014). *Mission-Statement.* http://www.policylink.org/about/mission-statement. [January 26, 2016].

Portland Mayor Charlie Hales Explains, (2015). Available from: http://voices.nationalgeographic.com/2015/10/29/portland-mayor-charlie-hales-explains-why-climate-action-is-about-both-planet-and-people/. [October 29, 2015].

Portland State University Institute for Sustainable Solutions, *SNI End of Year Report 2014-2015.* https://www.pdx.edu/sustainability/sites/www.pdx.edu.sustainability/files/SNI%20Report%202014-15_9.14.15.pdf. [October 10, 2016].

PSU Profile, *Snapshot of PSU*, (2015). https://www.pdx.edu/profile/snapshot-portland-state. [January 26, 2016].

Sustainable Neighborhoods Initiative, the right scale for impact, 2016 https://www.pdx.edu/sustainability/sustainable-neighborhoods. [January 26, 2016].

Vygotsky, L.S. (1978). *Mind in Society.* Cambridge, MA: Harvard University Press.

Wiek, A., & Kay, B. (2015). Learning while transforming: solutions-oriented learning for urban sustainability in Phoenix, Arizona. *Environmental Sustainability* 16:29-36

Wiek, A., Xiong, A., Brundiers, K., & Leeuw, S. (2013). Integrating problem- and project-based learning into sustainability programs: A case study on the School of Sustainability at Arizona State University. *International Journal of Sustainability and Higher Education.* Vol 14. No. 4. 431-449.

Williams, C. (2013, June 5th). *PSU receives national climate leadership award for innovation in sustainability.* https://www.pdx.edu/sustainability/news/psu-receives-national-climate-leadership-award-innovation-sustainability.

World Urbanization Prospectus, Highlights. 2014. http://esa.un.org/unpd/wup/Publications/Files/WUP2014-Highlights.pdf. 1-32.

Afterword

Jennifer H. Allen, David Ervin, B.D. Wortham-Galvin, and Jacob D.B. Sherman

As documented throughout this book, the development of PSU's sustainability programs and its community engagement in this context has been a process of ongoing learning and adaptation toward achieving our long-term aspiration to be a national leader in sustainability scholarship. While substantial progress has been made, challenges remain. Here we offer observations on the overarching lessons learned that emerge from the preceding chapters, in the hope that they may be useful to other institutions pursuing sustainability as an institutional priority. Many of these lessons also emerge in the case studies included in Volume II of this series, which will focus more specifically on relationships between the university and the community in furthering sustainability agendas.

It takes time. It took several years to lay the foundation among faculty, students and community partners that made it possible for PSU to articulate a shared long-term vision. It is important not to underestimate the time needed to build trust and social capital around such efforts. Similarly, it takes time and patience to establish trust and effective working relationships between faculty, students and community partners. However, the importance of taking the time to understand each others' priorities, interests, goals and culture cannot be underestimated.

Find and engage champions among faculty and staff. Key to the success of PSU's efforts to build its sustainability programs and to engage in meaningful ways with the community was the engagement of key faculty from a variety of departments who valued inter-disciplinarity and collaboration. The commitment of these faculty to working together across disciplinary lines and to taking the time to learn how to partner collaboratively with community members was essential to the success of sustainability initiatives. Similarly, the engagement of key university staff committed to sustainable practices laid the foundation for initiatives such as the Living Lab and other partnerships between academics and operations.

Give students responsibility and meaningful roles. PSU students have played a critical role since the beginning in advocating for sustainability efforts and in bringing energy and innovative ideas to the table. Offering mechanisms for student engagement and leadership can significantly leverage sustainability investments and ensure that sustainability programs are continually refreshed with new thinking and energy. Students are also able to provide a provocative voice to advocate for ideas staff and faculty may not be ready to champion, and they are extremely motivated to engage in problem-based opportunities that expose them to "real world" issues—an opportunity to enhance their learning as well as to contribute value to the community.

Top administrative support makes a big difference. PSU has benefited from the outset from a strong commitment to sustainability efforts, community-based learning, and engaged scholarship from university leadership, including the Provost, the Vice Provost for Graduate Studies and Research, and the President. While a sustainability effort could not succeed without faculty, student, and staff interest and investment, the importance of this high level validation played a critical role in allowing these efforts to move forward, even with what were at the time fairly limited resources.

Engage community partners early and in meaningful ways. From the beginning, the involvement of community members in research projects, strategic planning, and prioritization has enabled PSU to demonstrate the alignment between its work and community priorities, and allowed PSU to leverage resources to ensure projects would move forward. The track record that PSU had developed in terms of community engagement was one of the main reasons that the James F. and Marion L. Miller Foundation sought to invest in PSU's sustainability programs.

Demonstrate early success; winners beget more winners. During the start-up phase of developing PSU's sustainability programs, several activities received positive feedback from the administration, faculty, students and community partners; these are described in more detail in Chapter 1. These efforts helped establish a track record of innovation and success the encouraged ongoing investments of time and resources by all parties.

Target funding to projects that build core strategic areas of scholarship. There has been an ongoing tension between focusing resources on key areas in order to build institutional capacity and "peanut buttering" the resources too thinly across multiple areas. The Miller Foundation funding allowed PSU to invest in building capacity in key areas, including ecosystem services in urbanizing regions, urban sustainability, developing partnerships with the city of Portland on climate action issues, and brokering the development of community partnerships more broadly. Investing in laying a strong foundation in targeted areas that represent PSU's strengths has generally resulted in better outcomes over time. Only targeted investments can allow an institution to create a competitive niche in this rapidly expanding field.

Choose wicked problems that require the merging of tacit and explicit knowledge. Sustainability education and research is meant to tackle society's most complex problems. These "wicked" problems involve both known and uncertain feedback loops. As such, no definitive formulation, no stopping rules, and no true/false solutions exist (Rittel and Weber, 1973). Rather, wicked problems require interdisciplinary approaches and the engagement of community partners to combine frontier scientific and experiential knowledge, both explicit and tacit, in the search for constructive approaches, recognizing that adaptive management will be necessary to deal with uncertain forces and undesirable outcomes. Academia is the prime institution to foster and lead such approaches to finding solutions to society's vexing challenges that span environmental, social and economic realms.

Emphasize scholarship aspects to faculty. Because the concept of sustainability often raises issues of values and ethics, there can be concern among university communities regarding whether it constitutes an ideological agenda. Universities' unique contribution to this field is to bring the rigor of scholarship to the table, and emphasizing the scholarly aspects and opportunities in the field is critical to ensuring broad engagement of faculty

Stress problem solving to the community. PSU has a long-standing reputation for its community-based learning programs. Consistent with the approach of these programs, PSU's work with community partners has been most successful when joint work has responded to key needs and priorities in the community. As noted above, taking the time needed to understand these needs and priorities, and establish a foundation of trust with community members so that they understand their culture, priorities and needs are being taken into account is essential to successful partnerships.

Seek opportunities for public exposure. Universities in general are notorious for not publicizing their accomplishments to audiences outside of academia. The roots of this modesty likely extend back to the ethics and training of being a good scientist. In an emergent field such as sustainability science, humility is not a virtue—keeping the public and community partners informed of new initiatives and progress is imperative to build support for program growth, acquiring new resources, and to open the door to collaborative university-community partnerships.

Bridge the silos. Given the traditional disciplinary structure of universities, innovative administrative mechanisms and structures are needed to bridge these silos and to reward interdisciplinary scholarship and problem-based work. Similarly, having the capacity in the university to serve as a "broker" between faculty, students and community partners, and as steward of these partnerships over time, can significantly enhance the success of community-university partnerships. Targeting resources toward projects that bring groups of faculty together from multiple disciplines and that engage them and their students in co-production of knowledge with the community can send an important signal in this regard, as well as providing support for the development of social capital among faculty members and community partners.

Communicate, communicate, communicate. Communicating clearly and constantly is critical to fostering support for sustainability programs. This communication must be "two-way" in order to ensure that the good ideas that can come from anywhere are heard and reflected in institutional development. Communication is equally important whether resources are limited or substantial, in order to create an environment of trust, transparency and excitement.

Money is not the answer. While the receipt of the Miller Foundation gift raised PSU's sustainability programs and potential to a new level, the most important foundational elements for PSU's efforts were laid when resources were scarce and when faculty had to step out of their comfort zones without financial reward to make things happen. That the Miller Foundation made their gift to the sustainability programs in recognition of the investments of time and energy over the preceding eight years is a clear validation of these early efforts.

Many of the lessons highlighted here are relevant to the experiences showcased in Volume II of the Sustainable Solutions series: Community–University Partnerships. Volume II emphasizes methods, processes and outcomes for community-based projects with an eye toward physical, socio-economic and cultural agendas, as well as a focus on those people and systems left out of conventional approaches to sustainability.

PSU continues to glean lessons learned from its ongoing experience in advancing sustainability across campus and engaging in meaningful ways with community partners in the Portland region as well as nationally and internationally, and also seeks to learn from the experience of others. We hope this volume has offered some useful perspectives for others engaged in advancing this valuable work.

References

Rittel, H., & Webber, M. (1973). Dilemmas in a General Theory of Planning. *Policy Sciences,* 5, 155-169.

About the contributors

Editors

B.D. Wortham-Galvin, PhD, teaches studio, history and theory of architecture and urban design in the School of Architecture at Portland State University. Her research focuses on how theories of cultural sustainability and the everyday can be applied to the design and stewardship of an adaptable built environment. She is a Faculty Fellow with three PSU institutions: the Center for Public Interest Design, the Institute for Sustainable Solutions and BUILT (Building Science Lab to Advance Teaching), and she works with local and national communities on issues of equity and resilience in managing change in rural, suburban and urban places. The Daily Journal of Commerce named her one of Oregon's Women of Vision for 2015.

Jennifer H. Allen is Associate Professor of Public Administration in the Mark O. Hatfield School of Government and a Fellow at the Institute for Sustainable Solutions (ISS) at Portland State University. Her research focuses on sustainable economic development, collaborative approaches to reducing use of toxics and rural-urban connections. Jennifer served as the Director of ISS from 2012–2015 and has previously worked at the World Bank, Ecotrust and the Oregon Economic and Community Development Department. Jennifer holds a BA in American Studies from Yale University, a Master of Environmental Management from Yale School of Forestry and Environmental Studies and a PhD in Environmental Science and Public Policy from George Mason University.

Jacob Sherman is the Sustainability Curriculum Coordinator for the Institute for Sustainable Solutions at Portland State University. He leads many of the Institute's academic and student programs, which seek to use sustainability education and community-engagement to unleash higher education's ability to address society's complex problems. Jacob is co-editor of Sustainable Solutions (Greenleaf Publishing), and he previously worked for PSU's award-winning general education program, University Studies, to better integrate student research, engagement and creative activities into PSU's curriculum. Jacob holds a BA in English and a Master's Degree in Educational Leadership and Policy from Portland State University.

Contributors

Fletcher Beaudoin is the Assistant Director of Portland State University's Institute for Sustainable Solutions. He focuses on sustainability research, education and community engagement, working to build links between the PSU community and sustainability practitioners. He develops programs focused on scaling applied research and curriculum across the university, cultivates university-practitioner partnerships around topics of urban sustainability and ecosystem services and provides the day-to-day management of the Institute's activities and programs. He received his BA in English and Spanish from the University of Oregon and his Master's of Public Administration in Environmental Science and Policy and Energy Policy from Columbia University.

Darrell Brown, PhD, is the Les Fahey/KPMG Accounting Fellow in the School of Business Administration and a Fellow of the Institute for Sustainable Solutions at Portland State University. Holding a BS in forestry and a PhD in accounting, Dr Brown teaches and researches at the intersection of business sustainability and measurement. He teaches metrics for understanding the sustainability impacts of organizations and managerial and accounting systems classes. Current research interests include measurement issues related to organizational impacts on social and natural systems. He is interested in how organizational reporting practices influence sustainability-oriented behaviors, both internally and externally to the organization.

Heather Burns, EdD, is an Assistant Professor and Coordinator of the Leadership for Sustainability Education graduate program in the Educational Leadership and Policy department at Portland State University. She is also the PSU Coordinator of the Learning Gardens Laboratory, a garden-based education site. Dr Burns teaches courses on sustainability leadership, sustainability pedagogy, spiritual leadership and deep ecology. Her scholarship focuses primarily on teaching sustainability in higher education, including the roles of transformational learning, experiential learning, contemplative inquiry and community-based learning in creating sustainable change. Her work can be found in academic journals including the

Journal of Agriculture, Food Systems and Community Development, Journal of Sustainability Education, International Journal of Teaching and Learning in Higher Education and Teaching in Higher Education.

Monica Cuneo is the Health Equity Project Manager with the Institute for Sustainable Solutions. In this position she collaborates with PSU staff, faculty and community partners to develop projects that focus on addressing health equity in our region, convenes the Food is Hope, Food is Health Collaborative, a cross-sector group focused on developing food systems-based strategies to address the developmental origins of health and disease, and is developing an interdisciplinary graduate certificate in food systems. Monica holds a BA in Community Food Systems from The Evergreen State College and a Master of Public Health from Portland State University.

Alan DeLaTorre, PhD, is a Research Associate within the Institute on Aging at Portland State University. He has served as an instructor for undergraduate service-learning courses and graduate-level courses focused on gerontology in the Schools of Urban Studies and Planning and Community Health. His research has focused on age-friendly and sustainable communities and he aims to inform policy and practice in urban planning, development and other fields. Dr DeLaTorre has been involved in many community-based efforts since moving to Portland in 2002 and he currently serves as a Commissioner on the Portland Commission on Disability and as President of the Oregon Gerontological Association. He has been involved in the Age-Friendly Portland project since its inception on 2006 and is a current member of its Advisory Council and Chair of the Housing Committee.

Sally Eck is a radical, feminist activist. Her formal education includes bachelors in Sociology and Women's Studies, a Master's Degree in Education (emphasis on anti-racist and feminist pedagogies) and a certificate from the Social Justice Training Institute. She has been teaching at Portland State University for over fourteen years in Women's Studies, Social Justice Pedagogy and Service-Learning Courses, and as a social justice education consultant in Portland and nationally. She is also, most notably, independent Mama to twelve-year-old Isaac and ten-year-old Stella. She is committed to radicalizing education, recognizing the personal as political and co-creating a just and equitable world.

David Ervin is a Senior Research Faculty in the Institute for Sustainable Solutions and Professor Emeritus of Environmental Management and Economics at Portland State University. He was appointed the first Academic Sustainability Coordinator for Portland State in 2001. His current research program includes valuation of ecosystem services, managing the environmental effects of genetically engineered crops and factors affecting business sustainability. He has directed interdisciplinary research and education projects at universities, in government and with a non-profit think tank. His publications include multiple books and numerous articles from interdisciplinary investigations. He speaks to local, national and international audiences on sustainability topics.

J.R. "Jones" Estes, PhD, is Assistant Professor in University Studies and the Director of the Freshmen Year Experience in University Studies. Using a student-led curriculum model in her courses, Dr Estes focuses her students on solving difficult environmental and social problems, such as climate change and war/peace. A political ecologist, her research focuses on the intersection of the policy process, media and public participation in relation to the environment.

Todd Ferry is a Research Associate at the Center for Public Interest Design (CPID) within PSU's School of Architecture. He holds a BA in Philosophy from the University of Georgia and a Master of Architecture from the University of Texas at Austin. Before pursuing architecture, Todd worked for over a decade in the non-profit field leading him to seek opportunities to apply his skills as a designer toward public interest design efforts. To that end, he has been active in leading and participating in progressive design-build projects around the world. He is currently involved in many projects at the CPID, including a consultancy addressing the needs of underserved communities in Sacramento, design-build work for the Montesinos Orphanage and Environmental Technical School in Haiti, and the design of a community center in Inner Mongolia, China, to serve as a model of environmental sustainability in the region.

Celine Fitzmaurice is an Instructor in the University Studies Program at Portland State University where she teaches service-learning capstone courses. She received her MA in Anthropology from the University of Minnesota in 1995. Her research and teaching interests include reclaiming the commons, sustainable food systems and environmental advocacy. She also coordinates faculty development activities for the Capstone Program. She has facilitated experiential education programs in a variety of international, wilderness and higher education settings for over 20 years.

Jeffrey Gerwing, PhD, is an Associate Professor of Environmental Science and Management at Portland State University and a member of Living Cully Community Advisory Board that supports the collaborative work of non-profit organizations to increase access of residents in underserved Portland neighborhoods to economic opportunities and environmental assets. His research focuses on using adaptive management experiments and multi-party monitoring to improve the effectiveness of forest ecosystem restoration projects. In his teaching, Dr Gerwing uses interdisciplinary approaches and community-engaged learning projects to help students develop more complex understandings of sustainability issues.

William Jones, PhD, is Program Coordinator for, and teaches in, the School of Business Administration's Undergraduate Business Strategy/Capstone Program as well as advising capstone projects in the MBA, MIM, MSFA graduate programs. Dr

Jones has a consulting practice addressing investment risk and uncertainty, loss and damage and global equity/social justice related to climate change. He holds a Master of Urban Planning (University of Oregon) and PhD in planning and economics (Columbia University).

Sybil S. Kelley, PhD, is Assistant Professor of Science Education and Sustainable Systems at Portland State University in the Leadership for Sustainability Education program. She also teaches the Elementary Science Methods courses in the Graduate Teacher Education Program. Her work supports students and educators in underserved schools and neighborhoods to engage in authentic, project-based learning experiences that contribute to community problem solving. Her research focuses on investigating the impacts of these experiences on students and teachers. Prior to her work in education, Sybil worked as an environmental scientist and aquatic toxicologist. Dr Kelley has recently published in the Journal of Sustainability Education, Studies in Educational Evaluation and Teacher Education and Practice.

Robert Liberty has more than a third of a century's experience in working to implement plans and policies to create livable and sustainable cities and to conserve the rural lands and resources that provide food and fiber, and support natural systems. He has engaged in this work as a staff attorney and Director of 1000 Friends of Oregon, as a member of the Portland regional Metro Council, to which he was elected in 2004 and re-elected in 2008, and as a consultant advising governments and organizations in the US, China and other countries. Since 2012 he has been Director of the Urban Sustainability Accelerator at Portland State University. He has a BA from the University of Oregon Honors College, an MA from Oxford University, a JD from Harvard Law School and was a Loeb Fellow at the Harvard Graduate School of Design.

Nathan McClintock is Assistant Professor in the Toulan School of Urban Studies and Planning at Portland State University. A geographer and urbanist, he studies the relationships between urban agriculture, urban political economy, food systems planning, race, class and gender. His work appears in a range of journals, including Urban Geography, Land Use Policy and the Cambridge Journal of Regions, Economy and Society, and he is currently conducting research in Portland, with comparative work in Oakland, Vancouver and Montreal. He received his PhD in geography from UC Berkeley in 2011 and a MS in agroecology from North Carolina State University in 2004, and has worn a diversity of hats—researcher, trainer, journalist, Peace Corps volunteer, food policy council member and farmer—while working on sustainable agri-food systems in North America and the Global South.

Margaret B. Neal, PhD, is Director of the Institute on Aging and Professor of Community Health at Portland State University. She teaches graduate courses in gerontology and data collection methods and leads a service-learning program to

Nicaragua involving working with older adults. Her research has focused on the creation of age-friendly communities, transportation and neighborhood design for healthy aging, older workers, global aging issues and the challenges and opportunities of managing both paid employment and informal care to elders. Since 2006, she has been coordinating, on behalf of the City of Portland, the Age-Friendly Portland initiative, begun as a result of Portland's participation in the World Health Organization's Global Age-Friendly Cities project and its Global Network of Age-Friendly Cities and Communities. Dr Neal obtained her graduate degrees in urban studies specializing in gerontology and research methods from Portland State University and her bachelor's degree in Spanish from Indiana University.

Alex Novie is a multidisciplinary researcher investigating the dynamics of sustainable consumption. His research interests include food systems, energy systems and how notions of sustainability break down across cultural and socioeconomic groups. Alex has a background in data analytics, research design, community engagement and program management with experience in the academic, non-profit and private sectors. Alex holds a Master of Urban Studies degree from Portland State University and a BA in International Relations from the University of Redlands. He is currently an analyst implementing public policies to conserve energy use in buildings.

Sergio Palleroni is a Professor and Fellow and Director of the new Center for Public Interest Design at Portland State University. He has worked on sustainable architecture and community design in the developing world since the 1980s, both for not-for-profit agencies and governmental and international agencies such as UNESCO, the World Bank and government agencies worldwide. His work with students has received numerous national and international awards, including the 2011 NCARB Prize for Creative Integration of Practice and Education, the 2005 US National Design Award from the Smithsonian and White House, the first USGBC Education Award in 2008, in 2013 AIA's Latrobe Prize, and in 2015 a finalist for China's Tang Prize in Sustainability.

Rachel Samuelson, MEd, is the Coordinator of the Student Community Engagement Center at Portland State University. She received her Master's degree in Post-Secondary Adult Continuing Education in the Graduate School of Education at Portland State University. Since entering higher education administration in 2007, Ms Samuelson has specialized in student activities, leadership programming, community engagement and spiritual development of college students. Rachel works closely with dozens of community partners to maximize student impact and student learning. She loves serving alongside students and community partners, seeing first-hand efforts to promote positive change on both the individual and systemic levels.

Heather Spalding oversees the Sustainability Leadership Center and is finishing an MA in Educational Leadership and Policy with a specialization in Leadership for Sustainability Education at Portland State University (June 2015). She is a member of the Advisory Council for the Association for the Advancement of Sustainability in Higher Education (AASHE) and participates in sustainability activities through the North American Student Affairs Professional Association (NASPA) and American College Personnel Association (ACPA). She also holds a Permaculture and Whole Systems Design certificate.

Amy Spring is a Community Research and Partnerships Director at PSU and she received her Master's degree in Public Administration from Portland State University's Hatfield School of Government. Her emphasis of study was service learning and its impacts on students, faculty and community partners. She received her undergraduate degrees in Sociology and Urban Studies and Planning. Ms Spring works with PSU students, faculty, staff and community partners to facilitate and support community-based learning. She has been responsible for coordinating and facilitating assessment activities, faculty and student development workshops, student and faculty participation in community-based work, the development of community-based curriculum and all grant financial and programmatic reporting. On the national level, Amy has presented and published on a range of topics including: student leadership development in service learning; impact assessment of service learning on students, faculty and community partners and defining, documenting and evaluating the scholarships of engagement and teaching.

Jen Turner is the Agency Capacity and Education Coordinator for Oregon Food Bank, where she collaborates with anti-hunger and food systems sustainability stakeholders to address hunger and its root causes. She achieves this by shaping and providing educational opportunities and technical assistance to Oregon Food Bank's network of partner agencies, facilitating networks around resisting hunger and poverty, cultivating grassroots leadership and seeking out and sharing scalable models and proactive reduction interventions. Jen holds a Master of Urban Studies with an emphasis on equity and sustainability from Portland State University, and a BA in Communications and American Studies from American University.

Judy Walton is Program Administrator for the Urban Sustainability Accelerator. She was the founding director of the Association for the Advancement of Sustainability in Higher Education (AASHE) and an initiator of the American College and University Presidents' Climate Commitment (ACUPCC) as well as the Sustainability Tracking, Assessment and Rating System (STARS), the premier sustainability assessment system used by colleges and universities. Dr Walton's experience includes green building consulting, neighborhood planning, open space planning and teaching courses in sustainable cities and urban geography at Humboldt State University and Portland State University. While at Humboldt State, she helped develop an interdisciplinary MA program in Environment and Community. Her academic area of emphasis is urban geography, including downtown revitalization and sustainable cities. Dr Walton received her BA in political science with a minor in economics from the University of California at San Diego; an MA in geography from San Diego State University; and a PhD in geography from Syracuse University.

Dilafruz Williams, PhD, is a Professor and co-founder of the Leadership for Sustainability Education program and the Learning Gardens Laboratory in the Department of Educational Leadership and Policy, at Portland State University's Graduate School of Education. Dr Williams is co-author of Learning Gardens and Sustainability Education: Bringing Life to Schools and Schools to Life (Routledge), and coeditor of Ecological Education in Action: On Weaving Education, Culture, and the Environment (SUNY). In addition, she has authored dozens of chapters, journal articles and curriculum resource guides. Dr Williams has graduate degrees from Bombay, Syracuse and Harvard Universities in the sciences, public administration and philosophy of education. She was recently Principal Investigator for an NSF-funded project: Science in the Learning Gardens: Factors that Support Racial and Ethnic Minority Students' Success in Low-Income Middle Schools. Her areas of expertise are: Sustainability Education; Environmental Education, Learning Gardens: Curriculum Design; Research; STEM and Community-University-Schools Strategic Partnerships.

Vicki Wise serves as Director of Assessment and Research at Portland State University where she oversees assessment, planning and reporting for the Division of Enrollment Management and Student Affairs. Prior to PSU, she held the positions of Director of Assessment and Evaluation for the College of Education, Assistant Director for Institutional Research and Assistant Professor/Research Administrator in the Center for Assessment and Research Studies all at James Madison University. She earned her PhD and MA degrees at the University of Nebraska in Psychological and Cultural Studies and Educational Psychology, respectively.